# MY DEAR BOY

## Gay Love Letters through the Centuries

edited by

RICTOR NORTON

*My true love hath my heart, and I have his,*
*By just exchange one for another given:*
*I hold his dear, and mine he cannot miss,*
*There never was a better bargain driven:*
*My true love hath my heart, and I have his.*
—Sir Philip Sidney, *The Bargain*

Leyland Publications
San Francisco

First edition 1998

Introductions and all arrangements of letters in this edition copyright © 1998 by Rictor Norton.

Acknowledgments: These begin on page 279 and are to be considered as part of this copyright page for legal purposes.

Front cover: Ralph Hall (1913–1987) in a photo of *ca.* 1930s taken by Montague Glover (and interior photos of Glover/Hall—p. 240) from *A Class Apart* by James Gardiner (Serpent's Tail Press, London).
Front and back cover design/layout by Stevee Postman.

Photos by Steve Jensen (frontispiece, 8, 9, 10, 22) are copyright © 1998 by Steve Jensen.

Library of Congress Cataloging-in-Publication Data

My dear boy : gay love letters through the centuries / edited by Rictor Norton. — 1st ed.
   288 p. 23 cm.
   Includes index.
   ISBN 0-943595-70-3 (cloth : alk. paper). — ISBN 0-943595-71-1 (pbk. : alk. paper)
   1. Gay men—Correspondence.  2. Gay men's writings.  3. Love letters. I. Norton, Rictor, 1945–  .
HQ76.25.M9  1998
305.38'9664—dc21                    97-28335
                                          CIP

Leyland Publications
PO Box 410690
San Francisco, CA 94141
Write for free catalogue of books available.

# CONTENTS

## ILLUSTRATIONS

Personal letters have very rarely survived from the ancient world. The oldest letter containing a testimonial of gay love is a fragment of a letter sent in 334 BC from Alexander the Great's boyfriend Hephaestion to Alexander's mother Olympias, who had been nagging Alexander to find a wife: "Stop quarrelling with me; not that in any case I shall much care. You know Alexander means more to me than anyone." Hephaestion and his tutor Aristotle wrote many letters to one another, none of which have survived. Letters of assignation have been exchanged between men for centuries, about which we have some tantalizing hints. According to Suetonius, the prominent ex-praetor Claudius Pollio brandished a letter in the emperor Domitian's own handwriting offering to engage in homosexual acts with him. Juvenal in one of his satires refers to love letters sent to a hustler:

> . . . If your stars go against you
> The fantastic size of your cock will get you precisely nowhere
> However much Virro may have drooled at the spectacle
> Of your naked charms, though love-letters come in by the dozen
> Imploring your favours . . .

The mollies in early eighteenth-century London frequently wrote letters of assignation to one another and even used messenger boys for that purpose. Joseph Powis, who was convicted of breaking and entering, and hanged at Tyburn in 1732, in his confession and dying words said that once when he picked open a locked drawer in the Chancery Office he discovered letters belonging to the Clerk of the Masters addressed to Dear Miss Sukey Tooke, and signed Molly Soft-buttocks, appointing an assignation under the Piazza in Covent Garden. In the 1730s John Cooper, a butcher who called himself Princess Seraphina, earned money acting as a runner carrying messages between sodomitical gentlemen. In 1757 an effeminate male prostitute earned a good living by sending letters to wealthy men, offering his services. After receiving such a letter, the Earl of Tankerville helped the police to capture the rascal—who was found to have many such letters in his pocketbook, with blank spaces left for names to be filled in, and a list of names and addresses of prominent men. The spy Alfred Redl (1864–1913) received perfumed letters from men, together with their nude photographs.

Oscar Wilde facetiously said that he never wrote anything but for publication, but in fact his notorious letter to Bosie was intended solely for the recipient, and is known today only because it was stolen and used for blackmail. Noel Coward's play *A Song at Twilight* concerns a packet of homosexual letters used for blackmail, and was written partly to support

England's Criminal Law Amendment Bill being debated in 1957. Several films and novels have turned upon the discovery of gay love letters, and the whole of Margaret Yourcenar's *Alexis* is a fictional gay love letter.

Most gay love letters have not survived, often because blackmailers were paid, or because the family took steps to suppress such material after the death of the writer. Madame, second wife of Monsieur, Philippe de France, duc d'Orleans (1640–1701), admitted that on his death she immediately burned "all the letters the boys [*die Buben*] wrote him." When Mathilde Verlaine sued her husband for divorce, she showed her lawyer letters from Rimbaud to Verlaine which conclusively proved the homosexual relations between the two men. The letters were not used as evidence in court, because charges of physical abuse were sufficient for her to obtain the divorce. Later she destroyed these letters so that they would never be seen by her son. When Henry Maas edited *The Letters of A. E. Housman* (1971) he was refused permission to include Housman's letters to Moses Jackson, the great love of Housman's life, with whom he lived intermittently for five or six years between 1877 and 1885. Maas was allowed to see but not summarize these letters, which he found to be "of the greatest interest," and said "they will certainly form a valuable supplement to the present collection." The family continues to refuse permission for publication. Yukio Mishima's wife will not allow the publication of her husband's letters. T. S. Eliot's widow in 1988 allowed the publication of some letters from Jean Jules Verdenal, with whom Eliot lodged in Paris in 1910–11 and to whom he dedicated *The Love Song of J. Alfred Prufrock*; they are full of youthful enthusiasm and devotion to "mon cher ami," but there are said to be others that are franker, and Eliot's replies have not been published.

Family censorship and self-censorship (Henry James burned his papers to foil biographers) are exacerbated by institutional censorship. The South Caroliniana Library in 1978 tried to prevent Martin Duberman from publishing gay love letters written by Thomas Jefferson Withers in 1826. However, I must acknowledge that publishers, literary agents and curators of archives have been very generous and helpful during the compilation of this present anthology, with one exception. The Fellowship of the School of Economic Science, London, and their publishers Shepheard-Walwyn, refused to grant permission to include any selection from their English translation of the letters of Marsilio Ficino, despite being advised that such a refusal would lay them open to charges of homophobia. I cannot otherwise account for why a modern academic institution would wish to prevent a sixteenth-century philosopher from appearing in a gay context.

Some cultural historians believe that anthologies of "gay literature" and compendiums of "gay biographies" give a false impression of a unified gay experience which masks wide variations in different cultures and epochs. Most of the material collected in the present anthology comes from Europe and America, and is less than two thousand years old, so it is already part of a fairly well unified culture. But I would nevertheless contend that this anthology documents a fundamental human emotion that is transcultural and transhistorical. When one man says to another "I love you more than anyone else in the world" it means exactly the same thing whether it is uttered by the sophisticated twentieth-century American literary critic F. O. Matthiessen, or by the seventeenth-century Japanese samurai Mashida Toyonoshin, or by the fifteenth-century Dutch scholar Erasmus, or by the eleventh-century saint Anselm, or by the second-century emperor Marcus Aurelius. The love of one man for another is the fixed root or core value upon which a gay identity is constructed within historical constraints. It may be true that modern gays have characteristics of a recognizably modern personality, but it is an absurd exaggeration to say that "the homosexual" was invented in the late nineteenth century. In 1852 Magnus Huss discovered something he called "alcoholism"—but no one seriously contends that "alcoholics" did not exist prior to being labelled. A host of "deviant conditions" were classified in the late nineteenth century in order to bring them within the control of the expanding medical profession, but "sadists," "masochists," and even "heterosexuals" existed long before they were "discovered."

Some of the men in this anthology, even some who fully acknowledged being infatuated with other men, would not identify themselves with a label describing themselves as "men-who-love-men," whether that label be "sodomite" or "molly" or "Urning" or "queer" or "homosexual" or "gay," and I hesitate to force it upon them. Nevertheless I do not hesitate to label their ardent correspondence "gay love letters." Homosexuality is desire as well as act, and desire can be self-hidden as well as self-conscious. But in any case, most of the writers selected are confessedly head-over-heels in love with another man, and no phrase so satisfactorily describes their correspondence as "gay love letters." Too often, the debate about how to label a romantic masculine friendship is not an attempt to define experience, but to evade stigma. In most cases the debate about the term "gay" is not a genuine intellectual argument, but a linguistic red herring thrown out to escape a label that is felt to be denigrating. Virtually all the labels covering this area of experience are profoundly negative, and it is not surprising that they are felt to be incompatible with something that the participants regard as the most positive emotional experience in their lives. One could of course evade the issue by using the fashionable term "homosocial" whenever one cannot prove beyond the shadow of a doubt that a relationship between two men finds expression in genital activity, but in such instances "homosocial" is merely "homosexual" with a fig leaf.

It is often asserted that male sexuality is genitally focused while female sexuality is more peripheral, i.e. more affected by other bodily stimulation and by mood. But these love letters provide evidence for precisely this kind of peripheral eroticism within the male gay sensibility: even the chastest of the correspondents readily kiss, embrace and caress one another; the beauty of the physical male body is seldom obscured, and the longings of the correspondents are expressed in sensuous images that are erotic without necessarily being phallic. A passionate declaration of love is at the very least subliminally erotic, for there is a single continuum from lust to devotion. It has been remarked that spiritual friendship is sentimental sodomy. Amongst these correspondents the love itself is never subconscious, and its intensity is never in question, only our conceptual terminology is problematical. The nineteenth-century critic Edmund Gosse was very happily married and loved his children; he also loved the sculptor William Hamo Thornycroft and spent most of his holidays with him; when Lytton Strachey was asked if Gosse was a homosexual, Strachey replied "No, but he's Hamo-sexual." The wisdom of this anecdote could be applied to many of the selections in this anthology, for we are dealing with individual love affairs rather than life styles.

Romantic love letters by a host of writers during the Renaissance through Victorian periods have been dismissed as merely part of a literary tradition of masculine friendship. This is a bogus argument, for this was a specifically *homosexual* literary tradition, created for the classical world in the *Symposium* and *Phaedrus* by Plato whose boyfriends included Agathon and Aster, and in *De Amicitia* by Cicero who freed his lover Tiro from slavery, revived for medieval Christians in *De spirituali amicitia* by St. Aelred of Rievaulx who admitted that during his adolescence "the sweetness of love and the impurity of lust combined to take advantage of the inexperience of my youth," and re-revived for the Renaissance in *De Amore* by Marsilio Ficino who loved Giovanni Cavalcanti and who was called a sodomite by his enemies. Literary traditions are seldom "merely" literary: this tradition was a vehicle used by gay men to render eloquent the expression of a genuine emotion.

Are we justified in using a modern perception to read between the lines of sentiments of masculine affection expressed earlier than, say, 1920? Yes, of course we are. Freud was not the first person to recognize that no firm line can be drawn between love and desire: Marsilio Ficino in the fifteenth century emphasized that there was no essential difference between *amor* and *amicitia*: we are "naturally aroused for copulation whenever we judge any body to be beautiful. . . . It often happens that those who associate with males, in order to satisfy the demands of the genital part, copulate with them." It is wildly inaccurate to dismiss passionate endearment between men as being "typical" of the medieval period, or the Renaissance, or the early eighteenth century, and therefore not susceptible to "Freudian" erotic interpretation. The writers of such correspondence themselves acknowledged that it was *not* typical: Lord Hervey says of his letters to Stephen Fox in 1730 "I have often thought, if any very idle Body had Curiosity enough to intercept & examine my Letters, they would certainly conclude they came rather from a Mistress than a Friend.'' And Aelred also knew how his love for a certain Simon would be construed in the twelfth century: ''some may judge by my tears that my love was too carnal. Let them think what they wish.''

''Les amitiés particulières'' has been used to describe male-male love relationships in anthropological studies since the late seventeenth century; it is derived from medieval literature on ''special friendships'' that exceed the conventional bounds of brotherly love. An awareness of being different is supposedly typical of the modern gay identity, but an awareness that such friendships are different has existed for many centuries.

The literary tradition was also used to sanction a forbidden desire, and is sometimes cruelly exposed. Oscar Wilde's letter chastely addressing Lord Alfred Douglas as a slim gilt soul eventually contributed to Wilde's conviction and imprisonment. At Wilde's trial at the Old Bailey in 1895, Mr. Justice Wills described the document to the jury as ''a letter from the prisoner, of which it is difficult for me to speak with calmness, as addressed from one man to another. It is for you, however, to consider whether or not that letter is an indication of unclean sentiments and unclean appetites on both sides. It is to my mind a letter upon which ordinary people would be liable to put an uncomfortable construction.'' As recently as 1980, two young corporals in Ireland were charged with ''gross indecency'' and their sentimental love letters were read out in court, helping to convict them. Ultimately it is for the readers of this anthology to put their own constructions upon the letters that are included.

There are some important cultural differences between the periods represented here. The Japanese penchant for cutting off the thumb and presenting it as a gift to one's beloved is difficult to get to grips with (as it were). A more important difference is the rise of anti-gay legislation and attitudes in the west since the thirteenth century, and the ''medicalization'' of homosexuality since the late nineteenth century, so that modern American Christians are more likely to be guilt-ridden than ancient pagans or non-Europeans. Modern identities have been increasingly linked to exclusive sexual behaviour, but it is also true that many centuries of gay love letters document exclusive attachment to single individuals. Up until the end of the nineteenth century married men could be discreetly, or even indiscreetly, gay, but from the 1890s the maintenance of one wife and many boyfriends (a common pattern before then) became more difficult. For almost a century, 1870–1960, easygoing ''bisexuality'' was steadily replaced by the use of marriage as a route from homosexuality to heterosexuality, causing untold anguish to thousands of women as well as men. Stanley Haggart wrote to Harry Hay that his ''marriage was and is a perfect setup . . . wrong in every way. The reason is that I belong with you, and you with me." Several of the letters here illustrate the struggle of modern "bi-sexual" men to sort themselves out. Neal Cassady is rare in dealing with his "non-queerness"; usually the struggle involves coming to grips with an essentially homosexual identity in a heterosexual society. And yet there is still a similarity of emotional experience across the centuries.

As Erasmus wrote to his beloved Servatius: "Love, believe me, has its tears, and has its joys." Letters by their very nature document the separation of the correspondents. People normally write letters not while they happily live together, but when they are sadly apart from one another, so love letters are often skewed towards longing for reunion, dejection rather than celebration. The pain of loss and fear of rejection are substantial themes in many of these letters, as they are in heterosexual love letters. Heartbreak and longing are the stuff of romance. Tears trickle down the cheeks of many of the writers—and no doubt will occasionally blur the vision of many readers of these letters. The course of true love never did run smooth, and some of the stories are heartbreaking. Love followed by marriage—the complacent formula of heterosexual affairs—is not an option available for gay men, although in three or four instances the correspondents have managed to settle down together and live happily ever after—Montague Glover and Ralph Hall for fifty years.

There aren't a lot of saccharine hearts-and-flowers in gay love letters, though some of the more cuddly *billets doux* may make hard-hearted readers cringe. Love letters between men are often tender, but they often also have a blunt frankness—even a shocking brutality—that is seldom seen in heterosexual love letters. Tchaikovsky says to his nephew-lover Bob, who had not been writing to him lately: "If you do not want to write, at least spit on a piece of paper, put it in an envelope, and send it to me." Allen Ginsberg begs for the psychological whip and acknowledges that "my own love is one compounded of hostility & submission." Many of the more recent correspondents are matter-of-factly sexual. Peter Orlovsky tells Allen Ginsberg "I miss the shoe shine you'd give my cock!" Colin Spencer is so unhappy without John Tasker that he hasn't come for a week. W. S. Burroughs talks about "stiffening organs reaching out to touch warm flesh."

There is a sub-category of gay letters, largely ignored in this anthology, written between gay men describing the boys they have known, serving partly as a tool for vicarious masturbation. The boy-lovers Henry de Montherlant and Roger Peyrefitte have discussed their *garçons* and *gamins* in enormous, sometimes tedious, detail. Only a very few of their letters are actually *addressed to* the boys, Doudou or Edmond, "Chère petite tête," and the rest consist of wide-ranging cultural-historical-literary analyses of boy-love, particularly during 1938–41 after Montherlant was arrested for caressing the knees of a fourteen-year-old boy in a cinema. Typical of this genre is a letter from Michael Davidson to Colin Spencer on May 20, 1972 about a seventeen-year-old Irish lad he picked up in Leicester Square, whom he took home: "Not a hair on his body save for a slight flourish of delicate tracery about the pubic— . . . What quality of flesh and skin: silk spun from butterfly's wings—oh, the feel of that skin's texture and the flavour of it! And, my dear, that cock. An obelisk of dazzling loveliness, of astonishing perfection—breathtaking—consummately circumcised, of course, immaculate in appearance and proportion and impeccably lickable, kissable and suckable." This is all very interesting—and the relationship described did last for nearly one whole month—but it is not quite what I mean by "love letters," and I have included only a few examples of this category (Beckford writing to his pimp, and Baron Corvo offering to be a pimp).

I should perhaps add that despite the title *My Dear Boy*, very few of the relationships between the correspondents consist of boy-love. Marcus Aurelius was eighteen years old at the time Marcus Fronto addressed him as "Beloved Boy," George Villiers was twenty-one when he was King James's "sweet and dear child," the Earl of Sunderland's "dearest Boy" Captain Wilson was twenty-two, Whitman's "Dear Boy and Comrade" Peter Doyle was eighteen, Henry James's "dearest Boy" Hendrik Andersen was twenty-seven. And so it goes. "My Dear Boy" is really an *icon* of the gay imagination: the infatuation of the lover quite naturally transforms the beloved into the image of Eros. Most of the correspondence in this anthology demonstrates the truth of Wagner's perception that classical friendship "sprang directly from delight in . . . the material bodily beauty of the beloved comrade." Mythological Apollos and statues of nude youths are often referred to in these letters, part of an ideal pastoral idyll. Hart Crane describes his lover as having the crisp pointed ears of a faun; Heinrich von Kleist's lover is called "the fairest young bull ever sacrificed to Zeus"; the frequency with which Chester Kallman is picked up by rough trade is likened by W. H. Auden to the worship of the Three Shepherds. Many of the boys are angels: Samuel Hase looks "so like an angel" in his cassock that Brother Augustine worships him; Cocteau's Jean Marais is *mon bel ange*; the envelope containing one of John Fiske's letters is addressed *À un ange qu'on nommé Ernie Boulton, Londres*. Photographs are frequently requested, and in many cases surviving paintings and photographs testify that some of the beloved young men were very good looking indeed.

Most relationships—heterosexual as well as homosexual—have been "transgenerational" until fairly recently. Child-brides are common among indigenous peoples. Modern western men usually marry women who are younger than they, and have extramarital affairs with girls who are *much* younger than they. Society is mildly amused at "May-December" marriages, but raises its hands in horror at the "corruption" of a twenty-year-old "boy."

In many of the relationships represented in this anthology there is a wide difference of ages between the correspondents. Some of the men are separated by only two or three years, and their relationships are egalitarian, fraternal and matrimonial. But the pattern that is most common is avuncular or paternal: uncle–nephew, father–son, teacher–pupil, and especially protector/benefactor/patron–protégé. There are combinations such as paternal–matrimonial (King James signs his letter to Villiers "Thy dear dad and husband"), and sometimes the patron is the younger of the two men (as was Michelangelo's Cavalieri, Müller's Bonstetten, Wagner's King Ludwig). Such classification, however, is only mildly illuminating: the key feature is that all of these relationships are *romantic*.

For the most part I have limited my selections to the whole *raison d'être* of the love letter: the passionate affirmation of love. As with heterosexual love letters, this runs the gamut from caring devotion to stormy passion, from affectionate endearment to blind possessiveness, from tenderness to raging jealousy, sometimes over a woman, but usually over another man. In the selections I have concentrated upon the initial blossoming of the love affair, the awakening of love in oneself and the urging of the beloved to seize the day. The self-recognition and commitment that are part of intimacy sometimes lead to coming out within a large community, though usually the lovers are so absorbed in one another that the outside world is seen as a distraction. Conventional society and its laws are often the enemy of gay love; Rev. John Church's letters to his former boyfriend Ned document the same bitter sense of betrayal that is found in Oscar Wilde's "De Profundis."

Contrary to the view that only "modern homosexuals" wish to set up house together, the lover's request that the beloved will "come live with me and be my love" can be traced back through several centuries. In the 1570s Hubert Languet would have liked to have adopted Sir Philip Sidney; in the 1470s Ficino lived with Cavalcanti; in the 820s Bo Juyi and Yuan Zhan made a pact to live together as Taoist recluses. The records of the Inquisition in Spain, Portugal and Brazil; the police archives of early eighteenth-century Paris; the records of the Italian courts from the fourteenth through the sixteenth centuries—all turn up cases of men who lived together in long-term relationships that included intimacy and tenderness as well as "sodomitical sin." During the period between the two world wars self-conscious homosexual couples felt, as did F. O. Matthiessen, that it was an "uncharted, uninhabited country," whose rules they had to create both for themselves and for gay men who came after them. Twentieth-century lovers often write to one another about how they can make gay relationships work despite "infidelity." Cocteau writes to his young lover Jean Marais that although he wishes for them to live together, he has no desire to inhibit his freedom and in fact much of his pleasure lay in helping Marais to "feel freer than you would with a daddy or a mummy." Some men, like Ackerley seeking his "Ideal Friend" among Guardsmen and street boys, never quite found fulfilment, while others, like Burroughs among junkies and expatriates in Tangier, celebrated everything that middle-class America despised. As the 1970s approached, the modern gay *modus vivendi* entailed rejection of social "norms." Thus Colin Spencer abandoned "the game adaptability": "Love is rare enough after all, for one to tear one's own guts out in order to get it."

The importance of the love letter as a physical object in itself is not often sufficiently noticed. A love letter bears a symbolic meaning of greater importance than the written message it conveys. It is a love-token, a pledge of love, as well as a transmitter of sentiment. Baudri of Bourgueil in the twelfth century eagerly awaits a "tablet" from his beloved: a board covered with wax for writing, which in some cases could be made of ivory and serve as an elaborate gift. Federico García Lorca always carried with him the letters sent to him by his lover Rafael Rodríguez Rapún. One day Lorca failed to show up for a rehearsal of *Blood Wedding* to be performed in Barcelona, and his friend Rivas "found him sitting alone, deeply depressed, in a café, his head in his hands. It transpired that the previous night, after a binge in a downtown flamenco joint, Rapún had left with a Gypsy girl and failed to return to the hotel where he was staying with Lorca. Federico was in despair, believing that Rapún had abandoned him; and . . . pulled a wad of Rafael's letters out of his pocket to prove the passionate nature of their relationship" (Ian Gibson, *Lorca*, 1989). Many recipients of love letters have carried them next to their hearts and read them over and over again; all day, Russell Cheney would slip his hand into his pocket to hold the letter received from F. O. Matthiessen, or hold it against his cheek to achieve the sense of being with his lover. Tchaikovsky wrote to Bob Davïdov in May 1893, "I am writing to you with a voluptuous pleasure. The thought that this paper is going to be in your hands fills me with joy and brings tears to my eyes." Sir Philip Sidney was delighted to receive a letter from Hubert Languet: "for while I read, I fancy that I have the very Hubert himself before my eyes and in my hands." Hans Christian Andersen wrote to the Grand Duke of Saxe-Weimar-Eisenach: "When this greeting reaches your hands, may you feel in it the pulsations of my heart." Wilfred Owen told his beloved Siegfried Sassoon: "for anything in any envelope of your sealing, I give thanks and rejoice." In short, love letters are magical talismans of transcendence, protective amulets, touchstones of the power of love to unite, to exalt, to fulfil, to heal. As Jean Cocteau said to his lover Jean Marais: "Write me two lines. Your short letters are my fetishes." Gay love letters are the manifest emblems of the primordial self, what Pasolini called the "fossil" of homosexual love.

I have not included any letters by women. This is not simply because of limitations of space, but because I feel it is clearly preferable to have separate anthologies, the present collection of Gay Love Letters and a companion anthology of Lesbian Love Letters edited by a lesbian feminist press. It is only during relatively modern times that gay men and lesbians in Europe and America have shared similar concerns (identity, coming out, overcoming oppression). Prior to the 1850s gay men and lesbians experienced separate cultures, separate concerns, separate traditions. Gay and lesbian circles freely intermixed in the later nineteenth century, and there is even a sub-genre of letters between gay men and lesbians. But to bring gay and lesbian love letters together in a comprehensive anthology, striving for roughly equal parity, would be to dilute and to distort many of the issues of importance to each of them.

Anthologies inevitably include many selections from professional "men of letters," but I have taken pains to include substantial material from "ordinary" and "uneducated" men such as F. Holland Day's nude model Nardo, Civil War soldier Lewis Brown, clergyman John Church, and especially the cheerful working-class lad Ralph Hall. I have selected love letters by kings and aristocrats, musicians and artists, military men and monks, farm labourers and herring merchants, political activists and aesthetes, drag queens and hustlers. Some of these love letters have been proudly published by their correspondents and some have been published in newspapers and pamphlets as part of political and religious attacks; some have been produced in court (from the Inquisition to the Old Bailey) and some have been discovered in a cardboard box after a house clearance; some are painfully personal and some have been written with an eye to future readers. I have relied mostly upon published English-language sources, but important letters by Marsilio Ficino, Federico Gonzaga, Heinrich von Kleist, Charles-Victor de Bonstetten, Johannes von Müller, Johann Joachim Winckelmann, and Jean Cocteau have been specially translated for this anthology. The short introductions to each selection are not intended as potted biographies, but focus upon the context in which the letters were written, with emphasis upon the specifically gay history of the correspondents, rather than an evaluation of the achievements for which they may be famous or notorious.

Personal letters are written less with an eye to future publication than other forms of writing. They are more sincere and closer to the heart, and their eloquence comes from simple passion rather than studied art. They have a truthfulness and immediacy lacking in more reflective autobiographies or analyses. Modern gay love letters, by Cocteau, Matthiessen, Colin Spencer, Allen Ginsberg, J. R. Ackerley, are of immense value in learning how gay men established their *modus vivendi* in modern homophobic society. Contemporary letters are more scarce, mainly because letters come last in a literary life-cycle: usually they are published by one's executors. I have given generous space to earlier periods, because such "historical" documents are less readily accessible than letters published during the past fifty years. Gay love letters are important and precious documents for the study of gay history, and are a resource for the nurturing of gay love. It is important to reclaim the older documents in order to demonstrate that love letters between men are not simply a phenomenon that has arisen as a result of modern gay awareness, but are testimonials of an enduring love.

# ▼ BREATH OF MY LIFE ▼

[EMPEROR MARCUS AURELIUS & MARCUS CORNELIUS FRONTO]

The Roman Emperor Marcus Aurelius Antoninus (121–180) is not cited as one of the "great queens of history," for he was noted as a model husband and father and an advocate of the virtues of heterosexual marriage. In his famous *Meditations*, written towards the end of his life, he recorded that he learned from his father "to suppress all passion for young men." But when he became Emperor he instituted no official sanctions against homosexuality, other than to refuse to acknowledge the existence of Antinous, boyfriend of his patron the Emperor Hadrian.

But Marcus's life was not always so earnest. Hadrian adopted Marcus in 138 AD after the early death of his father, and appointed Marcus Cornelius Fronto as his tutor. Fronto was born in Numidia around 95 AD, studied in Alexandria, and was to become a Consul in 143, becoming famous as an advocate and orator, and a teacher of literature and archeology upon his retirement from public life. He valued eloquence more highly than philosophy, but failed to persuade his serious pupil to follow that path. Marcus Aurelius's writings are moving in their simplicity, while Fronto's works often have more elegance than pith. (Walter Pater translated his beautiful apologue on sleep in *Marius the Epicurean*.)

Fronto loved children and the young men who lived with him as his pupils, but he was unlucky in having these affections cut short, for five of his own six children predeceased him, and he also lost a grandson for whom he composed a moving elegy. The relationship between the eighteen-year-old pupil and his middle-aged teacher seems to have been playfully passionate, and the letters which survive from this earliest period are characteristic of both the elder orator noted for his splendid rhetoric (*pompa*) and the young emperor-to-be whom Hadrian nicknamed Verissimus, most truthful of men. Marcus Aurelius kept a bust of Fronto amongst his own household gods, and erected his statue in the Senate upon his death in 176.

---

MARCUS AURELIUS TO FRONTO

*[ca. 139]*

Hail my best of masters.

If any sleep comes back to you after the wakeful nights of which you complain, I beseech you write to me and, above all, I beseech you take care of your health. Then hide somewhere and bury that "axe of Tenedos" [proverb for unflinching justice], which you hold over us, and do not, whatever you do, give up your intention of pleading cases, or along with yours let all lips be dumb. . . .

Farewell, breath of my life. Should I not burn with love of you, who have written to me as you have! What shall I do? I cannot cease. Last year it befell me in this very place, and at this very time, to be consumed with a passionate longing for my mother. This year you inflame that my longing. My Lady [i.e. his mother Domitia Lucilla d. *ca.* 155, or his adopted mother Faustina the Elder, d. 140] greets you.

---

MARCUS CORNELIUS FRONTO TO MARCUS AURELIUS AS CAESAR

*[ca. 139]*

Beloved Boy,

This is the third letter that I am sending you on the same theme. . . . But if the present treatise [*A Discourse on Love*, composed by Fronto in Greek] seems to you to be longer than those which were previously sent through Lysias and Plato, let this be a proof to you that I can claim in fair words to be at no loss for words. But you must consider now whether my words are no less true than new.

No doubt, O Boy, you will wish to know at the very beginning of my discourse how it is that I, who am not in love, long with such eagerness for the very same things as lovers. I will tell you, therefore, first of all how this is. He who is ever so much a lover is, by Zeus, gifted with no keener sight than I who am no lover, but *I* can discern your beauty as well as anyone else, aye, far more accurately, I might say, even than your lover. But, just as we see in the case of fever patients, and those who have taken right good exercise in the gymnasium, the same result proceeds from different causes. They are both thirsty, the one from his malady, the other from his exercise. It has been my lot also to suffer some such malady from love . . .

Money given by me you would be right in calling a gift, but given by a lover a quittance. And the children of prophets say that to gods also is the thank-offering among sacrifices more acceptable than the sin-offering, for the one is offered by the prosperous for the preservation and possession of their goods, the other by the wretched for the averting of ills. Let this suffice to be said on what is expedient and beneficial both to you and to him.

But if it is right that he should receive aid from you . . . you set this on a firm basis . . . you framed this love for him and he devised Thessalian love-charms . . . owing to his insatiable desire . . . unless you have manifestly done wrong. [mutilated passage in the manuscript]

And do not ignore the fact that you are yourself wronged and subject to no small outrage in this, that all men know and speak openly thus of you, that he is your lover; and so, by anticipation and before being guilty of any such things, you abide the imputation of being guilty. Consequently the generality of the citizens call you the man's darling; but I shall keep your name unsullied and inviolate. For as far as I am concerned you shall be called *Beautiful*, not *Darling* [*kalos*, not *ephebos*]. . . .

Your lover, too, as they say, composes some amatory writings about you in the hope of enticing you with this bait, if with no other, and attracting you to himself and catching you; but such things are a disgrace and an insult and a sort of licentious cry, the outcome of stinging lust, such as those of wild beasts and fed cattle, that from sexual desire bellow or neigh or low or howl. Like to these are the lyrics of lovers. If, therefore, you submit yourself to your lover to enjoy where and when he pleases, awaiting neither time that is fitting nor leisure nor privacy, then, like a beast in the frenzy of desire, will he make straight for you and be eager to go to it not the least ashamed. . . .

One thing more will I tell you, and if you will pass it on to all other boys, your words will seem convincing. Very likely you have heard from your mother, or from those who brought you up, that among flowers there is one [perhaps the sunflower or marigold] that is indeed in love with the sun and undergoes the fate of lovers, lifting itself up when the sun rises, following his motions as he runs his course, and when he sets, turning itself about; but it takes no advantage thereby, nor yet, for all its love for the sun, does it find him the kinder. Least esteemed, at any rate, of plants and flowers, it is utilized neither for festal banquets nor for garlands of gods or men. Maybe, O Boy, you would like to see this flower. Well, I will show it you if we go for a walk outside the city walls as far as the Illisus . . .

---

MARCUS AURELIUS TO FRONTO

*[ca. 139]*

Hail, my best of masters.

Go on, threaten me as much as you please and attack me with hosts of arguments, yet shall you never drive your lover, I mean me, away; nor shall I the less assert that I love Fronto, or love him the less, because you prove with reasons so various and so vehement that those who are less in love must be more helped and indulged. So passionately, by Hercules, am I in love with you, nor am I frightened off by the law you lay down, and even if you show yourself more forward and facile to others, who are non-lovers, yet will I love you while I have life and health. . . .

This I can without rashness affirm: if that Phaedrus of yours ever really existed, if he was ever away from Socrates, Socrates never felt for Phaedrus a more passionate longing than I for the sight of you all these days: days do I say? months I mean . . . [line missing in manuscript] unless he is straightaway seized with love of you. Farewell, my greatest treasure beneath the sky, my glory. It is enough to have had such a master. My Lady mother sends you greeting.

# ▼ R O S E S  A R E  M Y  H E A R T ' S  D E S I R E ▼

[FLAVIUS PHILOSTRATOS & VARIOUS BOYS]

*Translated from Greek by Allen Rogers Benner and Francis H. Fobes*

Virtually nothing is known about the Greek rhetorician, "Sophist" and biographer Flavius Philostratos (*c.* 170–245), who studied in Athens before settling in Rome. About half of his amatory Epistles are addressed to handsome boys, unnamed and perhaps idealized lovers. Many of the letters appear in pairs, for example one praising boyish purity being matched later by one praising male prostitution. Although the letters may therefore be literary exercises, and although they have been characterized as "continuous cooing in a hot-house," they nevertheless have great charm and contain more truly poetic images than a good many heterosexual cliches about rosy-fingered maidens.

All readers agree that the letters addressed to the lads are less artificial than those addressed to the girls, and seem more likely to reflect the writer's genuine sentiments. His letters take it for granted that *paiderastia*—best translated as ladslove rather than boylove (as the beloved's age can range from thirteen to eighteen years)—is the natural state of affairs in any civilized society. They have often been plundered for material to enrich modern heterosexual love letters and love lyrics.

Philostratos also wrote a life of Apollonius of Tyana, written at the request of the Empress Julia Domna, which is full of homosexual gossip although this mystical philosopher and seer is praised for his chastity, and held up as a pagan rival to Christ.

---

FLAVIUS PHILOSTRATOS TO A HANDSOME BOY

*[3rd century AD]*
*Letter 1*

The roses, borne on their leaves as on wings, have made haste to come to you. Receive them kindly, either as mementos of Adonis or as tinct of Aphrodite or as eyes of the earth. Yes, a wreath of wild olives becomes an athlete, a tiara worn upright the Great King, and a helmet crest a soldier; but roses become a beautiful boy, both because of affinity of fragrance and because of their distinctive hue. You will not wear the roses: they will wear you.

---

*Letter 11*

How many times, do you think, have I unclosed my eyes to release you, even as hunters open their nets to give their quarry a chance to escape? And you sit fast, like those vexatious squatters who, when once they have seized on other people's land, will not hear of moving off again. Lo, once more, as so often in the past, I raise my eyelids; not at long last, I pray you, fly away, and raise the siege, and become a guest of other eyes. You are not listening, not you! You are pressing ever farther on, into my very soul! And what is this new fiery heat? In my perilous plight I cry for water; but no one assuages the heat, for the means of quenching this flame is very hard to find, whether one brings water from a spring or from a stream; yes, for love's fire sets even the water ablaze.

---

*Letter 13*

The handsome boy, if he is wild and cruel, is a fire; but if he is tame and kind, a shining beacon. Therefore do not consume me with flame, but let me live; and keep the altar of Compassion in your soul, gaining a firm friend at the price of a short-lived favour; and take time by the forelock— time which alone makes an end of handsome boys even as the populace makes an end of princes. For I fear—yes, I will speak out my thoughts— lest, while you linger and hesitate, your beard may make its advent and may obscure the loveliness of your face, even as the concourse of clouds is wont to hide the sun! Why do I fear what one may see already? The down is creeping on, and your cheeks are becoming fluffy, and over all your face the hair begins to grow. Ah me! In hesitating we have waxed old—you because you would not divine my love sooner, I because I shrank from asking. So before your springtime quite departs and winter comes upon you, grant springtime's gifts in the name of Love, I pray, and of this beard by which I must swear tomorrow.

---

*Letter 46*

You have done well to use the roses for a bed also; for pleasure in gifts received is a clear indication of regard for the sender. So through their agency I also touched you, for roses are amorous and artful and know how to make use of beauty. But I fear that they may actually have been restless and oppressed you in your sleep, even as the gold oppressed Danae. If you wish to do a favour for a lover, send back what is left of them, since they now breathe a fragrance, not of roses only, but also of you.

# ▼ FOR ALL TIME ▼

[PAULINUS OF NOLA & AUSONIUS]

*Translated from Latin by Thomas Stehling*

Saint Paulinus (*c.* 353–431) came from a wealthy family of Bordeaux, where he was a student of Ausonius (*c.* 310–*c.* 394), a teacher of rhetoric in Bordeaux from 334–64. Ausonius is said to have possessed in his library a collection of homosexual literature which shocked even the Romans (unfortunately these works have never been identified). He is best noted for having translated a famous Greek riddle posing the question how three men could engage in four sexual positions (correct: one in the middle both gives and receives).

Paulinus went to live near Barcelona, and later lived in Italy where he became bishop of Nola in 409. Ausonius retired to Bordeaux in 383, and in a letter to Paulinus imagines his friend travelling from Barcelona to Bordeaux, summoned by Ausonius's prayers: "Hurry while you are still a youth and while my old age, to please you, preserves its strength undrained." Paulinus replied from Barcelona that they would never be separated in spirit.

---

PAULINUS OF NOLA TO AUSONIUS

*[ca. 385]*

You and me: for all time which is given
And destined to mortal men,
For as long as I am held in this confining, limping body,
No matter how far I am separated from you in the world,
You will be neither distant from me nor far from my eyes:
I will hold you, intermingled in my very sinews.
I will see you in my heart and with a loving spirit embrace you;
You will be with me everywhere.
And when released from this bodily prison
I fly from earth
To the spot in heaven where our universal Father places me,
There too I will keep you in my spirit;
Nor will the end which frees me from my body
Release me from your love.
For the mind, once it has survived loss of limbs,
Continues to grow out of its heavenly root,
And therefore must keep both its understanding and affections
Along with its life.
And just as it experiences no death, it will experience no loss of memory
But remain forever alive, forever mindful.
    Farewell noble master.

# ▼ JOINED DELIGHT ▼

[BO JUYI & YUAN ZHEN]
*Translated from Chinese by Howard S. Levy and Arthur Walley*

China has a very ancient and honorable homosexual literary tradition, and gay love poems are contained in the country's earliest surviving anthology. Most gay men fulfilled their kinship interests (still the major factor in Chinese life today) by getting married, but they also maintained romantic homosexual affairs. The two major tropes for homosexual love—sharing peaches, and the passion of the cut sleeve—come from the story of Mizi Xia who gave a half-eaten peach to his lover Duke Ling of Wei (534–493 BC), and the story of how the Emperor Ai (reigned 6 BC to 1 AD) cut off his sleeve rather than wake his sleeping favorite Dong Xian.

These ancient images demonstrate that male-to-male *love* rather than just sex was important for establishing a specifically gay identity, and how imaginative metaphors are at least as important as pejorative labels. For two hundred years the Han Dynasty was ruled by ten openly bisexual emperors, and detailed biographies were written about their favorites. During the Tang Dynasty, more records survive describing gay life and romantic friendship outside of imperial circles.

The Chinese poet Bo Juyi (772–846) was one of the scholar-officials who served in the vast Chinese civil service, and became Governor of Suchow in 825. His fellow bureaucrats often were sent to provincial towns in the widespread empire, and he exchanged with them poems or verse-letters which are full of the expressions of romantic love. To his friend Qian Hui he sent a poetic souvenir of one winter night they spent together. His friend Yu Shunzhi sent him a bolt of patterned purple silk as a token of remembrance, and Bo Juyi replied how he would make this gift a symbol of their friendship.

His greatest love was his fellow student Yuan Zhen (779–831). They were both Collators of Texts in the Palace Library at the northern imperial city of Ch'ang-an, and they exchanged intimate poetry for several decades when different careers separated them and Yuan Zhen was sent to the eastern city of Lo-yang. Bo Juyi wrote to his beloved, "Who knows my heart as I think of you? It's a captive falcon and a caged crane." Even after a long separation—they both became commissioners in different provinces, and it could take almost a year for their letters to reach one another—Bo Juyi would sometimes dream that they were still together: "Awakening, I suspected you were at my side, reached for you but there was nothingness."

Both poets got married; Yuan Zhen loved his wife but she died after only a few years; Bo Juyi's wife "read no books" and he seems to have had no special intimacy with her; he built a cottage near a monastery where he would go to be alone. In his poem "Night Rain" (812) Bo Juyi speaks of

29

白樂天

Calligraphic drawing of the Chinese poet Bo Juyi (772–846).

his longing for Yuan Zhen: "There is one that I love in a far, far land; There is something that harrows me, tied in the depths of my heart. So far is the land that I cannot visit him; I can only gaze in longing, day on day. So deep the sorrow that it cannot be torn away; never a night but I brood on it, hour, by hour."

In 814 Bo Juyi sent Yuan Zhen a sum of money equivalent to half a year's salary, "Not that I thought you were bent on food and clothes, but only because I felt tenderly towards you." They were reunited briefly in 819, when both carved a poem on the rock outside a cave; they met again in 821–22 and in 829. The two men had made a pact to live together as Taoist recluses in their retirement, but Yuan Zhen died after a sudden illness before this plan could be put into effect. Bo Juyi wrote two formal dirges to recite at his beloved's funeral and three songs for the pall-bearers to sing.

---

BO JUYI TO QIAN HUI

*[early ninth century]*

Night deep—the memorial draft finished;
mist and moon intense piercing cold.
About to lie down, I warm the last remnant of the wine;
we face before the lamp and drink.
Drawing up the green silk coverlets,
placing our pillows side by side;
like spending more than a hundred nights,
to sleep together with you here.

---

BO JUYI TO YU SHUNZHI

Thousand leagues, friend's heart cordial;
one strand, fragrant silk purple resplendent.
Breaking the seal, it glistens
with a rose hue of the sun at eve—
The pattern fills in the width
of a breeze arising on autumnal waters.
About to cut it to make a mattress,
pitying the breaking of the leaves;
about to cut it to make a bag,
pitying the dividing of the flowers.
It is better to sew it,
making a coverlet of joined delight;
I think of you as if I'm with you,
day or night.

BO JUYI TO YUAN ZHEN

[805]

Since I left home to seek official state
Seven years I have lived in Ch'ang-an.
What have I gained? Only you, Yuan;
So hard it is to bind friendship fast. . . .
We did not go up together for Examination;
We were not serving in the same Department of State.
The bond that joined us lay deeper than outward things;
The rivers of our souls spring from the same well!

YUAN ZHEN TO BO JUYI

[816]

Other people too have friends that they love;
But ours was a love such as few friends have known.
You were all my sustenance; it mattered more
To see you daily than to get my morning food.
And if there was a single day when we did not meet
I would sit listless, my mind in a tangle of gloom.
To think we are now thousands of miles apart,
Lost like clouds, each drifting on his far way!
Those clouds on high, where many winds blow,
What is their chance of ever meeting again?
And if in open heaven the beings of the air
Are driven and thwarted, what of Man below?

BO JUYI TO YUAN ZHEN

Last night the clouds scattered everywhere,
for a thousand leagues the same moon color.
At dawn's coming I saw you in dreams;
it must be you were thinking of me.
In my dream I grasped your hand,
asked you what your thoughts were.
You said you thought of me with pain,
had no one to send a letter through.

When I awoke, I still had not spoken in reply.
a knock-on-the-door sound, rap rap!
Saying, " A messenger from Shangzhou,"
he delivered a letter of yours.
From the pillow I rose sudden and startled,
putting on my clothes topsy-turvy.
I opened the seal, saw the hand-letter,
one sheet, thirteen lines.

# ▼ BEST BELOVED BROTHER ▼

[SAINT ANSELM & GUNDULF & WILLIAM]

Anselm was born in Italy in 1033 and joined the Benedictine monastery of Bec in Normandy in 1056. He became its prior in 1063 and then its abbot in 1078. In 1093 he became Archbishop of Canterbury, where he died and was buried in 1109. In 1494 he was canonized.

Most of the following letters were written during his early residence at Bec, though he was already becoming noted for his scholarship and philosophy, infectious enthusiasm, and spiky personality. There is little reason to doubt the purity of Anselm's theological concept of friendship, or even his celibacy, but neither can we deny the erotic force behind his yearning and frustrated desire, his heartbreak and even jealousy. The intensity of his emotional experience with his pupils and the "beloved lover" (*dilecto dilectori*) to whom he addresses his epistles makes clear his gay sensibility.

Gundulf (*ca.* 1024–1108) was Anselm's immediate superior at Bec; at the time of the letters selected, Anselm feared for Gundulf's participation in the Crusades, but Anselm successfully persuaded Gundulf to go with him to Canterbury in 1070; he became Bishop of Rochester in 1077. Little is known of Brother William, a young monk at La Chaise-Dieu, near St. Etienne.

The Council of London in 1102 wanted to enact ecclesiastical legislation which declared—for the first time in English history—that homosexual behaviour was a sin, and they recommended that offending laymen be imprisoned and clergymen be anathematized. But Anselm as Archbishop of Canterbury prohibited the publication of their decree, advising the Council that homosexuality was widespread and few men were embarrassed by it or had even been aware it was a serious matter; he felt that although sodomites should not be admitted to the priesthood, confessors should take into account mitigating factors such as age and marital status before prescribing penance, and he advised counselling rather than punishment. St. Anselm's letters appeared during the last flowering of homosexual love before fanatical anti-gay prejudice swept across Europe in the thirteenth century, as documented by John Boswell in *Christianity, Social Tolerance and Homosexuality* (1980).

---

ANSELM TO GUNDULF

*[ca. 1071]*

*Greeting from brother Anselm to his honoured master,*
*best beloved brother and most attached friend, Master Gundulf.*

Though I desire to write to you, soul most beloved of my soul, I know not how best to begin my address. For whatever I know about you is sweet and joyous to my spirit: whatever I desire for you is the best which my mind

33

can conceive. For I saw you such that I loved you as you know; I hear you to be such that I yearn after you, God knows how much: wherever you go, my love follows you; and wherever I remain, my longing embraces you. And since you eagerly ask me by your messengers, exhort me by your letters, and urge me by your gifts, to have you in remembrance: "Let my tongue cleave to the roof of my mouth" if I have not held Gundulf first among my friends. I do not here mean Gundulf the layman, my father [his natural father by kinship], but my friend, Gundulf the monk. Now how could I forget you? How could he fade from my memory who is impressed upon my heart as is a seal upon wax? Also, why do you, as I hear, complain with so much sadness that you never receive a letter of mine, and why do you ask so affectionately to have one frequently, when in the spirit you have me always with you? When therefore you are silent, I know you care for me; and when I make no sign, "you know that I love you." You are a sharer in my existence, for I have no doubts of you; and I am witness to you that you are sure of me. Since therefore we are mutually sharers in each other's consciousness, it only remains that we should tell each other what concerns us, that we may alike either rejoice or be anxious for each other. But as to my affairs, and the reasons why I would have you rejoice or be anxious with me, you will learn better from the bearer of this letter than from the writer of the letter. Greet Master Lanfranc, the young nephew of our revered lord and master, Lanfranc the archbishop, and present to him my faithful desire to do him service. For since he is so near and dear to him whom so I venerate with affection and love with veneration as that I would love what he loves; and since I hear that he is of an amiable character: if he should allow it, I both offer him my service and ask for his friendship. Salute Master Osbern who is with you for my dear dead Osbern; for I would impress on you and on all my friends in as few words as I know how, and with the greatest earnestness I can, that wherever Osbern is, his soul is my soul. I therefore while alive would receive for him whatever if dead I might hope from your friendship, lest you be negligent when I am dead.

Farewell, farewell, my beloved [*mi charissime*]; and, to repay you according to your request, I pray and pray and pray, remember me, and forget not the soul of Osbern my beloved. If I seem to burden you too heavily, forget me, and remember him.

---

ANSELM TO GUNDULF

*[not later than 1077]*

*His own to his own, friend to friend,*
*Anselm to Gundulf, wishes through love of bliss perseverance in holiness,*
*and for the reward of holiness an eternity of blessedness.*

And now, this Gundulf and Anselm is witness that you and I are never so in want of each other as that we have to prove our mutual affection by letters. For since your spirit and mine can never bear to be absent from each other, but unceasingly are intertwined; we mutually need nothing from each other, save that we are not together in bodily presence. But why should I write on paper of my affection for you, since you carefully keep its exact image in the cell of your heart? For what is your love for me but the image of mine for you? Therefore your known wish induces me to write somewhat to you on account of our bodily separation; but since we are known to each other by the presence together of our spirits, I know not what to say to you, save—may God do with you as shall please Him, and be profitable to you. Farewell.

---

ANSELM TO WILLIAM

*[ca. 1074/75]*

*Brother Anselm, called Abbot of Bec,*
*to his loved and longed-for (would it were loving and longing) William:*
*despise dangerous and miserable vanities, and seek the secure and blessed*
*truth.*

So completely, oh my beloved whom I yearn after, has Almighty God filled my soul (by His grace, not through my own merits) with love of you, that, agitated between the longing for your salvation and the fear of your peril, being excited day and night by anxiety for you, it cannot rest; blessed be God for His gifts, and would that He might take away your hatred for your own soul even as He has given me the yearning for your salvation. Bear with me, dear friend, and endure him who loves you, should I appear to you importunate, and speak to you more sternly than you might wish. For the love of your soul compels mine, nor allows it to suffer that you should hate that which it loves with an ever-present love. Receive, therefore, most dear one, with a love which I pray God to impart to you, the sayings of him who loves you. Dearly beloved, you are what love says with pain, and grief says lovingly, who (which may God put away from you) have hated your soul, beloved of mine; for "whosoever loves iniquity hates his own soul" (Ps. xi, 6). Iniquity of a truth, and many iniquities are they with which you so eagerly make yourself happy, oh my beloved. Iniquity, and many iniquities are they whither the force of worldly things, rushing to ruin, impels you, my loved one. For the bloody confusion of war is iniquity. The ambition of worldly vanity is iniquity. The insatiable desire for false advantages and false riches is iniquity. Towards these, alas! I see him whom I so long to keep back by loving him, drawn by the subtle enemy deceiving his heart. Oh God, friend and deliverer of man, let not the enemy draw your servant away!

You tell me, beloved brother: "I do not love these things, but I love my brother who is entangled in them: and therefore I hasten to be involved therein with him, that I may help and guard him." Alas! wretched grief from the miserable error of the sons of Adam! . . . Answer me, brother: who shall help and guard you helping and guarding him? God, whom you care less to follow than that brother of yours! Christ, who calls you, you scorn to follow in peace and in your own country and among your relations and friends that as "heir of God" and "joint-heir with Him" you may possess the kingdom of heaven; and by such and so many difficult rugged ways, through rough seas and stormy tempests you hasten to your brother amid the confusion of war, that you may see him (to suppose something great) bearing rule over the Greeks . . .

Delay not your so great good, and fulfil my yearning for you, that I may have you for my companion in following Christ; and that we may strive together so that as you see me, so I may see you a companion in Christ's inheritance, which He gives. . . . Fear not to become the soldier of so great a King, for the King Himself will be beside you in every danger. Delay no longer to enter in this life on the road which you have chosen . . . I advise, counsel, pray, adjure, enjoin you as one most dear to abandon that Jerusalem which now is no vision of peace, but of tribulation, where with bloody hands men contend for the treasures of Constantinople and Babylon: and to enter upon the road to the heavenly Jerusalem, which is the vision of peace, where you shall find a treasure only to be received by those who despise the others.

I end this long letter unwillingly, since out of the abundance of the heart my mouth desires to speak much to you. . . . God direct your heart according to His will, and gratify my desire of you according to His mercy. Amen.

# ▼ TAKE UP RIPER PRACTICES ▼

[MARBOD OF RENNES & A YOUNG LOVER]
*Translated from Latin by Thomas Stehling*

Many medieval monks gave vent to suppressed homoerotic desires in love lyrics and love letters couched in the language of spiritual friendship, derived from Cicero's *De Amicitia* and the *Epistles* of St. Jerome. Egbert would write to Saint Boniface (716–720) with feelings more passionate than *caritas*: "I avow the bond of your love; when I tasted it in my inmost being a fragrance as of honeyed sweetness entered into my veins. . . . believe me, the tempest-tossed sailor does not long for his haven, the thirsty fields for their rain, the anxious mother waiting at the bend of the shore for her son, as much as I long to delight in seeing you." The last sentence is taken practically verbatim from a published letter from St. Jerome to Rufinus, which influenced most of the letters expressing the longing of Christian *amicitia*. The degree to which such documents may provide evidence of gay love rather than passionate friendship frankly depends upon the sexual sympathies of the interpreter.

Most medieval scholars start with the male heterosexual prejudice against homosexuality that blinds them to the evidence. Indeed, John Boswell in his ground-breaking study *Christianity, Social Tolerance, and Homosexuality* (1980) has documented many cases of censorship, suppression and deliberate distortion by such scholars. Critics are slowly adopting the view that the medieval gay sensibility is not an accident of literary imitation, but that the literary artifice (allusion to both pagan and biblical sources) was a vehicle for legitimizing such love.

The abbot Alcuin (*ca.* 735–804), head of Charlemagne's school at Aachen, gave his pupils nicknames derived from Virgil's *Eclogues*, and wrote to Arno, Bishop of Salzburg (*ca.* 750–821), "abduct me with your prayers [*precibus rape me*]." Is this allusion to the rape of Ganymede just an awkward poetic convention? Few can reject the genuine and homoerotic feelings behind the beginning of his letter to Arno: "I think of your love and friendship with such sweet memories, reverend bishop, that I long for that lovely time when I may be able to clutch the neck of your sweetness with the fingers of my desires. Alas, if only it were granted to me, as it was to Habakkuk, to be transported to you, how would I sink into your embraces, . . . how would I cover, with tightly pressed lips, not only your eyes, ears, and mouth but also your every finger and your toes, not once but many a time" (trans. John Boswell).

Dozens of gay verse letters are now fairly well known, most notably those by Walafrid Strabo (*ca.* 808–849), Notker Balbulus (*ca.* 840–912), Salamo (*ca.* 860–920) and Waldo, as well as those by the three clerics whose work follows: Marbod, Baudri and Hilary.

Marbod of Rennes (*ca.* 1035-1123) was born at Angers in France, where he was first a student, then a teacher, and finally *ca.* 1067, master at the cathedral school. In 1096 he became bishop of Rennes in Brittany.

---

MARBOD OF RENNES TO A YOUNG LOVER

Horace composed an ode about a certain boy
Who could easily enough have been a pretty girl.
Over his ivory neck flowed hair
Brighter than yellow gold, the kind I have always loved.
His forehead was white as snow, his luminous eyes black as pitch;
His unfledged cheeks full of pleasing sweetness
When they gleamed bright white and red.
His nose was straight, lips blazing, teeth lovely,
Chin shaped after a perfectly proportioned model.
Anyone wondering about the body which lay hidden under his clothes
Would be gratified, for the boy's body matched his face.
The sight of his face, radiant and full of beauty,
Kindled the observer's heart with the torch of love.
But this boy—so beautiful, so extraordinary,
An enticement to anyone catching sight of him—
Nature had molded wild and stern:
He would sooner die than consent to love.
Rough and thankless, like a tiger cub,
He only laughed at the gentlest words of a suitor,
Laughed at attentions doomed to have no effect,
Laughed at a sighing lover's tears,
He mocked those he himself caused to die.
Wicked indeed, this one, and as cruel as wicked,
Who with this vice in his character keeps his body from being his glory.
A handsome face demands a good mind, and a yielding one,
Not puffed up but ready for anything.
The little flower of youth is fleeting and too brief;
It soon withers, falls, and knows not how to revive.
This flesh is now so smooth, so milky, so unblemished,
So good, so handsome, so slippery, so tender.
Yet the time will come when it will become ugly and rough,
When this flesh, dear boyish flesh, will become worthless.
Therefore, while you flower, take up riper practices.
While you are in demand and able, be not slow to yield to an eager lover.
For this you will be prized, not made less of.
These words of my request, most beloved,
Are sent to you alone; do not show them to many others.

# ▼ THIS BOY MY HEART CARESSES ▼

[BAUDRI OF BOURGEUIL & VARIOUS LOVERS]
*Translated from Latin by Thomas Stehling*

Less well known (in English) until fairly recently are hundreds of love poems and letters by abbot Baudri of Bourgeuil (1046–1130), who studied under Marbod (see previous selection) at the cathedral school of Angers. In 1097 Baudri lost out on the bishopric of Orleans to John, nicknamed "Flora," the lover of the archbishop of Tours. But in 1107 he became archbishop of Dol near Mont St. Michel, though he spent most of his time in Normandy.

---

BAUDRI OF BOURGEUIL TO A FRIEND AFTER HIS OWN RETURN

I have owed you a reply for a long time, and now in return
For your many verses I write you these skimpy ones.
You know that responsibility for a long task detained me
And that stormy weather made my journey home difficult.
The journey was so difficult I could not write back to you;
It did not, however, make me forget you.
You were always friend and companion of my labor,
And it seemed to me that you shared in my journey.
Never did my soul forget you, neither while traveling
Nor while taking care of other things.
If I could do nothing else, I would daydream of you;
Many dreams created for me images of you.
Even when I was with counsellors, I was never far from you;
So strongly does love unite you to me.
It was as if some good thing touched us to each other
Or as if the charm of your conversation revived me.
Among my worries was always the weight of a heavier concern,
Heavier, but one I loved more than others:
I longed for my return; I would think about it panting
And wonder whether you could someday be restored to me.
And now I have returned; I visit you again through my letters.
I greet you and rejoice if you are well.
If you are well, so am I. Command of me what I command of you:
Quickly arrange to see me so that you can revive me.
O let us be restored to one another at last
So at least this feeble letter-writing may stop, for a long while.

## BAUDRI OF BOURGEUIL TO A CERTAIN WALTER

May an exchange of letters always unite us while we are apart,
And may this letter now bring me into your presence.
Let my letter now greet you, repeat my greetings,
And repeat them a third time to please you even more.
Lately I received a sweet poem from Walter
Which, since you wrote it, has touched your hand.
I received it with the honor it deserves
And immediately called you to mind with my love.
Now my poem gladly returns your visit,
And I pray that you cherish me with your love.
If you wish to take up lodging with me,
I will divide my heart and breast with you.
I will share with you anything of mine that can be divided;
If you command it, I will share my very soul.
You will be lodged completely within my breast
And will continue as the greatest part of my soul.
Meanwhile I will humbly pray for good fortune
Until conversation revive us.
A different garment—if you haven't considered it—
    would bring that about;
The name of monk would make such conversation endure forever.
So that you could long enjoy our true love,
Another life would change your visits,
Whether the love of God or fear of punishment or both
Commend monastic life to you.
In case you decide to come to us as such,
I have ordered our men to accompany you.
And if rumor has told you that I am about to visit you,
That hangs in doubt—it might be possible or it might not.
For now, therefore, hurry; "Procrastination harms the ready."
Anticipate tomorrow; do what you should today.

---

## BAUDRI OF BOURGEUIL TO A FRIEND TO WHOM HE HAD SENT A LETTER

O would that I had been my own messenger
Or been that letter which your hand softly touched;
And that I had had then the same power to feel I have now,
And that you could not recognize me until I wanted you to.
Then I would have explored your face and spirit as you read,
That is, if I could have restrained myself long enough.
The rest we would have left to nature and the gracious gods.
For God is readier than man to grant indulgence.

## Baudri of Bourgeuil to a Man Who Wanted to Leave Him

You prepare for your return—to revisit your homeland
And see your family—you prepare for your return.
You prepare for your return because duty requires it,
And yet I wish that the gods would turn you from duty.
O either let some event reunite the two of us,
Or let the work which keeps me here keep you too.
By going away you leave me now with nothing but tears,
And like mine your face flows with them.
But still, let what should nourish friends nourish us:
Before long a happy day will follow this sad one.
Let us always hope, and in hope repeat this:
Gracious gods will grant us better times.

---

## Baudri of Bourgeuil to Vitalis

O my song, send greetings to Vitalis,
Say to him what is appropriate and what will please him.
Endear me to him; I want to oblige him,
This boy my heart caresses and embraces.
More than all others, he alone has stayed in my heart;
More than all others, he alone has touched me deep inside.
If you want to know what singles him out—
His manners, nobility, appearance, dignity, honesty,
Shrewd simplicity along with simple shrewdness;
One thing is his beauty and the grace of another.
He is as cunning as a snake, simple as a cooing dove,
And with these two qualities he conquers age.
And more: eloquence has so inspired the boy
That Cicero scarcely measures up to Vitalis.
If he wanted to apprentice to the lyre or train his singing voice
Or both, he would be another Orpheus.
Therefore, Vitalis will nowhere be separated from me,
Indeed till the savage day which takes his spirit away.
And even then, if I can beg favor for me or for him,
Our two souls will become the breath of one spirit.
Meanwhile, let us embrace each other with our bright love,
And may both our souls thereby become brighter.
Let no one deprive us of the name of holy love.

# ▼ BEAUTIFUL BOY, UNPARALLELED BOY ▼

### [HILARY THE ENGLISHMAN & A BOY OF ANGERS & AN ENGLISH BOY]
*Translated from Latin by Thomas Stehling*

Hilary, apparently a cleric, was a pupil of Peter Abelard's in 1125 at the Paraclete Hermitage near Troyes. He may have later lived for a while near Angers, capital of Anglo-French Anjou by the mid twelfth century.

---

HILARY THE ENGLISHMAN TO A BOY OF ANGERS

*[ca. 1130/40?]*

Beautiful boy, unparalleled boy,
I pray look kindly
At this letter sent by your suitor,
See, read, and follow what you have read.

I have thrown myself at your knees,
My own knee bent, my hands joined;
As one of your suitors
I use both tears and prayers.

Face to face with you, I am afraid to speak:
Speech fails me and I am seized with silence.
But now at last in a letter I acknowledge my sickness,
And since I acknowledge it, I deserve health.

Miserable enough, I could almost endure it
As long as I wanted to hide my love.
When I could conceal it no longer,
I finally held up my hands in defeat.

Sick, I demand a doctor,
Stretching out my hands like a beggar.
You alone have the only medicine;
Therefore, save me, your cleric.

Long held in this grim prison,
I have found no one who wished to help me.
Since I cannot be freed with bribery,
I lead a life worse than death.

O my sadness, my ruin,
How I wish you wanted money!
But it is better that you have decided
Such bargaining is vice.

42

Nonetheless, boy, it is certainly stupid
To show such want of feeling,
[*line missing*]
Who acts out of modesty to handsome men.

The heavy theme of chastity
Condemned beautiful Hippolytus;
And Joseph almost came to his death
When he opposed the passion of a queen.

---

HILARY THE ENGLISHMAN TO AN ENGLISH BOY

Handsome boy, flower's beauty,
Shining gem, I want you to know
That your face's beauty
For me was the torch of love.

As soon as I saw you, desire
Struck me, but I despair,
For my Dido restrains me:
I dread her wrath.*

O how happy I would be
If, through a new replacement
As is the custom,
I could slough off this love affair.

I will succeed, I believe,
For I give myself to you as fair game;
I'll be the loot, you the robber—
To such a robber I surrender.

Even the ruler of the gods
Was once a ravisher of boys.
If he were here now, he would sweep away
So handsome a youth to his heavenly bed.

Then at last in the celestial palace
Ready for either duty—
Now in bed, now with the cup—
Two in one you would please Jove.

---

*In the *Aeneid*, Dido is the Carthaginian queen, lover of Aeneas. Their romance delayed Aeneas on his way to found Rome.

# ▼ WANTON SPORT ▼

[A Spanish monk]

*Translated from Latin by Thomas Stehling*

The following two letters come from the *Summa dictaminis per magistrum Dominicanum hispanum*, a late eleventh- or early twelfth-century treatise on composition collected by a Spanish Dominican monk preserved in the library of the cathedral of Beauvais. The manuscript contains a wide range of material, including many letters from the Knights Templars to the Pope defending themselves at the time of their persecution for heresy and sodomy (the Templars were virtually exterminated). These two items are genuine letters gathered for use, curiously, as "models" for how to reject an indecent proposition. They illustrate how important classical mythology was for the sanctioning of gay love, and how important Christian mythology was to its condemnation. They also provide additional support for John Boswell's theory that the word *ludus*—meaning game, sport, playfulness, "messin' about"—was a code word amongst gay men, an early instance of gay slang.

---

A MAN ENCOURAGES A BOY TO INDECENCY

*[ca. 1100]*

Jove's authority has published an edict that whatever gives pleasure should be considered in all situations to be honorable and free of sinfulness. When he went from Juno's slop to Ganymede's embraces, had he seen any shame in the boy's sport [*in ludo pueri*], he would have declined to associate himself with him. Their sport, as they say, was played out in the open. And in its wantonness [*ludi lascivia*] no one feared that the game's equipment would be ruined after the game. But when someone sticks his pole into the recesses of the labyrinth and finds no bottom to it, he fears he will lose everything he has thrust into it. And when it comes out he wants to be cut away from it. Doubtless troubled by this fear, men counted among their number today have sworn off the filth of dirty women and gone over to boys for the games of desire [*voluptatis ludos in pueros*]. That game transformed hyacinth into a flower and made a cupbearer out of the boy Ganymede (Hebe was removed from bearing Jove's wine cup); Cyparissus too was changed into a cypress. If I wanted to develop this theme of boys' honor, I would certainly begin with the delightful matter of their bodies. Since you have examples from such great authorities, you should not blush, my beloved, if I yearn to come to your embraces, if I aspire to become young again with a young man.

THE BOY'S REPLY

Nature's ancient law, which intended the different sexes to be intermingled, is terrified of contamination from your depravity. Nature, which should rejoice over young boys' pliant little hammers, did not set up shop in them; if opposite sexes mingle together in this age, the universal generation of things will be lost. Horrible man, I won't stoop to this filthy vice which displeases God. I am warned by the fall of Sodom and Gomorrah. And besides these, the fall of Orpheus, the harpist's metamorphosis, is warning enough for me. Therefore, I admonish your charity: do not try to arouse me and get me to leave other games for shame's sport [*ludum infamie*]. For if you keep doing this too persistently, you may regret it, when it turns out I make you notorious for your shameful behavior. If you want to follow the advice of someone who gives good counsel, you will swear off this wicked vice from now on, or you will end up just an old plough horse rotting in shit.

# ▼ P L A T O N I C   L O V E ▼

[Marsilio Ficino & Giovanni Cavalcanti]
*Translated from Italian by Rictor Norton*

Marsilio Ficino (1433–99) was the most powerful intellectual figure of the Renaissance, and his reconciliation of Classical with Christian ideals transformed philosophy, literature, and even painting for the following centuries. His teachings at the Platonic Academy inspired artists such as Michelangelo and Raphael (in fact he directed the painting of Botticelli's *Primavera*), while his translation of the complete works of Plato established the humanist basis of modern philosophy. This philosopher, scholar, doctor, musician and priest was not a dour "academic"; he was a vegetarian but enjoyed fine wine; he dressed modestly but enjoyed the visual arts; he preached but also played the lyre and sang lively Orphic hymns.

Ficino's letters were published in Latin in 1492, and in an Italian translation, probably by Ficino himself, in 1495. Those addressed to the young and handsome Giovanni Cavalcanti (1444–1509) are nothing less than ardent love letters. Whether or not the mantle of philosophy ever covered both men in bed is impossible to determine. After Ficino's death there were many rumours to that effect among his contemporaries, and his follower Benedetto Varchi was openly accused of being a sodomite. Ficino in one letter acknowledged that one can have "too great a love for the body, [but] that is not strange either, since the body is the companion and child of the soul. . . . the best hope is to remember that God understands how difficult and dangerous is the province which he has given us to live in and govern."

Giovanni Cavalcanti was the son of a Florentine nobleman, who went on to become a statesman and diplomat. Ficino loved his pupil from a very early age, and they lived together for many years at the villa at Careggio, given to Ficino by Cosimo de' Medici, where he supervised his Platonic Academy. Most of Ficino's works were written with Giovanni at his side, solacing him during periods of black melancholy, and his most important work *De Amore* is dedicated to his protégé. This is a commentary on Plato's *Symposium* within a framework in which members of Ficino's Academy read aloud and analyze the speeches of Plato's characters; Cavalcanti took the speeches of Phaedrus, the archetypal beloved in the canon of *amor Socraticus*, while the adolescent poet of the Academy, Carlo Marsuppini, played the part of the effeminate homosexual apologist Agathon. Ficino's translation (the first complete translation in any language) of Plato's *Phaedrus* (which was discovered in a Byzantine manuscript in 1423) was responsible for creating "platonic love," a term which he coined, which became a turning point in the history of love in the modern western world. He combined Neoplatonic and Christian ideals with images and phrases from Provençal and Tuscan love lyrics, which reestablished that *amor* was both source and goal of *amicitia*. Through the power of the god of love (Jupiter as well as the Christian God, for Ficino was also a student of Hermetic mysticism and astrology), lover and beloved are transformed into one another: he who gives himself unreservedly to his beloved ceases to be himself and becomes his beloved.

In order to foster a loving community of friends, Ficino deliberately elaborated the genre of the love letter as the manifest sign of love, and encouraged members of the Academy to exchange "epistola amatoria" with one another. Within a generation after his death platonic love—originally exclusive to male-to-male relations encouraged by Ficino's cult of friendship—was appropriated by the heterosexual hegemony under the name of "courtly love." Various conventional formulae were developed, which can be seen in the love letters Ficino received from his one-time pupil Lorenzo de' Medici, but no one has ever disputed that the letters to Cavalcanti—whom Ficino addressed as "Giovanni amico mio perfettissimo"—reveal genuine personal sentiment (seen as a "ridiculous attachment" by most classical linguists and historians). Most of the letters cannot be dated, for they were published in a "philosophical" rather than chronological order, but most of those to Cavalcanti were written during 1473–74 when they were separated for a short period.

---

MARSILIO FICINO TO GIOVANNI CAVALCANTI

*May 5, 1473*

Unique Friend,

The hand could not guide the pen, if it were not moved by the soul; similarly Marsilio could not write to a heroic and divine man if he had not first received an invitation from him. But the thing that troubles me most, is that you write to me as a result of your promise, so I cannot attribute your letter to love but to a bargain, whereas I wish for letters of love, and not sent for payment. Or perhaps you really are obligated to me by contract? Since I am bound to you by love, I wish you to be mine, but not by just a contract.

    Farewell
        M. Ficino

---

Unique Friend,

Yesterday at Novola we celebrated the holy day of St. James and St. Christopher—I would have called it a feast rather than just holy if you had been there: but without you there was no feast for me. See how dear you are to your Marsilio, who cares not (if one dare say so) even for heavenly things without you. That is appropriate, for he who has joined together St. James and St. Christopher in a single solemn festival has similarly united Marsilio and Giovanni in life. And the same spirit, or a similar genius, guides us both. I believe that God has ordained that we share one will and the same habits here upon earth, and that in heaven we shall live under the same rule, and with the same marks of happiness.

Farewell, O true companion of my voyage, the sweet reward [*dolce condimento*, literally "sweet sauce"] upon arrival at our destination.

M. Ficino

---

Unique Friend,

The Platonic philosophers, my dearest Giovanni, define true friendship as the stable union of the lives of two men. But I think that this united life is possible only for those men who work together and follow the same path towards a common goal. Basically I think that their friendship will be stable and firm only when the aim they have set for themselves is stable and firm.

Now the business of man is this, to strive for goodness. There are three kinds of goodness for mortal man: virtue, bodily pleasure and wealth [*beni d'animo, beni di corpo, e beni esterni*]. Only virtue is sure and everlasting; the pleasures of the body are mortal, and abundance of riches is transitory. Therefore that perfect union of two lives—which is true friendship—can be achieved only by those who seek not to accumulate wealth or to satisfy sensual pleasures, but those who . . . strive for virtue with equal zeal and who help one another to cultivate their souls. . . .

It is said that the ancient theologians, whose memory we revere, entered into sacred bonds of love and friendship with one another. Among the Persians it is said that Zoroaster, under the divine mystery of religious philosophy, chose Arimaspis as his companion. Hermes Trismegistus among the Egyptians similarly chose Aesculapius. In Thrace Orpheus chose Museus as his companion, and for such a union Pythagorus chose Aglaophemus as his companion. Plato in Athens first chose Dion of Syracuse, and after his death Xenocrates was dearest to him. Thus wise men have always felt it necessary to have God as their guide, with a man as their companion on their journey. Although I am not confident that I can follow in the footsteps of such men in their heavenly journey, there is nevertheless one thing I have acquired in full measure from the study of sacred philosophy, virtue and truth: the joyful company of the man most dear to me. For I think that the friendship of Giovan Cavalcanti and Marsilio Ficino as worthy of being numbered among those I have just named, and I do not doubt but that, with the guidance of God, who has so happily established and quickened our bond, this friendship will provide everything necessary to us for a life of tranquility and our investigation of the divine.

Marsilio Ficino

# ▼ O N L Y   R E T U R N   M Y   L O V E ▼

[DESIDERIUS ERASMUS & SERVATIUS]

*Translated from Latin by Francis Morgan Nichols*

The influential Dutch humanist Desiderius Erasmus (*ca.* 1466–1536) is best known for his satirical masterpiece *In Praise of Folly* (1509). Most biographers pass over his earliest letters which were written during his residence at the Augustinian monastery of Emmaus in Stein, near Gouda in Holland between 1482/3 and 1490. His countryman Servatius Rogerus was one of the youngest members of the Convent, slightly younger than Erasmus. The friends appear to have had limited access to one another, perhaps meeting only in Chapel. Servatius did not return Erasmus's devotion, at least not with the intensity desired by his would-be lover.

The following selections illustrate the passion of unrequited love, though by 1497 Erasmus found other friends who were more responsive, particularly William Hermann of Gouda, nephew of one of his former pupils, "between whom and me there is so intimate a friendship that you may say there is one mind in two bodies." Erasmus went off to conquer the courts of Renaissance Europe, while Servatius stayed on to become prior of the monastery. They never stopped writing to one another, though the correspondence became very cool.

In 1514 Servatius suggested that Erasmus (now aged about forty-eight) return to the monastery to live out his final years, which prompted a remarkable reply in which Erasmus summed up his life—a long list of achievements and books and honours—pointing out that he was desired by the great English universities, by the rulers of countries such as Spain and Italy, and had been received with honour by all the bishops and archbishops in Italy and England—and ended by saying thanks but no thanks.

I interpret his response as a deeply sarcastic revenge upon the man who once rejected him: "whereas you promise your assistance in finding me a place where I may live, as you say, with a good income, I cannot think what that can be, unless you would quarter me upon some convent of nuns, where I should be a servant to women, after having declined to serve Archbishops and Kings. . . . Farewell, my once sweetest companion, and now my reverend Father."

---

ERASMUS TO SERVATIUS ROGERUS

*[all letters 1482 through 1490]*

You are wondering perhaps, my Servatius, what has hindered me so long from writing to you, and it may be you suspect that I have dropped my intention or that my love for you has grown weak. Pray do not think that either of these obstacles has existed. It is not mind that has been wanting, but time; not will, but power. I wish the fates permitted me to enjoy that freedom of life, which Nature conferred; you would find me far more prompt to teach than to receive. But you see yourself in what a hubbub everything is, and I suppose you are not unaware how little leisure is left me among the anxieties of my life. Forgive therefore, I beseech you, our silence, and do for yourself all you can to come out a man. When a calmer state of things shall arise, we will resume our proposed work.

Farewell and love me, as you do.

---

What are you doing, my Servatius? For I suspect you are doing something great, which prevents your fulfilling your promise to me. You pledged yourself to send me a letter very soon; and see what a great interval has passed, and you neither write nor speak. What shall I guess to be the reason? You must certainly be either too busy or too idle; I suspect both, and that you are living in that leisure, than which nothing is more busy. For a state of desire implies leisure, since love is the passion of a vacant mind. You will therefore do what will please me and be of use to yourself, if you interrupt that leisure, and write to me without any delay. For the rest treat me with confidence, and you will be no more afraid of my conscience than your own. Speak with me about everything as with yourself. That will be what I should wish.

Farewell.

---

I should write more frequently to you, very dearest Servatius, if I knew for certain that you would not be more fatigued by reading my letters than I by writing them. And your comfort is so dear to me, that I had rather be tortured by what gives you rest, than fatigue you by what gives me pleasure. But since lovers find nothing so distressing as not to be allowed to meet one another, and we very rarely have that in our power, I cannot forego the opportunity of bidding this letter find its way to you in my stead. How I wish it may be some time our fortune to have no further need of letters, but to be able to meet face to face as often as we please. That joy is denied us; I cannot think of it without tears; but am I therefore to be deprived of all intercourse with you? . . .

So suspicious are those that love I sometimes seem to see, I know not what,—that you do not often think of me, or have even quite forgotten me. My wish would be, if it were possible, that you should care for me as much as I do for you and be as much pained by the love of me, as I am continually tormented by the want of you.

Farewell.

---

When my love for you, my dearest Servatius, has always been and still is so great, that you are dearer to me than these eyes, than this soul, than this self, what is it that has made you so inexorable that you not only do not

Erasmus (1466–1536), Dutch humanist, priest, and greatest scholar of the northern Renaissance. Painting by Hans Holbein.

love, but have no regard at all for him who loves you best? Are you so inhuman as to love those that hate, and hate those that love you? . . .

When you are away, nothing is sweet to me; in your presence I care for
nothing else. When I see you happy, I forget my own sorrows; if anything
painful has occurred to you, so help me Heaven, if my pain is not greater
than your own. Has this crime deserved so much hatred as you show me?
But now, my Servatius, I am not unaware what reply you will make to me.
It is what you often answer. You will say, "What on earth do you require
me to do for you? Do I hate you? What is it you want?" Can you ask this
question? I demand no costly presents. Only let your feeling for me be as
mine is for you, and you will make me happy. . . .

Farewell, my soul, and if there is anything human in you, return the love
of him who loves you.

---

It is no slight pleasure to me, my dearest Servatius, to see you are in good
health; for I cannot but rejoice at the good fortune of one who, though he
will not be my friend, is still most dear to me. But your long forgetfulness
of your loving Erasmus does indeed afflict me. So help me heaven, these
very few days that I have been deprived of your society have seemed to me
longer than a whole year. I have suffered such sorrow, been tormented with
such regrets, that I have sometimes prayed to be relieved from a life that
I hated. The very sadness of my face, the paleness of my complexion, the
dejection of my eyes, might easily show you the grief of my mind, if you
paid any attention to them. . . . There would be some excuse, if I asked
you for anything arduous, anything difficult, anything wrong. What is it
then? Only return my love. What more easy, more agreeable, more worthy of a generous mind? Only love, and I am satisfied. . . .

If, my dearest Servatius, I cannot have that friendship, which of all
things I most desire, I beg at least that the ordinary intercourse between
us may be resumed. If you think that also ought to be denied me, I have
nothing left to live for. Let me soon hear your decision by letter.

Farewell, only hope of my life.

---

Although, my dearest Servatius, I could not read your letter without tears,
still it not only chased away the grief which had afflicted me, but caused
me incredible and unexpected pleasure. Before, I had all day long wept
tears of grief; then the flood which moistened your letter flowed not from
sorrow of heart but from unutterable love of you. Love, believe me, has
its tears, and has its joys. And who, my Servatius, is of so strong a heart
that such a letter would not force him to weep? What sweet words! What
gracious sentiments! Nothing in it but is redolent of affection and of love!
Whenever I read it—and I read it every hour,—I seem to hear the sweet
voice, to see the friendly face of my Servatius. And when I am not allowed
to have any talk with you face to face, this letter is my comfort. . . .

But I entreat you throw me not again into the abyss of sorrows. Believe me, I suffer so much from your anger, that if I hear of it again it will kill me outright. I am of too tender a spirit to be able to bear repeatedly such cruel sport. . . .

Farewell, my hope, and the one solace of my life. Pray let a letter come from you as soon as possible.

# ▼ GRAND PASSIONS ▼

[FEDERICO GONZAGA & PIETRO ARETINO]
*Translated from Italian by Alexandra Trone*

Pietro Aretino (1492-1556) was notorious for a series of erotic sonnets, in one of which he declares himself to have been a sodomite from birth. His patrons included Popes Leo X (Giovanni de' Medici) and Clement VII, King François I and Emperor Charles V, and much of the nobility of Renaissance Europe, many of whom he blackmailed with threats to publish satires against them. He was called "the Divine Aretino" partly because his wit was so devilish. He himself was a bisexual libertine in the larger-than-life mode of Renaissance Italy, so outspoken as to be beyond any counterattacks. Gay themes are scattered throughout his poems and plays, notably in the comedy *Il marescalco*, in which a man is overjoyed to discover that the woman he has been forced to marry is really a page boy in disguise. In a letter to Giovanni de' Medici written in 1524 Aretino encloses a satirical poem saying that due to a sudden aberration he has fallen in love with a female cook and temporarily switched from boys to girls; but he concludes his letter with a reaffirmation of the sodomites' credo: "My Illustrious Lord, be absolutely certain that we all return to the ancient great mother, and if I escape with my honour from this madness, will bugger as much as much and as much for me as for my friends."

Aretino's letters to Giovanni de' Medici, for whom he acted as whoremonger, are well known. Much less well known are the following letters written by Federico Gonzaga (1500-1541), Marchese of Mantua (brother of Cardinal Gonzaga), who not only furthered Aretino's business and literary interests but also acted as his pimp for gay affairs, concerning some delicate negotiations.

---

FEDERICO GONZAGA TO PIETRO ARETINO

*Mantua*
*3rd January, 1528*

Magnificent and most learned maestro Pietro, dearest friend,

I very much regret your pain, torment and afflictions; and although I am very sorry to be deprived of the great pleasure that your virtues are wont to confer on me, the uncommon love I have for you nonetheless induces and constrains me to feel no small compassion for you. Thus I cannot do what you would not gladly consent to; how much I can do to cure your grand passions, wanting very much to be capable of abolishing all your troubles and of consoling you, depends on your intentions. And as for what will occur, I was very happy to command that it be done; and I ordered to be done all that of which you wrote, and if I can do anything else to please

54

and gratify you in relation to your work or to anything else that is close to your heart, I offer myself, etc.

---

The Magnificent, etc.

. . . I have had [a letter] written to Father di Carlo da Fano about your business with Thadeo, such that he should certainly seek you out, and I wanted to send one of my grooms for the purpose of delivering it had it not happened that one of my gentlemen had to go there at that time and I gave the letter to him; I have as yet had no answer, which surprises me, but perhaps it will not be very long in coming.

I would willingly satisfy your wishes regarding this kept boy who you write could remedy your trouble, if I knew who it was, but I do not know this boy of Bianchino's.

I only afterwards received your letter with the verses that you sent me, in which you lament that you have had no replies to your letters. Which, M. Pietro, you may be certain is for no reason other than that as I told you I was sending M. Francesco [Gonzaga] to My Lord [His Holiness Pope Clement VII] charged with speaking very warmly of your business, and waited for this intending to write everything in full; so you must not think that I am angry because I did not write or that you had caused me any trouble, for neither you nor your affairs shall ever weary me nor should you for this reason hesitate in any way to show the same confidence in me, who always wants to please you in every way. Similarly, this is the reason I did not write to [Monsignor the Most Reverend di] Monte earlier, for I was expecting the ambassador to do everything; but fearing that the delay might at times anger you I caused [a letter] to be written in the manner of which I have told you. . . .

There is nothing else to add at present except to thank you very much for the great pleasure that you give me every day with your most learned and delightful new compositions, all of which cannot tell you how dear you are to me, etc.

---

My Magnificent M. Pietro

There is nothing that is more agreeable and more pleasing to me and that gives me greater happiness than to have the good opinion of virtuous and learned persons; but it was most agreeable to have understood, from your letters which I have lately received, the memories you have of me and the regard you have for me, although you do this for a good friend. And truly I love you so much that I love you more than the others, and the fruits of your splendid intellect have so impressed you upon my memory that there is nothing that will suffice ever at any time to efface them from it. I have not forgotten to have [a letter] written on your behalf to the Most Reverend Monsignor my brother, and I ordered it to be written well. If I have thus been able to satisfy you in your desire for Bianchino I will also have done it gladly. But having understood his reluctance when Roberto spoke to him on your behalf, and as it seemed to me that I was unable to do justice to the work that I wanted to do in this regard, I did not think it fitting to plead with him or otherwise to exhort him, nor to have him exhorted in my name and I failed to think that I should command him, IT NOT BEING EITHER JUST OR HONEST TO COMMAND HIM IN THIS CASE. But pardon me if in this case I have not pleased you; if I can please you in any other way, as you know very well I am only too glad to do it and you will always find me ready. . . .

# ▼ CAPTIVE AND SLAVE CONFESSED ▼

[MICHELANGELO & TOMMASO CAVALIERI & FEBO DI POGGIO]
*Translated from Italian by John Addington Symonds*

Michelangelo (1475–1564) was a heroic masculinist in the great age of machismo. He regularly employed male models even for his female figures, including the famous statue of *Night* on the Medici Tombs, a figure whose breasts are obviously superimposed on a male torso. The gallery of nude youths, or *ignudi* in the Sistine Chapel outraged several pontiffs because of their wholly non-Christian associations; the recent controversial restoration of the Chapel makes these homoerotic images stand out even more clearly.

In 1623 Michelangelo's grandnephew published a collection of his poetry in which all the masculine pronouns were changed to feminine pronouns, which remained the standard edition for nearly two hundred and fifty years. John Addington Symonds's studies in the Buonarroti family archives in Florence brought this censorship to light for the first time in 1892, but it is only very recently that Michelangelo's homosexuality has become a generally accepted fact.

His earliest lovers included the handsome model Gherardo Perini who came to work for him around 1520, and, during the 1530s, the younger assistant Febo di Poggio, whom he called "that little blackmailer" because Febo steadily demanded money, clothes and love-gifts from him. In 1532 Michelangelo began wooing the Roman nobleman Tommaso Cavalieri, and became "An armed Knight's [Cavalieri's] captive and slave confessed." His love for Tommaso might have been wholly sublimated, but his love-gifts to his patron included drawings of the rape of Ganymede.

Michelangelo's contemporaries Leonardo da Vinci, Sandro Botticelli, Benvenuto Cellini and Giovanni Antonio Bazzi (Il Sodoma) were publicly charged with sodomy, and Michelangelo, like them, was offered "services" by the *ragazzi* who worked as apprentices in the art studios. But a powerful strain of neoplatonic puritanism in his complex personality, suggests that the conflict between desire and restraint was resolved more in his sculpture than in his life. "What from thee I long for and learn to know deep within me can scarcely be understood by the minds of men."

---

MICHELANGELO TO TOMMASO CAVALIERI

*January 1, 1533*

Without due consideration, Messer Tomao, my very dear lord, I was moved to write to your lordship, not by way of answer to any letter received from you, but being myself the first to make advances, as though I felt bound to cross a little stream with dry feet, or a ford made manifest by paucity of water. But now that I have left the shore, instead of the trifling water I expected, the ocean with its towering waves appears before me, so that, if it were possible, in order to avoid drowning, I would gladly retrace my steps to the dry land whence I started. Still, as I am here, I will e'en make of my heart a rock, and proceed further; and if I shall not display the art of sailing on the sea of your powerful genius, that genius itself will excuse me, nor will be disdainful of my inferiority in parts, nor desire from me that which I do not possess, inasmuch as he who is unique in all things can have peers in none. Therefore your lordship, the light of our century without paragon upon this world, is unable to be satisfied with the productions of other men, having no match or equal to yourself. And if, peradventure, something of mine, such as I hope and promise to perform, give pleasure to your mind, I shall esteem it more fortunate than excellent; and should I ever be sure of pleasing your lordship, as is said, in any particular, I will devote the present time and all my future to your service; indeed, it will grieve me much that I cannot regain the past, in order to devote a longer space to you than the future only will allow, seeing I am now too old. I have no more to say. Read the heart, and not the letter, because "the pen toils after man's good-will in vain."

I have to make excuses for expressing in my first letter a marvellous astonishment at your rare genius; and thus I do so, having recognised the error I was in; for it is much the same to wonder at God's working miracles as to wonder at Rome producing divine men. Of this the universe confirms us in our faith.

*P.S.:* It would be permissible to give the name of the things a man presents, to him who receives them; but proper sense of what is fitting prevents it being done in this letter.

---

MICHELANGELO TO TOMMASO CAVALIERI

*July 28, 1533*

My dear Lord,

—Had I not believed that I had made you certain of the very great, nay, measureless love I bear you, it would not have seemed strange to me nor have roused astonishment to observe the great uneasiness you show in your last letter, lest, through my not having written, I should have forgotten you. Still it is nothing new or marvellous when so many other things go counter, that this also should be topsy-turvy. For what your lordship says to me, I could say to yourself: nevertheless, you do this perhaps to try me, or to light a new and stronger flame, if that indeed were possible: but be it as it will: I know well that, at this hour, I could as easily forget your name as the food by which I live; nay, it were easier to forget the food, which only nourishes my body miserably, than your name, which nourishes both body and soul, filling the one and the other with such sweetness that neither weariness nor fear of death is felt by me while memory preserves you to my mind. Think, if the eyes could also enjoy their portion, in what condition I should find myself.

---

TOMMASO CAVALIERI TO MICHELANGELO

*Summer, 1533*

I have received from you a letter, which is the more acceptable because it was so wholly unexpected. I say unexpected, because I hold myself unworthy of such condescension in a man of your eminence. With regard to what Pierantonio spoke to you in my praise, and those things of mine which you have seen, and which you say have aroused in you no small affection for me, I answer that they were insufficient to impel a man of such transcendent genius, without a second, not to speak of a peer, upon this earth, to address a youth who was born but yesterday, and therefore is as ignorant as it is possible to be. At the same time I cannot call you a liar. I rather think then, nay, am certain, that the love you bear me is due to this, that you being a man most excellent in art, nay, art itself, are forced to love those who follow it and love it, among whom am I; and in this, according to my capacity, I yield to few. I promise you truly that you shall receive from me for your kindness affection equal, and perhaps greater, in exchange; for I never loved a man more than I do you, nor desired a friendship more than I do yours. About this, though my judgment may fail in other things, it is unerring . . .

Your most affectionate servant.

Thomao Cavalieri

---

MICHELANGELO TO FEBO DI POGGIO

*December, 1533*

Febo,

—Albeit you bear the greatest hatred toward my person—I know not why—I scarcely believe, because of the love I cherish for you, but probably through the words of others, to which you ought to give no credence, having proved me—yet I cannot do otherwise than write to you this letter. I am leaving Florence tomorrow, and am going to Pescia to meet the Cardinal di Cesis and Messer Baldassare. I shall journey with them to Pisa, and thence to Rome, and I shall never return again to Florence. I wish you to understand that, so long as I live, wherever I may be, I shall always remain at your service with loyalty and love, in a measure unequalled by any other friend whom you may have upon this world.

I pray God to open your eyes from some other quarter, in order that you may come to comprehend that he who desires your good more than his own welfare, is able to love, not to hate like an enemy.

Naught comforts you, I see, unless I die:
    Earth weeps, the heavens for me are moved to woe;
    You feel of grief the less, the more grieve I.
O sun that warms the world where'er you go,
    O Febo, light eterne for mortal eyes!
    Why dark to me alone, elsewhere not so?

---

FEBO DI POGGIO TO MICHELANGELO

*Florence*
*January 4, 1534*

Magnificent M. Michelangelo, to be honoured as a father,

—I came back yesterday from Pisa, whither I had gone to see my father. Immediately upon my arrival, that friend of yours at the bank put a letter from you into my hands, which I received with the greatest pleasure, having heard of your well-being. God be praised, I may say the same about myself. Afterwards I learned what you say about my being angry with you. You know well I could not be angry with you, since I regard you in the place of a father. Besides, your conduct toward me has not been of the sort to cause in me any such effect. That evening when you left Florence, in the morning I could not get away from M. Vincenzo, though I had the greatest desire to speak with you. Next morning I came to your house, and you were already gone, and great was my disappointment at your leaving Florence without my seeing you.

I am here in Florence; and when you left, you told me that if I wanted anything, I might ask it of that friend of yours; and now that M. Vincenzo is away, I am in want of money, both to clothe myself, and also to go to the Monte, to see those people fighting, for M. Vincenzo is there. Accordingly, I went to visit that friend at the bank, and he told me that he had no commission whatsoever from you; but that a messenger was starting tonight for Rome, and that an answer could come back within five days. So then, if you give him orders, he will not fail. I beseech you, then, to provide and assist me with any sum you think fit, and do not fail to answer.

I will not write more, except that with all my heart and power I recommend myself to you, praying God to keep you from harm.

    —Yours in the place of a son,
      Febo di Poggio

# ▼ FULL OF ANXIOUS FEAR ▼

[HUBERT LANGUET & SIR PHILIP SIDNEY]

*Languet to Sidney December 24, 1573 translated from Latin*
*by Charles Samuel Levy*
*All others translated from Latin by Steuart A. Pears*

The French diplomat and professor of law Hubert Languet (1518–81) in 1572 found that his life was in danger because of his support of the Huguenots, killed in the Massacre of Saint Bartholomew. He and Sir Philip Sidney (1554–86), fresh from Oxford on his tour of study, escaped France together, crossing the Rhine into Germany, and lived together in Frankfurt for a time. They then travelled together to Vienna, where Languet represented his patron Augustus, Elector of Saxony, at the Imperial court. Sidney remained there until November the following year, when he went to Venice with a certain Count Hannau.

This separation was the beginning of many years' correspondence (conducted in Latin) between the fifty-five-year-old diplomat and the nineteen-year-old courtier. Both men quote Cicero's *De Amicitia*, especially his dictum that "Friendship is the salt and spice of life." Sidney is more aloof, Languet more obviously infatuated: "my affection for you has somehow come to bewitch my soul." Languet would have liked to have set up house with Sidney, a situation precluded by Sidney's brilliant lineage and fortune: "But if I came upon a poor youth who resembled you in behaviour and character, I would certainly adopt him as my son and make him heir to my belongings, and I would not be at all concerned about his parentage."

Languet sent love poems to Sidney, and commissioned Veronese to paint a portrait of him, which has not been traced. It is fortunate that Languet died before Sidney, and was spared the grief over his beloved being tragically killed in the battle of Zutphen, when English poets poured forth the national grief in numerous epitaphs and elegies calling Sidney "the wonder of the age."

---

HUBERT LANGUET TO SIR PHILIP SIDNEY

*Vienna*
*November 19, 1573*

What care and anxiety, nay what fear had you spared me, if you had written to me only once or twice on your journey! I did not desire a laboured letter, only a word or two, as, "this day we arrived here in safety," or the like. You remember how earnestly I begged this of you when you were leaving me. But you will say, "it matters little to you whether you hear or not: when I arrive at Padua or Venice, then I will write to you." You might have done both, and if you had, I should have thought myself greatly obliged

61

by you. However, I would rather suppose that you have met no one to whom you could trust a letter for me, than either that you disregard your promises, or that your affection for me has begun to fail. That it was strong when you left me, I knew by the tears which hardly suffered you to say farewell. I forgive you this crime, and every other which you shall henceforth commit against me, if you will only be careful not to let your thirst for learning and acquiring information, lead you into danger. . . .

---

SIR PHILIP SIDNEY TO HUBERT LANGUET

*Venice*
*December 5, 1573*

Nay, but I do not say, "it matters little to you whether you hear or not," for I am well aware how that "love is full of anxious fear." But this I will say, and say with truth, that I met literally no one who was going towards Venice [i.e., to carry a letter]. But inasmuch as you tacitly charge me with some slackening of the affection with which I have regarded and ever shall regard you and all your noble qualities, while I acknowledge your kindness, I beg of you seriously and earnestly, that whatever be the distance which separates us, you will be satisfied of this, that I am not so possessed either with the folly of a boy, or the inconstancy of a woman, or the ingratitude of a brute, as not to seek eagerly the friendship of such a man, and hold it fast when I have gained it, and be thankful for it as long as I have it. I would I were sufficiently at home in Latin, or you in English; you should see what a scene I would make of these suspicions of yours. . . .

    Philip Sidney

---

LANGUET TO SIDNEY

*Vienna*
*December 4, 1573*

I was meditating a very sharp remonstrance when the letter came in, which you wrote on your arrival at Venice: that at once dispersed the cloud from my mind, and made me happy indeed, for I learned from it that you had reached your journey's end in safety, and had not forgotten me. I was delighted too with your promise not to lose any opportunity of writing to me. See that you fulfil it. . . .

    I beg you will not show any one the foolish letters I send to you. I write without selection all that my mind in its changing moods suggests to me, and it is enough for me if I succeed in making you believe that you are very dear to me. I hope you will tell me what you think of the persons to whom I gave you letters.

    —Farewell.

LANGUET TO SIDNEY

*December 24, 1573*

I was afraid that you wished to punish by silence the wrong you thought had been done to you. And you could hardly have inflicted a more severe punishment upon me than this. My very dear son (for I am now pleased to call you by that name), thus far I have coveted no riches and have taken no trouble to acquire any besides the friendship of those in whom I have seen the eager desire for virtue flourishing; and I have not failed in this, for I have formed very rewarding and gratifying friendships with more than a few persons. But my affection for you has entered my heart far more deeply than any I have ever felt for anyone else, and it has so wholly taken possession there that it tries to rule alone, and, as it were, to practice tyranny. . . .

---

SIDNEY TO LANGUET

*Padua*
*January 15, 1574*

To the most excellent and illustrious Hubert Languet,
Always my much esteemed friend, at Vienna.

Behold at last my letter from Padua! not that you are to expect any greater eloquence than is usually to be found in my epistles, but that you may know I have arrived here as I purposed, and in safety; . . . Here I am then, and I have already visited his excellency the Count, and the Baron Slavata your worthy young friends, and while I enjoy their acquaintance with the greatest pleasure to myself, I am perpetually reminded of your surpassing love of me, which you show in taking so much care not only for me, but for all my concerns and conveniences, and that without any deserving on my part. But you are not a man to be thanked for such a thing; for you are even now meditating greater kindness still, and, in truth, as far as I am concerned, much as I am indebted to you, I am only too willing to owe you more. But enough of this.

Your last letter, written on the 1st of January, reached me on the 13th. It brought me no news, for it was filled with instances of your affection, ever pleasant indeed, but long since known and proved, a kind of letter which is above all others delightful and acceptable to me, for while I read, I fancy that I have the very Hubert himself before my eyes and in my hands. . . .

The volumes of Cicero I will read diligently. There are some things also which I wish to learn of the Greeks, which hitherto I have but skimmed on the surface. But the chief object of my life, next to the everlasting blessedness of heaven, will always be the enjoyment of true friendship, and there you shall have the chiefest place.

    —Farewell, yours with all my heart,
       Philip Sidney

James I of England (and VI of Scotland) (1566–1625), son of the ever-famous Mary Queen of Scots. When he succeeded his cousin Elizabeth I on the English throne in 1603, one of his new subjects remarked wittily: ''Elizabeth was King; now James is Queen.'' Painting by John de Critz.

# ▼ THY DEAR DAD AND HUSBAND ▼

[KING JAMES I & VI & GEORGE VILLIERS]

King James (VI of Scotland, I of England) (1566–1625) was introduced to twenty-one-year-old George Villiers, son of an untitled and impoverished squire, in the summer of 1614. "Steenie," James's nickname for Villiers, is apparently derived from the biblical description of St. Stephen having "the face of an angel," for Villiers according to all contemporary accounts (and surviving paintings) was "the handsomest-bodied man in England." In November that year he was appointed the royal cupbearer, in April the following year he was knighted and by August 1615 he was James's bed-partner; the men spent a few days together at Farnham Castle that month, which Buckingham recalled in a letter to James years later, wondering "whether you loved me now . . . better than at the time which I shall never forget at Farnham, where the bed's head could not be found between the master and his dog."

His spectacular rise continued: he was created Master of the Horse and Knight of the Garter and given a Viscountcy in 1616, and made the Earl of Buckingham in 1617. In response to the Privy Council's remonstrations against such blatant favoritism, James defended himself: "I, James, am neither a god nor an angel, but a man like any other. Therefore I act like a man and confess to loving those dear to me more than other men. You may be sure that I love the Earl of Buckingham more than anyone else, and more than you who are here assembled. I wish to speak in my own behalf and not to have it thought to be a defect, for Jesus Christ did the same, and therefore I cannot be blamed. Christ had his son John, and I have my George."

Villiers became a Marquess in 1618, Lord High Admiral in 1619, and finally the Duke of Buckingham in 1623. In that year Buckingham wrote to James from Madrid, beginning "Dere Dad and Gossope" (gossip, from godparent, meaning chum) and closing "Your most humble slave and servant and doge [dog] Steenie." The two men were notorious for their kissing and caressing of one another in public, and their heedless contempt for public opinion contributed to the civil crisis enveloping the nation.

James suspended Parliament in 1621 and more or less lost control of the government. Their personal friend the Lord High Chancellor Sir Francis Bacon, well known for sleeping with his Welsh serving boys, in a politically motivated trial was convicted of accepting bribes, and Villiers was assassinated in 1628 three years after James's death. James had arranged Villiers's marriage to Lady Katherine Manners, daughter to the Earl of Rutland, on May 16, 1620, which of course was necessary for dynastic purposes. But the very day after his wedding night he found a letter from

James waiting for him, in which the king clearly staked his continuing claim upon his beloved:

---

JAMES I TO GEORGE VILLIERS, MARQUESS OF BUCKINGHAM

*[17 May 1620]*

My only sweet and dear child,

Thy dear dad sends thee his blessing this morning and also to his daughter. The Lord of Heaven send you a sweet and blithe wakening, all kind of comfort in your sanctified bed, and bless the fruits thereof that I may have sweet bedchamber boys to play me with, and this is my daily prayer, sweet heart. When thou risest, keep thee from importunity of people that may trouble thy mind, that at meeting I may see thy white teeth shine upon me, and so bear me comfortable company in my journey. And so God bless thee, hoping thou wilt not forget to read over again my former letter.

James R.

---

*[December 1622?]*

My only sweet and dear child,

I am now so miserable a coward, as I do nothing but weep and mourn; for I protest to God I rode this afternoon a great way in the park without speaking to anybody and the tears trickling down my cheeks, as now they do that I can scarcely see to write. But alas, what shall I do at our parting? The only small comfort I can have will be to pry in thy defects with the eye of an enemy, and of every mote to make a mountain, and so harden my heart against thy absence. But this little malice is like jealousy, proceeding from a sweet root; but in one point it overcometh it, for as it proceeds from love so it cannot but end in love. Sweet heart, be earnest with Kate to come and meet thee at Newhall [Buckingham's mansion in Essex] within eight or ten days after this. Cast thee to be here tomorrow, as near about two in the afternoon as thou canst, and come galloping hither. Remember thy picture and suffer none of the Council to come here [probably Theobalds, where he ordered on December 16 that none of the Lords were to trouble themselves to come]. For God's sake write not a word again and let no creature see this letter. The Lord of heaven and earth to bless thee, and my sweet daughter, and my sweet little grandchild, and all thy blessed family, and send thee a happy return, both now and thou knowest when, to thy dear dad and Christian gossip.

James R.

---

*Windsor*
*18 April [1623]*

My sweet Steenie gossip,

The bearer hereof had so great a longing to see you as I was forced to give him leave. . . .

For news, your bay Spanish mare with the black mane and tail hath an exceeding fair and fine horse-foal of ten days old, just of her own colour but that he hath the far foot white; and there is another of them ready to foal. God send my sweet baby the like luck with his Spanish breed before this time twelve-month. Thus hoping that ye will give a good advice to the bearer hereof to lead a good life in times coming, I pray the Lord send my sweet Steenie gossip a happy and comfortable return in the arms of his dear dad.

     James R.

---

*[December 1623?]*

My only sweet and dear child,

    Notwithstanding of your desiring me not to write yesterday, yet had I written in the evening if, at my coming out of the park, such a drowsiness had not come upon me as I was forced to set and sleep in my chair half an hour. And yet I cannot content myself without sending you this present, praying God that I may have a joyful and comfortable meeting with you and that we may make at this Christmas a new marriage ever to be kept hereafter; for, God so love me, as I desire only to live in this world for your sake, and that I had rather live banished in any part of the earth with you than live a sorrowful widow's life without you. And so God bless you, my sweet child and wife, and grant that ye may ever be a comfort to your dear dad and husband.

     James R.

# ▼ HEART TROUSER FLY ▼

[FRANCISCO CORREA NETTO & MANOEL VIEGAS]

*Translated from Portuguese by Luiz Mott and Aroldo Assunçao*

There was a well-established gay subculture in Lisbon and the larger cities of Portugal during the seventeenth century, in which effeminate gay men (*fanchonos*) kept assignations in special rooming houses, and danced together in public squares during festivals wearing women's clothes (*danca dos fanchonos*). Some gay men adopted nicknames such as "Rafael Fanchono," "Miss Turk," and "Miss Galicia."

The following letters were sent by "Francisquinha": Francisco Correa Netto, the sacristan of the Cathedral of Silves in southern Portugal, to Manoel Viegas, a guitarist and maker of musical instruments, who also served at the Cathedral. Viegas turned them over to the Vicar of Silves on March 29, 1664, who sent them to the Inquisition of Evora and denounced Correa for "sodomy."

Correa destroyed Viegas's letters to him, so we know only half the story. It seems that there was a courtship followed by jealousy, and Viegas may have betrayed his one-time lover at the instigation of the Vicar of Silves who had a grudge against Correa. Several people claimed that Correa was a notorious sodomite, but the Inquisition decided not to arrest or put him on trial for *neffandum peccatum* because they required proof of anal penetration and emission, which could not be obtained. The phrase *coração da barguilha*, which literally means "heart trouser fly," is a poetic euphemism for *caralho*, "cock." The archives of the Portuguese Inquisition contain other gay love letters, as well as these, awaiting translation.

---

FRANCISCO CORREA NETTO TO MANOEL VIEGAS

*[ca. March 1664]*

Senhor Manoel Viegas:

If men sleep with me, it is not to find a pussy. They place the cock between my legs, and there they have their way. I do not achieve it. If Your Grace [*Vossa Merce*] would wish the same, dispose of me, I am at your service, to whom I swear unto death, to offer what is needed, and the losses are mine.

Francisco Correa Netto

---

Tender gift to me and longing of my senses, the tranquillity of my thoughts about you is the proof of how much I desire and love you!

Now I shall not have peace nor hope of having you, because I see that not even with the best argument will my pledge serve you, heart wounded to death, heart never to be released from my affection for you.

My love and bounty: my feelings cannot rest an hour, either by day or night, without bringing to mind your companionship and your sweet words that are continually reflected in my memory.

Mirror of my sight and joy, if I have any right to you, bring peace to my heart and confirm the news I received this evening, that you were betrothed to a niece of Francisco Luiz last Monday. I would have said that by Easter you would be betrothed to me. You implied that often, and you gave your word on it. But do as you please: in spite of this I shall not stop doing what I can to be at your service. And remembering your arms and the kiss you gave me, that is what torments me most! And you know this subject well, in that heart trouser fly, it was that which desired me, with its craving to fly up. There was no Lent for that heart trouser fly, when I touched it with my fingers, and instantly it sprang up! And you, so evil, who did not want to do what comes so naturally!

Goodbye, my darling, my happiness, my true love!

My idea is that, even though you may be married, you do not have to break your promise to be the betrothed of your devoted Francisquinha. It seems to me you told Manoel da Costa that if I complied with your whims, even then you would not come to me, because you do not care, and it was all sham.

Here is paper to answer: Now you have no excuse not to write for lack of paper.

---

Manual [*sic*] Viegas:

Our Lord allow you to live as many happy years as you desire!

I was not so black-hearted that you should say publicly that I should not go to your house. If you wished to say that, you should write or tell me privately. However, not even for this affront will I become your enemy; and if you need something, advise me in writing.

I sent your clothes to be washed. Go to the house of Matias Araujo to order some shoes. And I will give you everything I have promised. And for the fiancee, thirty *alqueires* [ = 5 sacks, or 300 kilos] of wheat. As for my letters, tear them up, as I will destroy yours. Make me a guitar [*viola*] by your own hand, for which I will pay you. Heaven guard you all the years you desire, friend.

Francisco Correa Netto

---

False Traitor!

False deluded love: with what words can I express this sentiment? After Your Grace [*Vossa Merce*] left, news came to me that Your Grace intended to possess Maria Nunes, who does not conceal this from anyone, not even from me, saying that Your Grace gave her some beads and pin money, saying that you desired her much. And en route to the shoemaker's to repair some shoes, we talked about biscuits, and she said that Your Grace gave her some, and she said there were none so perfect. So it seems that Your

Grace has a great love for her, because she says that you come from your lovers, bringing her their gifts.

My destiny is wretched. I was confident until this, thinking that I possessed Your Grace. Better that I were put to death a thousand times than to live with something that I remember that I did to some person some time ago. But after all, if she goes around telling everyone that she saw what you gave me on my finger, my heart will burst within my chest, and I had to excuse this by saying that I had purchased the ring from Your Grace. *Vossa Merce* has left my heart besieged, with my sentiments manifest in my tears; and when I see the person I desire, I am sad and jealous, and so Your Grace grows happier. As the proverb says, "One remembers where the honey was" [*O mel faz por onde o lembrem*], and this is how I must be with Your Grace, inasmuch as Your Grace pays so little attention. Your Grace has so many, and one will be the worse for it, and I am that one, because I had such love for Your Grace, that just seeing you made me so happy that I could not eat. It is certain that "whoever loves more strongly deserves least" [*quem mais ama, menos merece*]. I will leave my heart afar, and I will look at the ground whenever I pass Your Grace.

Heaven protect Your Grace for the sake of your two lovers!

---

False and Flatterer:

If I could mock, scoffing at someone in love! But in the end, "whoever loves more strongly deserves least." For me there were only tears, tears caused by you and by so many skirts. Now she has what I desired. So often I have sent you word not to pay attention to me, but why do you dine with your women friends rather than with me, and then why do you send me notes that are lies? Those women were jealous of me because I wore someone else's ring. They said that I should return it to its owner. And here it is. I don't want anything of yours in my possession. Do the same with what you have of mine, and that will give me much pleasure. Do not ever speak to me or look at me again. I return the ring to encourage the hilarity of your lady friends.

# ▼ THE FLOATING WORLD ▼

[MASHIDA TOYONOSHIN & MORIWAKI GONKURŌ]
*Translated from Japanese by Paul Gordon Schalow*

Homosexuality was a fully integrated and non-stigmatized part of seventeenth-century Japanese culture, flourishing primarily within the Buddhist priestly tradition, among samurai (warrior) classes and in kabuki theater, where handsome young men dressed as boys or women (*onnagata*) onstage and functioned as courtesans offstage.

Gay love letters are often referred to in Japanese literature, notably in the collection of forty stories in *The Great Mirror of Male Love* (*Nanshoku ōkagami*) (1687) written by Ihara Saikaku (1642–93) describing (and advocating) love between adult men and youths. The onnagata Matsushima Han'ya, who retired from the stage in 1686, age twenty, was famous for the elegant style of his love letters to other boys. Boys could not resist the love letters sent to them by the master of martial arts Maruo Kan'emon. Dekijima Kozarashi, a popular boy actor in the 1670s, received hundreds of love letters from the men who watched him perform.

In the Great Temple in Naniwa where kabuki actors worshipped their patron saint Aizen Myō-ō, they would hang love letters on a sacred cherry tree, sometimes sealed, sometimes for all to read, praying to be united with the men they loved. In one of Saikaku's stories a wealthy monk's hermitage is covered by wallpaper which upon closer inspection turns out to be hundreds of gay love letters composed by kabuki boy actors and left as gifts as they departed his shelter. In addition to love letters, men would often prove their love for one another by slashing their arms or cutting their thighs or, quite common, slicing off the tip of their thumb and tossing it on the stage as if it were a bouquet of flowers. This kind of ritualized sadomasochism culminates in *seppuku* or ritual suicide at the slightest whisper of dishonor (notably in the suicide of Yukio Mishima in 1970, which shocked the West). The actor of boys' roles Togawa Hayanojō killed himself in 1686 not because he had a male lover—to whom he wrote a moving farewell letter—but because he could not pay for the expensive clothes required by his profession.

Similarly amongst the samurai homosexuality in itself was never a cause for shame. The following letter is reproduced in Saikaku's "Love Letter Sent in a Sea Bass," a story based upon a nonfictional account of a real incident involving a young samurai named Mashida Toyonoshin which took place in Bizen Province in 1667. Despite the semi-fictionalized context, it is clear that Saikaku is working from written sources, and the letter itself is essentially a genuine letter (the poem with which it concludes slightly modifies a poem written and published by Mashida Toyonoshin). Thirteen-year-old Toyonoshin (named "Jinnosuke" in the story), one of the most beautiful boys in Izumo Province, swears a vow of love with the twenty-eight-year-old samurai Moriwaki Gonkuro. But boys in the lord's personal service are forbidden to establish sexual relationships with outsiders not in the same service. The older samurai secretly sends love letters to the boy hidden in the mouth of a sea bass.

They first make love when Toyonoshin is fourteen years old, and they continue their secret meetings until his sixteenth year, when a minor retainer in the same lord's service, the guard Hanzawa Ihei, begins courting him. Toyonoshin refuses to answer the guard's love letters, and the guard challenges him to a fight to the death. Toyonoshin asks Gonkuro for help, but Gonkuro says he should find some way of placating Ihei and avoiding violence. Toyonoshin perceives this as cowardice, and decides to meet the challenge alone, but first he expresses his resentment in a letter to Gonkuro, reproduced below. But at the last minute Gonkuro proves his love by joining Toyonoshin in the duel, and they kill or wound most of Ihei's cohorts. They prepare to commit ritual suicide because they have killed the lord's retainers, but the lord forgives them because of their valor, and has the rest of Ihei's party rounded up and killed. Everyone flocks to see Toyonoshin's wondrous sword, and the love of Toyonoshin and Gonkuro becomes a model for all aspiring young samurai: "all yearned to sacrifice their lives for the sake of male love."

For more on this world read *Partings at Dawn: An Anthology of Japanese Gay Literature*, ed. by Stephen Miller, Gay Sunshine Press, 1996.

---

MASHIDA TOYONOSHIN TO MORIWAKI GONKURŌ

*[Bizen Province]*
*Kambun 7 [1667], third month, 26th day*

From the very beginning, when I first said, "this body is no longer my own," I understood that I would have to die if the nature of our relationship were ever revealed. Now that this situation has come about I feel no particular sorrow. Tonight, I shall fight to the finish at a mountain temple.

In view of our years of intimacy, I am deeply hurt that you should hesitate to die with me. Lest it prove to be a barrier to my salvation in the next life, I decided to include in this final testament all of the grudges against you that have accumulated in me since we first met.

First: I made my way at night to your distant residence a total of 327 times over the past three years. Not once did I fail to encounter trouble of some kind. To avoid detection by patrols making their nightly rounds, I disguised myself as a servant and hid my face behind my sleeve, or hobbled along with a cane and lantern dressed like a priest. No one knows the lengths I went to in order to meet you!

Remember last year, the twentieth day of the eleventh month? I was gravely ill (with worry about you, I am sure), and my mother stayed at my bedside all evening. I was convinced that I would not see morning, but the thought of dying without one last meeting with you was unbearable. I cursed the light of the rising moon and made my way in disarray to your door. Surely you recognized my footsteps, but my only welcome was to have you extinguish the lamp and hush your conversation. How cruel you were to me! I would love to know who your companion was that night.

Next: Last spring, I casually wrote the poem "My sleeves rot, soaked with tears of jealous rage, and with them, alas! rots my good reputation, ruined for the sake of love" on the back of a fan painted by Kano no Uneme in the pattern of a "riot of flowers." You took it and said, "The cool breeze from this fan will help me bear the flames of our love this summer." How happy you made me! But shortly it came to my attention that you gave the fan to your attendant Kichisuke with a note across the poem that said, "This calligraphy is terrible."

Again, when I asked you for your favorite lark as a gift (the one you got from the birdcatcher Jūbei), you refused and gave it to Kitamura Shōhachi instead. He is, of course, the most handsome boy in the household. My jealousy has not abated yet.

Next: On the eleventh day of the fourth month past, the lord ordered all of his young attendants from the inner chamber to practice horseback riding. Setsubara Tarōzaemon was kind enough to tell me that the back of my skirt was soiled and brushed it off for me. You were standing directly behind me, but did not tell me about it. In fact, I saw you exchange amused glances with Kozawa Kurōjirō. After our years of love together such a thing should never happen.

Next: On the eighteenth of the fifth month, you were angry with me for talking well into the night with Ogasawara Han'ya. As I explained to you that night, he came for recitation practice along with Ogaki Magosaburō and Matsuhara Tomoya. There were no other visitors. Han'ya is still a mere child, Magosaburō is my age, and Tomoya you know. There should be no problem with our getting together to practice every night if we wish, yet you are still full of suspicions. I find your frequent insinuating remarks very upsetting. By the gods of Japan, I swear that I still cannot forget my anger at your distrust.

Next: Since the time when we first became lovers, you never once saw me to my house when we bid each other farewell in the morning. In fact, in all these years, you only twice saw me as far as the bridge in front of Uneme's. If you love someone, you should be willing to see him safely home through wilds filled with wolves and tigers.

Though I hold this and that grudge against you, the fact that I cannot bring myself to stop loving you must be the work of some strange fate. To weep is my only comfort. For the sake of our friendship up to now, I ask you to pray, even if but once, for my rebirth in paradise. How strange to think that the impermanence of this world should also affect me.

[He closed the letter with a poem:]

> "While yet in full bloom,
> it is buffeted by an unexpected gale;
> the morning glory
> falls with the dew,
> ere evening draws nigh."

These are the thoughts I wanted to leave with you. Evening, my last, is drawing nigh, so I shall bid farewell.

# ▼ I BRING YOU MY HEART ▼

[A BUDDHIST PRIEST & OKAJIMA UNEME]

## The Monk from Kyoto Who Hated Cherry Blossoms*
### Ihara Saikaku
### Translated from Japanese by Paul Gordon Schalow

Homosexual love is said to have been "imported" into Japan by the Buddhist monk Kobo Daishi (also called Kukai, 774–835), and indeed the love of *chigo* (boy favourites) occurred as often among monks as among kabuki actors and the samurai. The following story is from Saikaku's *A Collection of Discarded Letters* (1696), published three years after his death. It is the only letter in the collection that treats the topic of male love and, as Saikaku suggests in his brief commentary following the letter, the connection between male love and Buddhist monks was strong enough that the letter's treatment of the topic could be called "typical."

The letter-writer refers to his susceptibility to the beauty of handsome young men as a "chronic" or "incurable" illness (*jibyo*), something one is born with and carries through life as an innate physical or mental disposition. One senses not only the pleasure the monk takes in his latest discovery but also the anguish, given his own humble background, that results from his unreasonable desire for such a high-born youth, who is the son of a local lord.

An abridged form of the story appeared earlier in English translation in *Comrade Loves of the Samurai* under the title "Letter from a Buddhist Priest telling his Friend that his Lover comes to him," translated by E. Powys Mathers (1928). A complete English translation is presented here for the first time.

---

FROM A BUDDHIST PRIEST

*[seventeenth century]*

I was weary of the cherry blossoms in the capital and decided to leave Kyoto while it was yet spring. Now someone tells me that he intends to see for himself the cherry trees at Higashiyama[1] and join in the music and singing that goes on behind the curtains spread under them, so I have asked

---

*Translator's note: The translation of this story is based on a modern-print version of Saikaku's text in *Yorozu no fumi hōgu* (A Collection of Discarded Letters) in *Teihon Saikaku zenshū*, vol. 8, pp. 275–279 (Tokyo: Chuo Koron-sha, 1950). Translated by Paul Gordon Schalow.

[1]The "eastern hills" that rise to the east of the ancient capital, Kyoto, are even now a favorite place to enjoy the cherry blossoms. The letter-writer's home is in this district of Higashiyama, and his decision to leave the capital was motivated by his desire to escape the noisy revelers who flocked there to view the blossoms in spring.

". . . My reverie was disturbed by the sound of footsteps of an approaching company of people."

"It was a certain high priest who had come to pay a call at the temple. Close by his side was a handsome youth of no more than sixteen years of age, the beauty of whose face was beyond anything I had ever seen in the capital."

him to deliver this letter to you.

First, rest assured that I am well; I was delighted to hear that you, dear monk, have given up the sobriquet "the drunken warrior," and that your commitment to the pursuit of the path of Buddhahood seems steadfast.

My humble home has no doubt become an assembly place for mice in my absence. But since I left behind not even a single dried sardine, the pests must be laughing among themselves at my utter poverty, so befitting my station as a monk.

Chrysanthemums and bush clover are probably blooming all by themselves by now in the gaps in my garden fence. It is sad that no one will be there to mourn them when the night frosts nip the fading blossoms.

I left my key with you so that you would feel free to enter there anytime. Should a handsome youth happen to pass by on his way down Higashiyama, by all means invite him in and show my garden to him. If you like, treat him to some chestnuts and potatoes, which you will find in the root cellar under the bamboo porch on the north side. (Don't tell anyone, but the reason I left them there was because they were a gift from Mr. Takenaka.)

My weakness for handsome youths seems to be an incurable one, for I have once again fallen in love with a young man, whose presence here makes me wonder if I will ever see the capital again.

It all started last spring when I left you in the capital and went to visit an acquaintance in Okayama, Bizen Province. For a time I was treated hospitably enough, but gradually I found it difficult to remain there. So, I boarded a boat that was fortuitously sailing on the very Sea of Seto at dawn that the great priest Saigyō had once so admired in a poem. I threw my fate to the wind, and it eventually brought me to Higo Province.[2] A fellow monk and poet of linked verse I knew at the temple of Kiyomasa[3] invited me to stay and enjoy my leisure with him for a while.

One evening, I rested in the cool breeze of his garden to escape the summer heat. Man-made hills gave the garden a sense of great depth, and water had been made to flow artfully over carefully placed rocks. The effect was most refreshing. I found myself envying the saintly pleasure my friend seemed to derive from the miniature landscape.

From within the thick forest of cedars surrounding the temple came the song of a single nightingale, strangely reminiscent of the capital. This was a moment that ought to be commemorated in verse, I thought, and I struggled to recall the rules of Chinese composition laid out in *The Threefold Rhyme*.[4]

---

[2]Modern-day Kumamoto, located at the southernmost end of the southernmost major island of Kyūshū in the Japanese archipelago.

[3]The temple of Kiyomasa is Honmyō-ji in the city of Kumamoto. It was supported by Katō Kiyomasa, lord of the region, as his familial temple.

[4]*Sanjūin*, a collection of Chinese poems in five volumes designed as an aid in poetry composition. It dates from 1412, but was still widely used in Saikaku's day.

Suddenly, my reverie was disturbed by the sound of footsteps of an approaching company of people. It was a certain high priest who had come to pay a call at the temple. Close by his side was a handsome youth of no more than sixteen years of age, the beauty of whose face was beyond anything I had ever seen even in the capital. How was it possible, I thought, for such a creature to exist in a place as remote as this western province? The longer one lives, the more suprising one's experiences are.

A shiver ran through my body as I thought of the irony of my plight: I had come to this remote place to escape the disquiet of the flowery capital, and had discovered instead the source of a very special agony. My heart burned inside me. After tea was served to the visitors, I could not bear the thought of allowing the youth to leave without a parting look, and so I stole a peek through a gap in the door. This only intensified my passion, of course.

After his departure, I asked someone the youth's name. He was the second son of a high-ranking nobleman, and his heartfelt desire was to become a monk. It was for that purpose that he had been entrusted to the high priest. I was in a dreadful state, and felt as if my body would burst from the feelings inside me.

"How sad that a simple monk like me should be possessed of such an extravagant love." I admitted to my friend how unreasonable my feelings were, but I could not accept his advice to simply forget the youth. Instead, I was determined to make him aware of the existence of my feelings. This is the letter I wrote to him.

Yesterday I glimpsed the in-born beauty of your face, and knew that this must have been how, in China, Emperor Wen felt when he saw Deng Tong wearing a purple cap, or how Emperor Ai felt when he saw Dong Xian dressed in imperial robes. Those who see you mistake you for the beautiful Madame Li; those who hear of you yearn for a glimpse of this veritable Yang Kuei Fei.[5]

All who see or hear of you are deeply moved, for the hearts of men are not made of wood or stone. I know that it is impossible to consummate my love, but I feel compelled to spell out in this humble letter exactly how I feel for you.

Ever since the moment I was granted a fleeting glimpse of your face, my breast has smoldered like the smoke billowing from Mt. Aso, and my tears have flowed like the river Shirakawa.[6] Your eyes resemble the circle of the

---

[5]The youth's beauty is compared to that of legendary imperial favorites from China, two male and two female. True beauty in a youth thus transcends boundaries of sex and gender.

[6]Mt. Aso is an active volcano in the center of the island of Kyūshū; the Shirakawa flows through the northern environs of the town of Kumamoto.

cinnamon tree, and your heart is like the thread of a willow.[7]

Upon my arrival at the port of Tsurugasaki, I was straight-away impressed with the peony-like splendor of Kyūshū, a place without rival in the four seas. But it was when I came to Kumamoto that I discovered the greatest beauty of all, one fragment of which is, like a drop of amber, the rarest of gems. Had I not seen it with my own eyes, I would not have believed that a beauty surpassing the cherry blossoms could exist in this world. You are a reincarnation, all in one, of Xi Shi, beloved consort of the Chinese King of Wu, the Japanese beauty Komachi, Yukihira in his youth, and his handsome brother Narihira.[8] Your image not only haunts my dreams but is with me when I am awake.

My only recourse is to offer prayers at the Fujisaki Shrine, or to throw myself into the Kikuchi River.[9] I would gladly give up my life for your sake. The enlightened mind knows that the life of a man, even if he lives a hundred years, is but a moment's dream. I would gladly give up a thousand nights of spring for a single night pillowed in your arms.

In my waking moments, not once do thoughts of you leave me. What sort of karmic bond must it be that links me so powerfully to you?

Thus, I wrote him of my true feelings. And, hard to believe, I just received his warm reply. I cannot begin to tell you how it made me feel. Pen and paper are inadequate to the task. In his reply, he stated that he would like to visit me in my traveler's lodgings one evening soon. I do not know what day it will be, but you can imagine my feelings as I await word from him. I spend my days in an agony of expectation. *This*, I realize, must be love.

The other day I tattooed six letters on my right arm; I hope that they have the desired effect.[10] If only you were closer at hand, I could tell you

---

[7]A commentary suggests that "the circle of the cinnamon tree" is the new moon. The metaphor may mean that the youth's eyes are shaped like the new moon, narrow and crescent-shaped, both of which are desirable traits; or, it may be a metaphor for the brightness of the youth's eyes. Commentaries do not offer an explanation for the image of "the thread of a willow." The willow is a common metaphor for a woman's or youth's slender waist.

[8]The youth's beauty is again compared to that of male and female legendary beauties, both Chinese and Japanese. Ariwara no Narihira (825–880) was especially famed for his beauty and prowess as a lover of women, although legends of his love of men and youths were in circulation by Saikaku's day.

[9]The Fujisaki shrine was located in Kumamoto and was dedicated to Hachiman, guardian deity of the warrior class to which the youth belonged. The Kikuchi is a river that flows through the northern district of Kumamoto.

[10]A commentary suggests that the six letters are probably the characters "na-mu-a-mi-da-butsu." These words of the sutra are intoned by believers as an expression of faith in the power of Amitābha Buddha to grant their hopes of rebirth in the western paradise. Here, the monk has tattooed the words into his flesh in the hope that he will be granted his wish for sexual union with the youth.

exactly how things go when he visits me.

His name is Okajima Uneme.

I shall end here. I just wish it were possible to talk all night with you over a cup of saké about this splendid turn of events. I would send the crows of this province to sing in the thickets of the capital at Gion so that morning would never dawn on our conversation.

Please do not tell Gensai's sandal-bearer, Matsunosuké, about this matter. I have written it down just to give you some news about me until my eventual return.

Ninth month, Eleventh day.

Keigan

Saikaku's commentary:

This letter is from a monk disgusted with the noise of cherry-blossom viewing in the capital who went to the western provinces [Kyūshū] where he unexpectedly fell in love with a handsome youth. The letter is sent to a friend in the capital to inform him of the affair, and includes a summary of a love letter that the monk sent to the youth. It is typical of a monk.

# ▼ THE EARL AND HIS BEAU ▼

[CHARLES SPENCER & EDWARD WILSON]

Charles Spencer, third Earl of Sunderland (1674–1722) [ancestor in the direct male line of Sir Winston Churchill] was accused by contemporaries with having been the first person to have set up molly houses in Britain— clandestine meeting places for gay men, often in the private back rooms of public taverns. In 1693 he began an intrigue with Captain Edward Wilson whose good looks earned him the sobriquet Beau Wilson, and in a short time Wilson's extravagance made it obvious he was a kept man. The diarist John Evelyn wondered at the "Mysterie" of how the younger son of a man of only middling wealth had managed to live "in the Garb & Equipage of the richest Noble man in the nation for House, Furniture, Coaches & 6 horses." Wilson became Sunderland's man-mistress, even dressing in women's clothes to please him, meeting him secretly by way of a house on Hyde Park Corner which had a secret back exit, not far from Sunderland's house on Piccadilly. At the time of their short-lived affair Sunderland was twenty years old, Wilson about twenty-two.

Sunderland was a typical libertine: as he wrote to his Beau, "one melting Extasy, thou alone can'st give, will recompense a thousand such Uneasinesses.—D—n this confounded Hurry of Business, which has debarr'd me of Thee these five Days, and forced me last Night to make use of my Pillow which was as insipid as a —." Wilson was interested in money as well as flattery, and he made a veiled threat of blackmail after he discovered that his lord had been cheating on him with a wench. Sunderland in turn was enraged when he saw Wilson acting as a harlot with other men, and threatened to cut him off. Wilson's wealth became so conspicuous that the two men spread a rumour that Wilson was being kept by Elizabeth Villiers, mistress of William III. She hired a spy to find out the truth, John Law, who one night accosted and captured the "lady" who came out of the house on Hyde Park Corner and discovered her to be Wilson in disguise. With a pistol held to his head, Wilson was forced to reveal the entire affair, but paid Law money to keep him quiet. Law then began to blackmail Sunderland as well. The intrigue—which Sunderland enjoyed at first—got out of hand, and I think Sunderland hired Law to kill Wilson.

In Spring 1694 Law found a trumped-up excuse to pull Wilson from his carriage on the Strand and engage in a "duel" on the spot, stabbing him to death. Law was convicted of murder but escaped from prison (probably with the aid of Villiers or Sunderland or both) and fled to France. In 1695 Sunderland married a wealthy heiress, and after her death he married another heiress, and in due course a third heiress. He became First Lord of the Treasury, i.e. Prime Minister, and was a powerful political intriguer. Law in the meantime became a famous economist and helped to found the

Bank of France, and Sunderland in England set up the South Sea Scheme based upon Law's Mississippi Scheme. The famous collapse of the economy in 1721—the South Sea Bubble—led to the imprisonment of several South Sea Directors, and Sunderland tried to defend himself against charges of conspiring to destabilize the nation for the Jacobite cause. Law returned to England and was granted a royal pardon in November 1721; Sunderland was at his weakest, and Law probably forced him to arrange the pardon.

In April 1722 Sunderland was found dead, just when all his crimes were coming home to roost; it was believed he had poisoned himself. A year later the great mystery of Beau Wilson's sudden wealth was revealed, with the publication of *Love-letters Between a certain late Nobleman And the famous Mr. Wilson*, a packet of nineteen homosexual love letters, plus one to Law, claimed to have been discovered in a cabinet in Wilson's room upon his death. Some think the letters are fictional, but in my book *Mother Clap's Molly House: The Gay Subculture in England 1700-1830* I argue the case for their authenticity, arguing that Wilson gave the key to the cabinet to his friend Captain Wightman just before he died, that Wightman passed the letters to the political writer John Trenchard, who passed them to his amanuensis Thomas Gordon who published them. Gordon also wrote in 1721 *The Conspirators: Or, The Case of Catiline* in which he attacked Sunderland as the head of a circle of sodomites within the government. Sunderland was a powerful and ruthless man, which is why the letters were suppressed until just after his death.

---

To Mr. Wilson

*[1693]*

Say, was it a cold Insencibility that caused you to shun a Challenge, where to give and receive excess of Pleasure, was to have been the only Combat between us; or conscious of your own matchless Charms, are you resolv'd with peevish, coy Pride, to be won at the Expence of a thousand Inquietudes and restless fond Desires, you Force me to endure?

If you are of a Turn insencible to Pleasure, I know Gold has the greatest ascendant over you; for all covet it for what it purchases: This Bill may convince you, I have that in my Power: I can be Fortune to you, and, with many Blessings I'll crown the chiefest Wishes of your Heart; only hasten to gratify the eager Impatience of mine, that longs to hold you in these Arms, where you may secure me, ever yours.

Greenwich-Park, be behind Flamstead's House [the Royal Observatory, Greenwich Park], and I shall see you to Morrow Nine at Night, don't fail to come.

To Mr. Wilson

I Had not above an hundred Pieces by me when I receiv'd yours, which made me send, swift as the Minutes, to the Bank to fetch this. I would have my Willy believe, I am never so delighted, as when I am doing that which may convince him, how very dear he is to his nown Love: Then come away, the Bath is ready, that I may Wrestle with it, and pit it, and pat it, and — it; and then for cooler Sport, devour it with greedy Kisses; for Venus, and all the Poet's Wenches are but dirty Dowdies to thee.

Put on the Brussels Head and Indian Atlass I sent yesterday. [i.e. Brussels lace headdress and Indian silk gown]

---

To Mr. Wilson

Did I not strictly charge my dearest Boy, at parting, not to omit one Opportunity of accquainting [*sic*] me with his returning Health by which alone my Joys can be restored? six Posts have past, and yet no Notice taken of its forlorn expecting dying Lover: Tell me the Cause of this, if thou art able; but I'm afraid thou can'st not, or dur'st not do it; either thy Illness is relaps'd with a malicious Bent to make eternal Separation, and thou hast too much Tenderness to kill me with the Knowledge of it; or I have been remiss or overfond, and cloy'd thee; that thou dost artfully withdraw thyself from these loathed Arms; or dost thou vilely descend to the low Subtilties of the inferiour Sex, who, to enhance their Price, play at fast and loose, insult and idly triumph over the Sot that does more idly suffer such a Drab to gain the ascendant. Forgive me, my dear Willy, if I wrong Thee; lay all the Blame on this unruly Passion: A Plague confound those lying Dogs of Poets, who to delude and torture all Mankind, would palm it on us as a Heaven of Pleasure—Damn'd Spite,—It's Hell to love and doat to Madness, as I do on Thee. Answer me quickly if thou canst; say something to me; if it be a Lye, let it be a well invented one; and it will please.

You see I'm mad to B— I had forgot to bid you inclose to Her at Park-Corner; direct mine for Mrs. Gray.

---

To the Lord —

My Lord,

After a long, long fruitless Expectation of your Command how to direct to you, which your Lordship may remember was not fix'd on, tho' I often urged it I have been so wretched to construct it as a Mark of your declining Favour: as the Tortures of my Soul are inexpressible under such bitter Affliction, so are my Joys as full to find them causeless: Those soft complaining passionate Expressions transported me beyond my Strength to bear, and then revived me with your kind Rebukes; what followed raised an Extasy too great: The past Conflicts of my Mind, under the imaginary Displeasure of my dearest Lord, made me regardless of the Disorders of my Body, which since your Lordship has enjoyn'd shall be more my Care; my Fate is wholly in your Power, and you have vouchsafed to bless me above all Men. Command me to be well and live; but not (for Oh! I cannot) live without you: Recall me from this restless Banishment, or honour me with your loved Presence here; the Beauties of the Place have such Enticements, which, with other Reasons, I am informd, have long detained some Persons of Distinction on odd Intreagues, perhaps, not unworthy your Lordship's Notice.

    I am,

        My Lord, &c.

---

To the Lord —

My Lord,

    Eager to acquaint your Lordship with my Return to Town, I dispatched a Messenger that Moment with a Letter, who failing of the wish'd Opportunity, to deliver it as usual, I went immediately to the Play, in Hopes to gratify my Impatience by seeing you there; but contrary to that, had the Mortification to find one Misfortune attended by a still greater; when as sometime to disguise my secret Affection, I survey Beauty with as much seeming Delight as other Men; Curiosity led me to make Enqiry of a fine dress'd Lady, I have never before observ'd to adorn any publick Place; but how was I confounded and what racking Thoughts possest me, when I understood she was a new favourite Mistress of your Lordship obtain'd, with much Difficulty; so that, my Lord, my missing you last Night, which then only seem'd Chance, may probably hereafter appear to be your Lordship's Choice: I refer to your own Judgment, which never errs in Matters of far higher Importance than my Happiness, and who are so well aquainted with all the Passions that can affect human Nature, that it would be Presumption to send you my feeble Discription, of what I suffer on this hateful Discovery. I only flatter myself with one Hope, attended by a thousand Doubts, which two or three Lines from your Lordship will confirm or disperse: I long, yet dread to have your Answer, which I am certain you won't fail to send, as soon as this comes to your Hands, If you have any Regard for,

  My Lord,

      Your most entirely,

          most passionately devoted Servant,

            W. Wilson.

To Mr. Wilson

Did it fret and tease itself because I have got a Wench, but don't let one
Fear perplex it: When I have Thee in my Arms, thou shalt see how I despise
all the Pleasures that changeling Sex can give compared to one Touch of
thine; it's true, I had her dirty Maidenhead which I took some Pains for;
not so much to amuse the dull Time in thy tedious Absence, which no consideration but your dear Health, could have made me comply with; as to
stop some good natur'd Reflections I found made on my Indifference that
way. But thou alone art every, and all the Delight my greedy Soul covets,
which is heigthned to such Excess, that even pains me, to find my dear
Willy has such a Tenderness for its nown Love; then hasten to my fond
Heart, that leaps and bounds with Impatience to see Thee, and devour thee
with greedy Kisses.

---

To the Lord —

My Lord,
    It is not to be express'd with how much Rapture I receiv'd your Lord-
ship's Commands to attend you, and if it were possible that could increase
with me, it is even now, when the different Transports of my Soul prevent
my ready Obedience to them. Can I support your adored Presence with the
Torture of not seeing you entirely on my own. No, my Lord, the Great-
ness of my Passion created and inspired by you, has disdained to share a
Pleasure with that base, low, dull, insinuating Sex; let not one of them presume to hope the least Thought, in your exalted Mind, or noble Appetites,
and contemn the idle medling insipid World; but I forget myself, and rave
with the distracting Thought, that any thing in Nature should be able to
interpose between us; pardon, my dearest Lord, when I assume to joyn myself with you; remember, it is a Crime you first descended to encourage
me in, and impute it to no other Spirit of Ambition, but that of being
inseparably,
        Your Lordship's
            most obedience Slave,
                W. Wilson

---

To Mr. Wilson

Is this thy Faith? Is this thy Return to all my foolish lavish Fondness? It
seems I have taught you a Trade, and Harlot-like you intend to be as common and as despicable as those abject Wretches [We must beg Pardon of
the Reader for omitting here some Lines which are in the Original of this
Letter, being too obscene to be inserted] May every Disease incident to
them infect and destroy thee. What, couldst thou find none but that old

nauseous Dog to kiss and slobber thee? Don't pretend to deny it, for by
— I saw him: Had not a little Regard to my self prevented, I had stabb'd
thee that moment.

I suppose you intend to hide your detested Head in some Hole, to escape
my Rage; but my Revenge shall find thee, and punish thy black Ingratitude:
an Ingratitude so vile, that thou deservest to be a terrible Example to all
that base Frye: Did not I take thee from a wretched necessitous Life, perplex'd with petty Duns, and have raised thee to be the Nation's Wonder?
Have I deny'd thee any thing? but have been so lavish to make thee (or thou
pretendest) to blush at my Excess of Bounty: But now I will be as boundless in my Hatred as I have been profuse in my extravagant Love. May all
——— torture thee, as thy Baseness does me.

---

To the Lord —

May all the detestable Curses your Lordship has been pleased to pronounce
with ten thousand more, inflict ——— if I know or can guess what you
mean.

Is it to try the Bent of my Mind, under the most calamitous of all Circumstances, your Lordship's dread Displeasure? as you have before done
the other Way, in raising me from that abject Fortune to your high Grace,
dispensing Favours beyond my own aspiring Hopes, or vainest Desires;
which when I cease most gratefully to acknowledge, as is my Duty, or give
just Cause of Offence, either by Action or Omission, may all the Valuable World, nay what is infinitely preferable to all, your Lordships self, continue to hate, despise, and brand me, for the most villanous of all that black
and loathsome Herd you have already rank'd me with.

Am I not the Creature of your Framing, to rise, to fall, to live or die,
to mould and fashion as you please? And should I dare to repine at, or
more basely endeavour to hide my self from the Fate you have allotted me?
Is it thinking too poorly of the Wretch, your Lordship once vouchsafed to
honour with your Love and Esteem, which, perhaps, you'll see was not
wholly misplaced, when I have an Opportunity to throw myself at your
Feet; in the mean Time, devise as many Tortures to rack this hated Body,
as at present my Soul endures, and let both fall a willing Sacrifice to gratify
your Pleasures.

    I am,
      My Lord
        Your Lordship's most
          faithfully most entirely
            devoted Slave,
              W. Wilson

# ▼ TOWN AND COUNTRY ▼

[JOHN, LORD HERVEY & STEPHEN FOX]

"The world," observed Lady Mary Wortley Montague, "consists of men, women, and Herveys." John, Lord Hervey (1696–1743) was satirized by Alexander Pope as "Sporus," Nero's catamite: "Now high, now low, now Master up, now Miss, / And he himself one vile Antithesis. . . . / Fop at the Toilet, Flatt'rer at the Board, / Now trips a Lady, and now struts a Lord." This archetype of "the third sex" painted his face to a fashionable pallor, was high-strung and fainted often, but was vigorous enough to engage in a duel, to marry and to father eight children. In fact his courting of Pope's mistress was what prompted the poet's malicious satire.

But not long after marrying, while recovering his health in Bath in 1727, Hervey began courting Stephen Fox (1704–76), a young country gentleman, and then visited his estate in Somerset. Hervey was thirty-one, Stephen twenty-three. The men spent so much time together that Lady Hervey protested that her estate at Ickworth had become "my hermitage." For fifteen months during 1728–29 Hervey and Stephen travelled Europe together on their Grand Tour. Exactly how close the two men became on that trip may be indicated by the fact that the first twenty-six pages of Hervey's volume of letters covering that period were torn out and destroyed by his grandson the first Marquess of Bristol.

On their return from the Continent, Hervey could not stand the separation: "I must see you soon; I can't live without You" (November 15, 1729). In August 1730 Hervey proposed that they live together: "why should we see one another by Visits, but never have a common home?" He arranged for Lord Bateman to lend his house in Windsor to Stephen so that they could see one another while Hervey was engaged in his courtly duties at Windsor Castle; the Earl of Sunderland (see preceding selection) had arranged for his daughter to marry Bateman, but he was forced to separate from her when his homosexual tastes became too public.

In November Hervey signed over the lease of his house on Great Burlington Street to Stephen, so they did achieve a common home even though technically Hervey moved into an apartment in St. James's Palace. The letters had reached their peak of intensity in late September 1730, when Hervey tells Stephen that it is impossible "had I time to write volumes, how warmly, how tenderly, how gratefully, how contentedly and unalterably I am Yours" (September 24), and that "Every Body has some Madness in their Composition, & I freely acknowledge you are mine" (September 25). Hervey and Stephen spent the next two months together. The letters now conclude with frank avowals of love: "Adieu, que je vous aime, que je vous adore: & si vous m'aimé de même venez me le dire" (September 25).

Stephen's descendant, the Earl of Ilchester, who edited the letters in

1950, cut out the frequent avowals of devotion which he considered to be mawkish and sentimental; obviously sensual passages were also suppressed. Hervey regularly closes with Mon cher, et très cher, carissime; caro et carissimo, et sempre caro; mea cara et sola voluptas; le plus aimable et le plus aimé qu'il y est au monde.

In August 1731, at a large dinner party in the presence of the Prince of Wales, the Lord Chancellor drank to Stephen's health, and Hervey told Stephen that "without the least affectation, I assure you, I colour'd and felt just as I imagine your favorite & fondest Mistress would have done upon the same Occasion." But Hervey was sophisticated and urbane, and Stephen felt himself to be provincial; in November 1733 he told Hervey he was unfit to keep him company and planned to live alone in the country, at which Hervey protested "I should like you rusty better than any other body polish'd," but their correspondence more or less ceased by the end of that year.

Hervey was appointed Vice-Chamberlain, i.e. master of court ceremonies, in 1730, and acted as a political propagandist under Walpole's ministry. He was frequently attacked by his enemies as a homosexual, e.g. an anonymous lampoon notes of his attendance at Parliament that he is "Lady of the Lords," and it was rumoured that he was the "pathick" of Frederick Prince of Wales, son of George II. They were undoubtedly close to one another (in later life they shared a mistress), and Stephen was jealous. Hervey arranged for Stephen's marriage to a child-heiress in 1736 (he became Earl of Ilchester in 1756), and turned his attentions to Francesco Algarotti, the young Italian scholar who had taken London by storm that year. Another series of billets doux ensued between the two men, and Algarotti moved into Hervey's apartment at St. James's in 1739. But that is another story, which does not quite match the intensity of Hervey's first love.

---

LORD HERVEY TO STEPHEN FOX

*Ickworth*
*June 1, 1727*

I can't help taking a malicious pleasure to hear the country affords you so few of any kind, and that your joys there are at so low an ebb that a sound horse and a big-bellied pheasant are the only ones you have yet experienced. You will easily believe me, when I tell you these are such as I shall never envy you; but you will not find it quite so easy to make me believe you, when you say you wish yourself in town again. If your wishes were very strong (since your horses are so very sound), what hinders the gratification of them? . . .

I won't tell you how I feel every time I goe through St. James's Street because I don't love writing unintelligibly; & the more faithful the descrip-

Stephen Fox (1704–1776), later Earl of Ilchester, as a young man.
Painting by Enoch Seeman.

tion was, the farther one of your temper & way of thinking would be from comprehending what it meant. I might as well talk to a blind man of Colours, an Atheist of Devotion, or an Eunuch of f[ucking]. That regret for the Loss of any body one loves & likes is a sort of Sensation you have merit enough to teach, tho' I believe you'll never have merit enough to learn it. You have left some such remembrance behind you that I assure you (if 'tis any satisfaction to you to know it) you are not in the least Danger of being forgotten. The favours I have received at Your Honour's *Hands* are of such a Nature that tho' the impression might wear out of my Mind, yet they are written in such lasting characters upon every Limb, that 'tis impossible for me to look on a Leg or an Arm without having my Memory refresh'd. I have some thoughts of exposing the marks of your pollisonerie [lewdness] to move Compassion, as the Beggers that have been Slaves at Jerusalem doe the burnt Crucifix upon their Arms; they have remain'd so long that I begin to think they are equally indelible. [These sentences are in Hervey's own handwriting, rather than that of his amanuensis.]

---

*Ickworth*
*June 27, 1728*

The little time other people allow me to write to you in, and the little time you allow me to think of other people, makes me perpetually absent from the thing I am doing, and often constrains me in the thing I would do. They have no good of me, nor I of myself. I am absent from them without being present to you; and very naturally (and consequently very simply) because I can't enjoy what I would I don't enjoy what I might; which is just as reasonable and as prudent a way of acting, as if I should cut off my legs because I have not wings: or should resolve never to eat when the thing I loved best was not in season. Yet so we are made, and so we act: at least the generality of mankind. But among many other peculiar blessings bestowed by Heaven upon you, you enjoy that negative one of this troublesome ingredient being left quite out of your composition. You have a proneness to be pleased, and are not only exempt from the pain of ever wishing for anything you do not possess, but have a capacity given you of extracting a joy out of everything you do, and to put your pleasures in the strongest light, are not capable of giving greater than you take. You are to your company, just what you are to your food: you can sit down to what I am sure you could never hunger after: can swallow what does not please your taste: and digest what one would imagine must have made anybody sick. Don't imagine I am modest enough to think myself such a sort of dish, for 'tis the least of my thoughts; and if I could, would certainly persuade you not only to have me always at your table, but to eat of no other.
    Adieu.

*November 18, 1729*

. . . I am grown already quite an English fine Gentlman. I do a hundred different Things of a Day & like none of them; yawn in the Faces of the Women I talk to; eat & drink with Men I have no friendship for; play despising the Court & live in the Drawing-Room; rail at Quid-nuncs & go hawking about for News; throw the faults of my Constitution upon the Climate; flatter awkwardly, rally worse, & in short make none of my Actions conducive to the pleasure or profit either of my-self or anybody else.

You are in part responsible for this. If I regretted less what I have lost, I should be less indifferent to what I possess: and if I had a worse opinion of you, perhaps I might have a better of other people: consequently, should be better pleased myself, and of course more industrious to please them. But as things now stand, I look upon you as my dwelling: and feel the inconveniences of these other animals as I did those of Italian inns, hate all their filth, and would no more make friends of the one, than I would my home of the other. . . .

Adieu. 'Tis three a clock. I am quite undressed, and expect Mr. and Mrs. Pulteney every moment to dinner. The Dr. is already here, and says, "Oh! you have writ enough." I should be of his mind, if I thought anything I have said had explained to you how affectionately, entirely and unalterably, my dear, dear creature, I am your's.

---

*August 26, 1730*

. . . You are my Eau de Barbade, that intoxicates my spirits without vitiating my taste, and are so much superior to common draught in every particular that one need not blush for being drunk with you. At least I dont, and own I languish as much for want of the daily dose of you which I have been so long used to, as Lord Scarsdale can do for his three flasks of claret, and feel as sensible a decay of spirits in a transition to any other company, as he could do upon being reduced to water.

---

*Windsor*
*September 16, 1730*

. . . I have persuaded Ld. Bateman to be at Old Windsor [at his house] when you are here. Not that I will lend you for a moment of the day or night that I can have you; but in order, if I can so contrive, that the hours you are not with me may not lie as heavy upon your hands, as I always find those in which I can not be with you; . . . I have made it impossible for me to live without You. I have often thought, if any very idle Body had Curiosity enough to intercept & examine my Letters, they would certainly conclude they came rather from a Mistress than a Friend; but it must be people that were unacquainted with You who made that Conclusion; other-wise, they might know that Reason would make one as fond of your Society as passion could make one of any other Body's. . . . Lord Bateman is grown quite a courtier. Adieu, mon bien aimable, mon bien aimé.

*Hampton Court*
*August 23, 1731*

The people who are about the Prince (I have not seen him these three days) say he is better, though weak beyond imagination for so short an illness. He has this morning begun the bark, and cut off his hair. I should say many things to you if you were here, which I shall not trust even to a cipher. Solomon you know says, "Speak not in Palaces for the walls have ears; nor of Princes for the birds of the air will reveal it." . . . I have been blooded to-day, so cannot use my arm to write any more.

Adieu. I love you & love you more than I thought I could love any thing. I have received a Letter from you to-day which no body who loved you less could deserve.

Adio carissimo.

*August 31, 1731*

[Hervey apologized for having said he wished he could love Frederick, Prince of Wales as much as he loved Stephen, which led to a lover's jealousy and misunderstanding.] The Tears you speak of are at this Distance so infectious that I hardly see the Words I write. . . . I am as incapable of wishing to love any Body else so well, as I am of wishing to love You less. God forbid any Mortal should ever have the power over me you have, or that you should ever have less. . . .

Adieu, if I was to fill a thousand Reams of paper it would be only aiming in different phrases & still imperfectly to tell you the same thing, & assure you that since I first knew you I have been without repenting & still am & ever shall be undividedly & indisolubly Yours.

# ▼ LOVE AT THE OUTER LIMITS ▼

[JOHANN JOACHIM WINCKELMANN & REINHOLD VON BERG]
*Translated from German by Alexandra Trone*

Johann Joachim Winckelmann (1717–68) in his monumental *History of Ancient Art* established Greek art as the touchstone for all art irrespective of place or time. His ideal of beauty, which had a tremendous effect upon neoclassical artistic taste and art theory for more than a century, was grounded in his gay sensibility: "those who are observant of beauty only in women, and are moved little or not at all by the beauty of men, seldom have an impartial, vital, inborn instinct for beauty in art."

In 1740 Winckelmann was the tutor to Frederick Wilhelm Peter Lamprecht, son of the Dean of the Chapter of Magdeburg Cathedral. Lamprecht went with Winckelmann to Seehausen, where the latter got a job as a teacher, and where they shared the same room (not simply the same apartment) until their highly emotional break-up in 1746. Lamprecht went on to become a dull Prussian civil servant. In 1748 Winckelmann escaped the provinces and became librarian and secretary to the diplomat Count Heinrich von Bünau in Saxony. In due course he entered the service of Cardinal Passionei in Dresden, a noted art collector.

In 1754 he experienced an inner struggle, with physical symptoms such as night sweats and loss of weight and insomnia, and left Dresden in 1755, determined to devote his life to the study of art in Rome. There he freed himself from German puritanism and embraced Italian sensuosity. In his correspondence he became fairly open about his liaisons with, for example, Franz Stauder, a pupil of Anton Raphael Mengs, the young Florentine Nicoló Castellani, and an unnamed "beautiful young eunuch."

By 1761 he had completely recovered his health and vitality—clearly because he stopped repressing his sexuality and came out: "I can be satisfied with my life. I have no worries other than my work, and have even found someone with whom I can speak of love: a good-looking, blond young Roman of sixteen, half a head taller than I am." He settled into the Villa Albani on the outskirts of Rome, cataloguing the collection of antiquities of Cardinal Albani, chief librarian to the Vatican. There he wrote a series of famous "Reflections" on Greek art and culture, blending principles of political freedom and education with aesthetic theory. He produced scholarly studies of archeology and antiquities, and issued a sequence of celebrated interpretations of famous Greek sculptures, notably the Laocoön group, the Apollo Belevedere, the Belevedere Torso, and Antinous in the Vatican collections.

His ideal of beauty was embodied in his beloved Friedrich Rheinhold von Berg, to whom he dedicated his most famous essay *On the Nature and the Cultivation of Sensibility to the Beautiful in Art*. Berg was twenty-six,

Johann Joachim Winckelmann (1717–1768) in a painting by Anton Raphael Mengs.

Winckelmann forty-five when they met in 1762. Winckelmann wrote to another friend, "I have fallen in love, and how! with a young Livonian." He even carved Berg's initials on the bark of a sycamore in Frascati. But Berg eventually deserted Rome for the livelier social life of Paris, and they separated; eventually he lived out an undistinguished life on his estates at Riga.

In 1768, at the height of an internationally acclaimed career, Winckelmann enigmatically decided to return to Germany. But he broke off his journey after a nervous breakdown, probably due to an onslaught of Germanic guilt which he thought he had forever left behind, and began his return, stopping briefly at Vienna for an audience with Empress Maria Theresa. Travelling incognito, he arrived in Trieste on June 1, 1768, and checked into the largest inn, to wait until a suitable ship departed for Rome. There he fell in with Francesco Arcangeli, an unemployed cook or café waiter and small-time thief, who went to Winckelmann's room every night for the next few days. Arcangeli was astonished not only by Winckelmann's collection of gold and silver medals and his stories of life at the great courts of Europe, but by Winckelmann's odd clothing: white linen shirt with gold buttons inlaid with cornelian, and black leather trousers.

On June 7 Arcangeli bought a knife and a rope. The following day, in Winckelmann's room after dinner as usual, he threw the knotted rope around Winckelmann's neck; Winckelmann pulled away; Arcangeli drew the knife and they struggled, Winckelmann grasping the knife by the blade to unsuccessfully ward off the blows. In Arcangeli's confession he pointedly notes that he spread Winckelmann's legs apart and stabbed him not only in the chest but "lower down." I interpret this as a record of a frenzied sexual attack. Arcangeli fled, Winckelmann staggered out of the room and down the stairs, crying "Look what he did to me!" In the remaining few hours of life left to him, Winckelmann made his will and forgave his enemy. Arcangeli was nevertheless captured, condemned to death, and broken on the wheel in the plaza in front of the inn. Though neither young nor beautiful—thirty-one and pockmarked—Arcangeli was obviously a bit of rough trade with whom Winckelmann had decided to celebrate his return to the life of the senses.

---

JOHANN JOACHIM WINCKELMANN TO
F. W. PETER LAMPRECHT                              *[Seehausen, summer 1746]*

What words of affection shall I use to answer your charming lines? How I have pressed them to lips and breast. If only you could see what is going on in my soul! My very dearest brother, if life and honour were at stake, my heart would sacrifice them for your sake. Such friends as you should be displayed to the world as models. Heaven should repay us for our honesty. But who would bewail my fate? It has put my soul into such a state that it is not at peace without the charms of an invaluable friend (if I could only embrace him) yet keeps me apart from him. To me all is lost, honour and pleasure, peace and quiet, unless I see you and enjoy you. . . . I am not lucky in love. My eyes weep only for you. I am in a state not unlike that of Diogenes as described by Lucian, utterly alone, an enemy of the people, without friends or company. My spirit breaks its bounds when I think of you, as was said by Plato to Dion. You ask to see me: but I cannot. How I wish that I could sense the feelings behind the written word. Now I recognize the power of love. But perhaps no one can any longer love a friend with such sincerity and yearning. My fate, however, has declared itself against me quite, it will tear me away or else torment me with a futile delay. If only it could give me the disposition of the unfeeling stoics! I shall love you without hope. Would to God my happiness were bound to yours, which I can foresee. May God provide good aspects for it. I am desolate and my only consolation is that there must be something in me that binds me so firmly to you. That must be the only thing in me that is exceptional. I shall love you as long as I live and even as I expire . . .

---

JOHANN JOACHIM WINCKELMANN TO
REINHOLD VON BERG                                         *Rome*
                                         *the 9th of June, 1762*

Noble friend!

As a loving mother weeps inconsolably over a beloved child torn from her by a violent prince who sends it to its death on the battlefield, I lament my parting from you, dear friend, with tears that flow from my very soul. From the moment I first saw you I was unaccountably drawn to you, not solely to your outward appearance, and this gave me a feeling of the harmony that is beyond human comprehension and which is struck up by the eternal affinity of things. In the 40 years of my life this is the second time this has happened to me, and it will presumably be the last. My dear friend, no one else in the world can love you so: for such a complete accord of souls is only possible between two; all other inclinations are only branches off this noble main stem. But this divine impulse is unknown to most people, and is therefore badly misconstrued by many. The power of love in its extreme form must be expressed in all possible ways

> I thee both as Man and Woman prize
> For a perfect love implies
> Love in all capacities.
>                                         Cowley

and that is the foundation on which the undying friendships of the ancient world, those of Theseus and Pirithous, of Achilles and Patroclus, were built. Friendship without love is only acquaintance. The other, however, is heroic and sublime above all else; it humiliates the willing friend till he grovels in the dust and it drives him to the day of his death. All virtue is in some measure weakened by other proclivities and in some measure capable of false pretences; a friendship that extends to the outer limits of humanity bursts forth with violence and is the highest virtue now unknown to mortals, and is thus also the greatest good they can possess. Christian morality does not teach this; the heathens, however, prayed to it, and the greatest deeds of antiquity were accomplished through it.

Only one month of your extended stay in Rome and more leisure in which to talk with you, my friend, alone, would have set our friendship on solid foundations, and all my time would have been devoted to you. This notwithstanding, I should have explained myself in strong words unmentionable in writing had I not realized that this would be an unusual way for me to speak to you. You may thus believe that I do not wish to be paid [for my book]; your good opinion, however, retains all its worth without that, and I kiss your hands as in thanks for a great treasure that you would have liked to give me. The genius of our friendship will follow you from a distance as far as Paris, and will there leave you in the abode of foolish pleasures; here, however, your image will be that of my saint.

Convey my respects to the dear Count von Münnich, who inspires well-merited regard and love in everyone. My best wishes follow him on the road to the honour, of which he may feel assured, of one day being a great and virtuous man of whose acquaintance I, in my later years, may speak with pride.

I kiss you with heart and soul, my noble friend, my beloved, and I expire
Your

     obedient servant and your own
     and eternal friend
     Johann Winckelmann

# ▼ I NEVER SAW SUCH A BOY ▼

[THOMAS GRAY & CHARLES-VICTOR DE BONSTETTEN]

The English poet Thomas Gray (1716–71), most famous for his "Elegy Written in a Country Churchyard," was dubbed "Miss Gray" when he went to Peterhouse College, Cambridge, because of his mincing manners. He abandoned his degree course when an inheritance left him independent, but nevertheless acquired a reputation for his knowledge about English medievalism, especially Druidic history so popular in the 1750s. His school friend Horace Walpole—creator of Strawberry Hill and popularizer of the "gothick" style—was the first great love of his life, and many of Walpole's letters to him illustrate a "sentimental sodomy" characteristic of the many bachelors in Walpole's circle. He and Walpole travelled together for two years, and Walpole became his literary patron, but they had a falling out in 1745 which has never been quite understood.

Gray's second great love was the unfortunate Henry Tuthill, also a friend from school, who became a Fellow of Peterhouse in 1749, but who was dismissed in 1757 because of a homosexual scandal, and who eventually drowned himself as a result of his disgrace. Some of Gray's correspondence from this period has been selectively destroyed, but what survives (including letters where Tuthill's name can still be seen behind the erasures of Gray's first editor and biographer William Mason) suggests that he and his friend Thomas Wharton conspired to suppress public knowledge of these events and particularly Gray's involvement in the affair, which has never been adequately researched due to scholarly homophobia. The episode cast a permanent pall of melancholy upon Gray's character.

But several years before his death, in December 1769, his confidant Rev. Norton Nicholls introduced him to the young Swiss aristocrat Charles-Victor de Bonstetten (1745–1832), who had come to London to improve his English. By the end of the month Bonstetten returned with Gray to Pembroke Hall, Cambridge, where he lived close to Gray's lodgings and ate every day in Gray's rooms. Gray wrote to Nicholls in January 1770: "I never saw such a boy: our breed is not made on this model." But Bonstetten had to return to Switzerland at the end of three months, and there was a painful parting. Bonstetten was a young Apollo, charming, volatile and romantic, and provided for the frail and aging poet-historian an Indian summer.

Gray wrote to Nicholls in March 1770 several days before taking his friend to the boat in Dover: "He gives me too much pleasure, and at least an equal share of inquietude. You do not understand him so well as I do, but I leave my meaning imperfect, till we meet. I have never met with so extraordinary a Person. God bless him!" Bonstetten invited Gray to come to Switzerland the summer of the following year (1771), and plans were made for the holiday, but Gray was too unwell to travel, and died in July. The two men wrote regularly for over a year, although hardly any of Bonstetten's letters have survived. (Bonstetten went on to become the beloved of the historian Johannes von Müller, whose passionate letters to him appear in the next selection.)

---

CHARLES-VICTOR DE BONSTETTEN TO
NORTON NICHOLLS                                        *Cambridge the 6. Jan. 1770*

*Hence vain deluding Joys* [Milton's *Il Penseroso*] is our motto hier, written on every feature, and ourly spoken by every solitary Chapel bel; So that decently you cant expect no other but a very grave letter. I realy beg you pardon to wrap up my thoughts in so smart a dress as an in quarto sheet. I know they should apear in a folo leave, but the Ideas themselves shall look so solemn as to belie their dress.—Tho' I wear not yet the black gown, and am only an inferior Priest in the temple of Meditation, yet my countenance is already consecrated. I never walk but with even steps and musing gate, and looks comercing with the skyes; and unfold my wrinkles only when I see mr. Gray, or think of you. Then notwithstanding all your learnings and knowledge, I feel in such occasions that I have a heart, which you know is as some others a quite prophane thing to carry under a black gown.

I am in a hurry from morning till evening. At 8 o Clock I am roused by a young square Cap, with whom I follow Satan through Chaos and night. He explained me in Greek and latin, the *sweet reluctant amorous Delays* [*Paradise Lost*] of our Grandmother Eve. We finish our travels in a copious breakfeast of muffins and tea. . . .

---

THOMAS GRAY TO CHARLES-VICTOR DE BONSTETTEN

*Cambridge*
*April 12, 1770*

Never did I feel, my dear Bonstetten, to what a tedious length the few short moments of our life may be extended by impatience and expectation, till you had left me: nor ever knew before with so strong a conviction how much this frail body sympathizes with the inquietude of the mind. I am grown old in the compass of less than three weeks, like the Sultan in the Turkish Tales, that did plunge his head into a vessel of water and take it out again (as the standers-by affirm'd) at the command of a Dervish, and found he had pass'd many years in captivity and begot a large family of children. The strength and spirits that now enable me to write to you, are only owing to your last letter, a temporary gleam of sunshine. Heaven knows, when it may shine again! I did not conceive till now (I own) what it was to lose you, nor felt the solitude and insipidity of my own condition, before I possess'd the happiness of your friendship.

I must cite another Greek writer [Plato, *Republic*] to you, because it is very much to my purpose. He is describing the character of a Genius truly inclined to Philosophy. It includes (he says) qualifications rarely united in one single mind, quickness of apprehension and a retentive memory; vivacity and application, gentleness and magnanimity: to these he adds an invincible love of truth, and consequently of probity and justice. Such a soul (continues he) will be little inclined to sensual pleasures, and consequently temperate; a stranger to illiberality and avarice being accustom'd to the most extensive views of things and sublimest contemplations . . . But these very endowments so necessary to a soul form'd for philosophy are often the ruin of it (especially when join'd to the external advantages of wealth, nobility, strength and beauty) that is, if it light on a bad soil; and want its proper nurture, which nothing but an excellent education can bestow. . . . and remember, that extraordinary vices and extraordinary virtues are alike the produce of a vigorous Mind: little souls are alike incapable of the one or the other.

If you have ever met with the portrait sketch'd out by Plato, you will know it again: for my part (to my sorrow) I have had that happiness: I see the principal features, and I foresee the dangers with a trembling anxiety. But enough of this, I return to your letter: it proves at least, that in the midst of your new gaieties, I still hold some place in your memory, and (what pleases me above all) it has an air of undissembled sincerity. Go on, my best and amiable Friend, to shew me your heart simply and without the shadow of disguise, and leave me to weep over it (as I now do) no matter whether from joy or sorrow.

*19 April 1770*

Alas! how do I every moment feel the truth of what I have somewhere read: *Ce n'est pas le voir que de s'en souvenir* [remembering him is not the same as seeing him], and yet that remembrance is the only satisfaction I have left. My life now is but a perpetual conversation with your shadow.—The known sound of your voice still rings in my ears.—There, on the corner of the fender you are standing, or tinkling on the Pianoforte, or stretch'd at length on the sofa.—Do you reflect, my dearest Friend, that it is a week or eight days, before I can receive a letter from you and as much more before you can have my answer, that all that time (with more than Herculean toil) I am employ'd in pushing the tedious hours along, and wishing to annihilate them; the more I strive, the heavier they move and the longer they grow. I can not bear this place, where I have spent many tedious years within less than a month, since you left me. I am going for a few days to see poor Nicholls invited by a letter, wherein he mentions you in such terms, as add to my regard for him, and express my own sentiments better than I can do myself. "I am concern'd (says he [letter not extant]) that

I can not pass my life with him, I never met with any one that pleased and suited me so well: the miracle to me is, how he comes to be so little spoil'd, and the miracle of miracles will be, if he continues so in the midst of every danger and seduction, and without any advantages, but from his own excellent nature and understanding. I own, I am very anxious for him on this account, and perhaps your inquietude may have proceeded from the same cause. I hope, I am to hear, when he has pass'd that cursed sea, or will he forget me thus *in insulam relegatum*? If he should, it is out of my power to retaliate.''

Sure you have wrote to him, my dear Bonstetten, or sure you will! He has moved me with these gentle and sensible expressions of his kindness for you. Are you untouch'd by them?

You do me the credit (and false or true, it goes to my heart) of ascribing to me your love for many virtues of the highest rank. Would to heaven it were so; but they are indeed the fruits of your own noble and generous understanding, that has hitherto struggled against the stream of custom, passion, and ill company, even when you were but a Child, and will you now give way to that stream, when your strength is increased? Shall the Jargon of French Sophists, the allurements of painted women *comme il faut*, or the vulgar caresses of prostitute beauty, the property of all, that can afford to purchase it, induce you to give up a mind and body by Nature distinguish'd from all others to folly, idleness, disease, and vain remorse? Have a care, my ever-amiable Friend, *of loving, what you do not approve*, and know me for your most faithful and most humble Despote.

---

*9 May 1770*

I am return'd, my dear B., from the little journey I had made into Suffolk [to see Nicholls] without answering the end proposed. The thought, that you might have been with me there, has embitter'd all my hours. Your letter has made me happy; as happy as so gloomy, so solitary a Being as I am is capable of being. I know and have too often felt the disadvantages I lay myself under, how much I hurt the little interest I have in you, by this air of sadness so contrary to your nature and present enjoyments: but sure you will forgive, tho' you can not sympathize with me. It is impossible with me to dissemble with you. Such as I am, I expose my heart to your view, nor wish to conceal a single thought from your penetrating eyes. All that you say to me, especially on the subject of Switzerland, is infinitely acceptable. It feels too pleasing ever to be fulfill'd, and as often as I read over your truly kind letter, written long since from London, I stop at these words: *La mort qui peut glacer nos bras avant qu'ils soient entrelacés* [Death may freeze our limbs before we embrace].

# ▼ FRIENDSHIP AND PHILOSOPHY ▼

[JOHANNES VON MÜLLER & CHARLES-VICTOR DE BONSTETTEN]
*Müller to Bonstetten translated from German by Alexandra Trone*
*Bonstetten to Müller translated from German by Rictor Norton*

The fact that Charles-Victor de Bonstetten (1745–1832) received passionate love letters from two great men (see the letters from Thomas Gray, previous selection) is ample testimony of the attractiveness of his personality. Johannes von Müller (1752–1809) met Bonstetten in Hapsburg in May 1773 at the start of his research for his magnum opus, a five-volume history of Switzerland. He was instantly bowled over by the accomplished man of the world, seven years younger than he, who seemed to possess all the graces, good taste, numerous languages and wide-ranging knowledge. The insight which Bonstetten provided into the Swiss people was invaluable to the historian. Their friendship was intimate for twelve years, and they continued writing until Müller's death.

Müller's philosophical companion and servant Bonnet wrote to Bonstetten in November 1, 1774 that Müller "loves you like one loves a mistress. One would have to return to the golden age to find a parallel friendship. You are indispensable to his happiness." They travelled together on various occasions, for example in the Alps in 1777, though never as frequently as Müller wished, for they were often separated due to the former's social obligations and the latter's scholarly pursuits.

Müller always travelled with young male companions, and even set up house together in the Alps with the American Francis Kinlock, though they were separated by the American War of Independence. Goethe discussed Müller's homoerotic relationships with a friend of his. Müller fulfilled his various posts as history professor and tutor with exceptional sagacity; in 1786 he became librarian to the Archbishop-Elector of Mainz, chief librarian of the Imperial Library in 1800, royal historiographer in 1804, and in 1807 the Emperor Napoleon appointed him secretary of state for Westphalia. He died two years later, still a bachelor.

But for all the brilliance of his career, from the moment he met Bonstetten he realized that all the achievements of world ambition were sterile in comparison to the pleasures of the private life, as he explained to Bonstetten in 1775, going on to quote passages from Cicero's *De Amicitia* as the classical basis of the "unending love" he felt for his friend. There was a crisis in their relationship in 1793, when Bonstetten began courting Frederike Brun whom he eventually married. Müller seems to have wished to end their correspondence, but Bonstetten protested that their love need not cease: "The memory of you moves me so deeply, we have grown so intimately together that the drying up of your heart has blighted my soul. . . . As for me I cannot at all let our friendship disappear; however it may be for your soul, it is even more necessary for my sake."

They now wrote much less frequently, although in the last year of his life Müller still addressed Bonstetten as "my good, my tender, my eternal friend." Bonstetten was an important member of the intellectual and literary circle of Geneva which included Mme. de Stael, and he wrote studies of ancient literature and history, and philosophical studies of, for example, the imagination. His most famous work *L'homme du Midi et l'homme du Nord*, a study of the different temperaments of the north and the south, e.g. the melancholy of the north versus the animated passions of the south, can be seen as a paradigm of his northern friends Gray and Müller and himself. In his last years he was active in political writing regarding the Swiss confederation and republicanism.

---

JOHANNES VON MÜLLER TO CHARLES-VICTOR DE BONSTETTEN

*Geneva*
*26th of December, 1774*

I feel very well. All my bodily maladies and maladies of soul derive from ennui when I have no work. Work is the foundation of friendship, and a book in my hand. My friend, you are absolutely right. Only these two things can make me happy and useful to others. My vitality cannot wait out Fortune's slow pace. My very virtues would be my undoing, because the ill-repute of the unemployed, the ignobility that brings advantage, some of the moral weaknesses of the great would make me angry and would torment me. It seems to me that peace and happiness, pleasure and inner merit are far more easily, more surely and for me more properly achieved through scholarship. . . . I cannot tell you what peace, what cheerfulness, what intellectual pleasure I get from philosophy.

What makes contact with the circles which I have quit this last hour especially pleasant is not only that they enable me to increase the number of my acquaintances, it is also my happiness in these circles, and I am far better rewarded by the company of Trembley Polype, of Bonnet [his servant and factotum], of Clason than by the smiles of the most enchantingly beautiful women. A natural sympathy binds me to these people, these Englishmen are genuinely kind to me and give me as much of their time as I want. Trembley Polype has offered to provide me with introductions that could be useful to me in England.

What do you say? *avec un bon esprit on a beaucoup de peine à être bon homme*. You, who know Bonnet? Do not say "que les études donnent des défauts cu caractère," but "Eloquent spokesmen for idealist philosophy or for political chimeras make the world unbearable for young men who see it quite differently, and make these young men, for whom it has no use, unbearable to the world. The study of detailed histories and the desire to please those whom one wants as friends will save one from this."

*Cologne*
*5th April, 1776*

I have as little doubt as you that I will not be happy anywhere in the world where I cannot follow my academic pursuits and cultivate friendship in absolute peace and independence, and that no one is better able than you to grant me this happiness, my dearest B. I will use all the means at my disposal so to control the circumstances of the strange destiny to which human affairs are subject that we may achieve this excellent goal. I shall not postpone anything that depends on hard work and virtue, that I may earn the independence that my heart and mind so urgently need. The rest, my dear friend, is not in my hands: economics may force me—not to sell my freedom, but to go to another country. I shall deal with this matter in a manner worthy of a friend of yours; I perceive where true happiness lies: in the pleasure of the mind in observing and reasoning and in the pleasure of the heart in avowing its feelings. . . .

*Genthod*
*8th August, 1776*

Any mistakes I may make in the future will be your fault; that is only if you neglect your letter-writing—your friendship can never grow cold— might I let myself be surprised by a passion. Tell me why I love you more as time passes. You are now incessantly in me and around me. My dearest friend, how much better it is to think of you than to live with the others! How is it possible to desecrate a heart that is consecrated to you? I need you more than ever; over and above these immutable, laudable plans for a useful life and an immortal name I have forsworn everything that is considered to be pleasant and delightful—not only pleasure but love, not only revels, but good living, not only greed, but ambition. B. is everything to me, you make all my battles easy and all abstinence sweet. Thus you live in my mind and especially in my heart. You write to me often, but it does not seem enough to me; you often address only the historian, and do not embrace your friend often enough.

CHARLES-VICTOR DE BONSTETTEN TO JOHANNES VON MÜLLER

Ah! Mully,                                                          *May 20, 1802*

Allow me still to call you by that sweet name. I wish to see you, I sigh for your friendship. Is it still alive, do you wish to keep our longstanding vow? Ah! you and my love are my consolation, my life. Do you still love me? Oh! what would I not give to embrace you! . . . I read your letters with a transport which I cannot describe to you. All my youth appears before my eyes, but with the bitter sentiment of my eternal uncertainty. I realize too late, alas, the route that I ought to have taken, the road along which your eloquence wished to lead me.

# ▼ REVOLUTIONARY LOVE ▼

### [ALEXANDER HAMILTON & JOHN LAURENS]

Alexander Hamilton (1757–1804) was a pamphleteer in support of Colonial freedom, and fought in the American Revolutionary Army under George Washington and Lafayette. He served in the Continental Congress 1782–83, then began a law practice in New York. After the war he helped to found the Federalist Party (writing many noted essays in *The Federalist*) and influenced national politics. His long-time adversary Vice President Aaron Burr killed him in a duel in 1804.

The aristocratic Southerner John Laurens (1754–82), also an aide to General Washington, once fought a duel to defend Washington's honour. In 1780 he was held prisoner of war by the British at the defeat of Charleston, South Carolina. On his release, he went to France to raise funds for the Revolutionary Army, which he rejoined on his return. He was killed in a minor foraging party on August 27, 1782.

Hamilton wrote to Laurens while Laurens was organizing black slaves to fight the British in South Carolina in 1779, and after Laurens's capture in 1780. Laurens had married in 1776, but his letters were passionate on the subject of friendship, as when he wrote to his friend Richard Meade: "Adieu: I embrace you tenderly. . . . My friendship for you will burn with that pure flame which has kindled you your virtues." Hamilton, who had not yet married, playfully raises the subject of marriage as a substitute or displacement for his own love of Laurens, as an opportunity to explore his own feelings and to gauge the other man's response.

---

ALEXANDER HAMILTON TO JOHN LAURENS

*[April, 1779]*

Cold in my professions—warm in my friendships—I wish, my Dear Laurens, it were in my power, by actions rather than words, to convince you that I love you. I shall only tell you that 'till you bade us Adieu, I hardly knew the value you had taught my heart to set upon you. Indeed, my friend, it was not well done. You know the opinion I entertain of mankind, and how much it is my desire to preserve myself free from particular attachments, and to keep my happiness independent of the caprice of others. You should not have taken advantage of my sensibility, to steal into my affections without my consent. But as you have done it, and as we are generally indulgent to those we love, I shall not scruple to pardon the fraud you have committed, on one condition; that for my sake, if not for your own, you will always continue to merit the partiality, which you have so artfully instilled into me. . . .

And Now my Dear as we are upon the subject of wife, I empower and command you to get me one in Carolina. Such a wife as I want will, I know, be difficult to be found, but if you succeed, it will be the stronger proof of your zeal and dexterity. . . .

If you should not readily meet with a lady that you think answers my description you can only advertise in the public papers and doubtless you will hear of many . . . who will be glad to become candidates for such a prize as I am. To excite their emulation, it will be necessary for you to give an account of the lover—his *size*, make, quality of mind and *body*, achievements, expectations, fortune, &c. In drawing my picture, you will no doubt be civil to your friend; mind you do justice to the length of my nose and don't forget, that I [about five words here—presumably in praise of his penis—have been mutilated in the manuscript].

After reviewing what I have written, I am ready to ask myself what could have put it into my head to hazard this Jeu *de follie*. Do I want a wife? No—I have plagues enough without desiring to add to the number that *greatest of all*; and if I were silly enough to do it, I should take care how I employ a proxy. Did I mean to show my wit? If I did, I am sure I have missed my aim. Did I only intend to [frisk]? In this I have succeeded, but I have done more. I have gratified my feelings, by lengthening out the only kind of intercourse now in my power with my friend. Adieu

Yours.

A Hamilton

---

*South Carolina*
*September 11, 1779*

I acknowledge but one letter from you, since you left us, of the 14th of July which just arrived in time to appease a violent conflict between my friendship and my pride. I have written you five or six letters since you left Philadelphia and I should have written you more had you made proper return. But like a jealous lover, when I thought you slighted my caresses, my affection was alarmed and my vanity piqued. I had almost resolved to lavish no more of them upon you and to reject you as an inconstant and an ungrateful —. But you have now disarmed my resentment and by a single mark of attention made up the quarrel. You must at least allow me a large stock of good nature. . . .

Have you not heard that I am on the point of becoming a benedict? I confess my sins. I am guilty. Next fall completes my doom. I give up my liberty to Miss Schuyler. She is a good hearted girl who I am sure will never play the termagant; though not a genius she has good sense enough to be agreeable, and though not a beauty, she has fine black eyes—is rather handsome and has every other requisite of the exterior to make a lover happy. And believe me, I am lover in earnest, though I do not speak of the perfections of my Mistress in the enthusiasm of Chivalry.

Is it true that you are confined to Pensylvania? Cannot you pay us a visit? If you can, hasten to give us a pleasure which we shall relish with the sensibility of the sincerest friendship.

Adieu God bless you. . . .

A Hamilton

The lads all sympathize with you and send you the assurances of their love.

---

*September 16, 1780*

That you can speak only of your private affairs shall be no excuse for your not writing frequently. Remember that you write to your friends, and that friends have the same interests, pains, pleasures, sympathies; and that all men love egotism.

In spite of Schuylers black eyes, I have still a part for the public and another for you; so your impatience to have me married is misplaced; a strange cure by the way, as if after matrimony I was to be less devoted than I am now. Let me tell you, that I intend to restore the empire of Hymen and that Cupid is to be his prime Minister. I wish you were at liberty to *transgress* the bounds of Pensylvania. I would invite you after the fall to Albany to be witness to the *final consummation*. My Mistress is a good girl, and already loves you because I have told her you are a clever fellow and my friend; but mind, she loves you *a l'americaine* not *a la françoise*.

Adieu, be happy, and let friendship between us be more than a name

A Hamilton

The General & all the lads send you their love.

William Beckford of Fonthill (1760–1844) in middle age. Painting by John Hoppner.

# ▼ DEAREST IMPRESARIO ▼

[WILLIAM BECKFORD & MASTER SAUNDERS]
*Translated from Italian by Boyd Alexander*

The great art collector William Beckford (1760–1844), the wealthiest man in England, was forced to spend many years travelling abroad due to a homosexual scandal involving twelve-year-old William "Kitty" Courtenay in 1784 (the future Earl of Devon), young son of Viscount Courtenay. He spent much of his time in Lisbon, Portugal, where he met Gregorio Fellipe Franchi (1770–1828), a young, attractive and lively musician in the choir of the Patriarchal Seminary. In short order Franchi became Beckford's protégé, and Beckford brought "the Portuguese orange" back with him to England in 1789.

As Franchi grew older he became Beckford's confidant and agent, travelling to London and the Continent collecting paintings, objets d'art and books to fill his master's astonishing home, the gothic extravaganza of Fonthill Abbey in Wiltshire. In this mansion of cathedral proportions— whose central tower was nearly 300 feet high, and whose series of interconnecting reception rooms had an uninterrupted vista of 300 feet—Beckford lived an outcast and a recluse from respectable society, surrounded by a harem of boy-servants to whom he gave nicknames such as "pale Ambrose, infamous Poupee, horrid Ghoul, insipid Mme. Bion [his valet Richardson], cadaverous Nicobuse, the portentous dwarf, frigid 'Silence,' Miss Long, Miss Butterfly [slang for catamite], Countess Pox, Mr. Prudent Well-Sealed-up, The Monkey, The Turk."

Beckford once observed "it's cruel to hear talk of fair boys and dark Jade vases and not to buy them." Many of Beckford's jade vases, paintings and books now grace the finest museum collections in Europe, though his boys have been largely forgotten. The following letters are from a period when Franchi not only negotiated the sale of two paintings by Claude Lorraine, but also acted as Beckford's pimp, eventually succeeding in arranging an assignation between Beckford and Master Saunders, celebrated equestrian performer and tightrope walker at the Circus Royal, who was about eighteen when Beckford laid eyes on him. Franchi insinuated himself into the household of "the Leg family" (i.e. wearers of tights, upon which Beckford played many puns), offering sweets to Abraham Saunders' other children and giving them small sums of money, and wrote back descriptions for Beckford to savour. (The correspondence is in Italian, with some obscene passages omitted by the translator.)

Beckford fantasized about leaving England for Portugal: "It seems to me that a withdrawal into the paradise of Don Fagundes with a copious detachment of artistes etc. gathered together by the Boy of Boys will be the best course to take. Let us get the whole troupe to emigrate, along with the audience gallery, dressing room, stalls and wigs etc. What a *levée en masse*! If I were at my last gasp I would rise for this one. *Gloria in excelsis* (full organ) *et in terra papale Pax, non Pox*—I hope . . .''

---

WILLIAM BECKFORD TO GREGORIO FRANCHI

*Tuesday 8 September [1807]*

. . . If it is at all possible, go to see an angel called Saunders who is a tight-rope walker at the Circus Royal and the certain captivator of every bugger's soul. Ah!

Farewell . . .

---

*Friday [11 September 1807]*

. . . I am afraid that the angel is no longer at the Circus. Highest heaven is where he exists. Ah what a blessed creature! How happy I would be if I could save such a beautiful soul! . . .

---

*Pissing Wednesday 23 September*

. . . It is wretched weather with fog everywhere, and in this lovely sky there are no cherubim to be seen except the dwarf, the Ghoul and pale Ambrose. I can hear nothing except Mr. Wyatt [James Wyatt his architect] lamenting like a Prime Minister at the Court of the most watery and pissful Tertian Fever. He is of a deathly cadaverousness and stinks as only those beneath ground do. Ah, when will more favourable times come? Ah, when shall I be able to see the long desired * [invented pederastic symbol of three interleaved Cs, representing Saunders]. In the meantime, find out what you can about the site of the Earthly Paradise. Many have sought it in vain: some in Syria or Mesopotamia, some in Abyssinia, others in Ceylon, but I (according to the latest information) in Bristol.

---

*[Sunday] 27 September*

I am condemned by cruel Destiny to run a hospital and to hear of nothing but the maladies of that Bagasse Queen Charlotte and the Bagasse Wyatt—how much better it would be to have some sweet invalid to dose with cordials. So if young S[aun]d[e]rs wants a change of air (and perhaps of habits too) let him come to this bosky shade "to cool his fever."

Just Heaven! how interesting the news from Duke Street is! Ah, if you could but act as Impresario to the Court of Maria I [Queen of Portugal], and look out some valiant youth who could dance the tight-rope in the royal presence, as the saintly David, the king of harpists, was sought out in order to appease the furies of Saul. If only you could (and I don't see why not), it would make me so happy. *"Je sens un grand voide dans mon coeur,"* as the Marchioness Lepri used to say to me; and in the way that one frequently says one thing and does another, it was a little lower than the heart that the sentimental lady pointed [to]. But such a pantomime is of small consequence to me. What matters to me is—but you know already what it is, and while you are carrying out so many commissions, execute one for me anyway. Dearest Impresario, have no fear of obstacles; the moment the beatific vision appears before your eyes, all fear (save that of God) will cease to trouble you. In view of your sympatheticness, I think you will find me not only the most charitable of human beings but also the most steadfast and reasonable.

A visit to his father, a proposition for a journey to foreign parts, and even a life-annuity—all this is possible.

> tighti tighti tighti ti
> titi tighti, tighti tighti ti

Celestial harmony, music of the spheres, you make my heart leap! Oh how I despise all the chords of all the lyres of all the poets! Give me only one *cord (garni de son ange)* and . . . ! [a phrase too scabrous to quote]

I descend and touch ground, and here I am at the door of the china shop. Twenty-four plates at twenty-one a piece is some price, and we haven't much money, as you know. What the devil are the plates anyway? Chinese or Japanese? God knows. Why not send one, or put them aside until I can see them? How can I judge without seeing them! What are the other trifles? And the two cups with their covers so different from any I have in my power. Ah my power, my power! It were better to be impotent, better to fall into the secure sleep of total dissolution, than to rage in vain. For pity's sake go to Duke Street and see how he is. Whisper sweetly some proposition of a flight (why not to Brazil?!) with the whole Court, in splendid vessels all glittering with gold, diamonds and carbuncles. There, above the deck my little angel will be poised whilst little zephyrs play and clarinets, oboes and hunting-horns sound. Rings of brilliants, wondrous bracelets and golden coins will rain down in abundance . . .

---

*Tuesday 29 September*

. . . If your cold had not obscured your lucid intellect you would not find it so difficult to seek out the object—the loveliest under heaven. Ah what an object! What harm would there be in paying a visit to Duke Street to find out whether or not *Monsu* [pun on *Monsieur* and *mon çu*, my arse] the son of the house would be agreeable to an engagement abroad. Would this be impossible? I don't see why.

*Thursday 8 October*

I see clearly that poor Barzaba [Syriac for voluptuary, boy-lover] must die of grief and sorrow just as dawn was breaking for him. The infamous cruelty of tormenting his delicate creature with exertions so little suited to his tender years must distress every charitable soul. If you have the least compassion or inclination to serve an honest and pitiable old man, do see if it will not be possible, before this cruel and fatal departure for Ireland, to sow the seed of a friendship; and then, when he returns (if indeed the poor dear rascal survives), who knows whether he may not remember you and a certain kind soul full of the most human compassion who is interested in him and only seeks to discover how much would be asked should any occasion arise for his making a profitable trip. That is all—an all which should in no way be so difficult or dangerous for you to perform. One exposes oneself to no trouble or risk in making an enquiry of this kind with decency. Who is a firmer friend of decency than Barzaba? None to my knowledge. And it would make Barzaba so jubilant, so content if he could ease the destiny (hitherto not very kind) of a charming unfortunate.

My dear Gregory, I cannot live in peace until I know something more positive about this interesting creature. For heaven's sake see him, make his acquaintance, visit his wretched hovel in Duke Street, ask after his dear health, make friends with his father—and you will restore me to life. He cannot leave yet, he cannot leave so soon after a fever for fever-ridden Ireland. If you wish to please me, to oblige me, to enchant me it is in your power. One hour spent on these commissions will enable you to help me in the only thing in which I really need help. Nothing else matters. But this does matter so *very, very, very* much that unless you wish to fail in all the duties of friendship and Christian charity you will find some plausible excuse for going where my beloved has his haunts. One moment of this beatific vision will suffice to show you that I am right, and provide sustenance for a thousand conversations between us when terrible Ireland swallows up my treasure.

Happy you, to be able, in the easiest and simplest way in the world, to gild my days and breathe new life into the miserable carcass of poor, love-sick, drooling, sorrowing Barzaba.

. . . I would forgive everything if only you would give proof of your ability by going there—where I live, where I breathe—for elsewhere I do not exist. Ah! Ah! Ah!

---

*Alleluia Saturday [10 October]*

. . . How lovely to see that dear name! Duke Street! Duke of my soul, lead me [*conducetemi*] beneath your banners and I will follow you faithfully where you will, how you will, when you will. Let us march to victory, to military glory. But if sweet peace be more the order of your days let us live in peace in some obscure corner. I submit to whatever is required. . . . You are not deaf to my laments.

---

### The Sunday of the Return to Life [11 October]

. . . In a room at Brunet's Hotel [Leicester Square]—he is going to appear. Ah, how my heart beats! For God's sake, be careful, risk nothing. Shall I kiss? No, for God's sake, not yet; be discreet, moderate, collected, cold—if that's possible in the rays of the sun in full —. Talk of this and that, of a contract, of parrots, oranges and lemons etc. Make yourself his friend, but not a lover—nothing suspicious [rest deleted as being too scabrous]. Decency, decency! . . . But I'm not sure that without witnesses present the risk isn't great—discussing this face to face, alone with the angel himself in his own room in furnished apartments. Passing into the presence of God without the mediation of His saints is too rash, too —. My dear Gregory, my revered and esteemed Acheron, do not expose yourself to any peril—remember me, but at the same time remember the cursèd country in which, for my extreme misfortune, I live!

# ▼ FAIR YOUNG BULL ▼

[HEINRICH VON KLEIST & ERNST VON PFUEL]

*Translated from German by Alexandra Trone*

Bernd Heinrich Wilhelm von Kleist (1777–1811) resigned his commission from the Prussian army in 1799 because he was by nature a musician, a writer, an enthusiast. For several years he travelled restlessly across Europe experiencing a series of obscure intellectual and emotional crises. A personal "dark night of the soul" around 1801, Napoleon's defeat of Prussia from 1806, and his imprisonment as a spy in France in 1807, culminated in a fanatical patriotism as the basis for a purpose in life and literary inspiration. His poetry, short stories and plays are excellent examples of the medievalism and Apollonianism of the high German Romantic movement.

He is most noted for his unrelenting psychological realism in describing characters obsessed by an unsparing sense of justice which becomes a personal desire for revenge, in a malign medieval universe where tragedy prevails. His writings exhibit in fact the single-minded intensity of the sado-masochist: in his finest play *Penthesilea* the heroine tears her lover Achilles limb from limb with her teeth and bare hands, and in several short stories he describes in graphic detail how the hero blows out his own brains after first killing the heroine.

Kleist threatened to kill himself on several occasions, inexplicably broke off an engagement to be married, and loved secrecy and disguise and mysterious trips with male friends. At the age of thirty-four, Kleist entered into a suicide pact with Henriette Vogel—not as doomed lovers, simply as doomed individuals, she doomed by terminal cancer, he by poverty and disillusion—and one day in November 1811 on the shore of the Wannsee he shot her and then himself.

Kleist's characters are subject to states of high excitement and violent turmoil, and finally a desire to be damned. The early psychoanalysts were fascinated by his bizarre life and monomaniacal characters. A homosexual conflict is obviously the key to unlocking his inner life, but his biographers tend to refer vaguely to "the mysteries" of his emotional and sexual life. An astonishing letter survives to Ernst von Pfuel, written while Napoleon was ravaging the country and separating the two men who were obviously lovers; Pfuel was destined to become the Prussian War Minister. Most of Kleist's letters are addressed to his close friend Rühle von Lilienstern, his confidant rather than his lover, but that relationship also seems to have begun in similarly intense circumstances.

HEINRICH VON KLEIST TO ERNST VON PFUEL

*Berlin*
*7th January, 1805*

With your eloquence, dear boy, you wield a strange power over my heart, and although it is I myself who gave you full insight into my state of mind, yet at times you show me an image of myself so close to my very soul that I start as before the newest phenomenon in all the world. I shall never forget that festive night when, in the worst hole in all of France, you abused me in a manner that was truly awe-inspiring, nearly as the archangel abused his fallen brother in the Messiad [epic poem by Klopstock]. Why can I no longer venerate you, whom I still love above all, as my master? How we rushed into one another's arms a year ago in Dresden! How boundlessly the world opened out, like a racetrack, before our beings trembling with desire for the contest! And now we lie there, flung across one another, ending with our glances the race that never seemed so splendid to us as now, enveloped in the dust of our fall. The fault is mine, mine, I entangled you in this, oh I can't tell you this as I feel it. My dear Pfuel, of what use are all these tears to me? To pass the time minute by minute as they fall, I would, like the bereft [literally "naked"] King Richard, hollow out a grave with them and in that grave bury you and me and our endless pain. So we shall embrace no more! Not even if one day, recovered from our [i.e. our country's] plunge into ruin—for what is there from which man does not recover—we meet again, old and hobbling along on crutches. What we loved in one another then were the highest qualities of mankind; for we loved to observe our natures unfolding through a few fortunate gifts that were only then developing. We felt—or at least I did—the delightful enthusiasm of friendship! You brought back the times of ancient Greece to my heart, I could have slept with you, dear boy; thus all my soul embraces you. Often, as you went to bathe in the Lake of Thun, I would gaze at your beautiful body with truly girlish feelings. An artist might well use it for a study. Were I an artist, it might perhaps have inspired me with an idea for a god. Your small, curly head set on a sturdy neck, two wide shoulders, a sinewy body: the whole a model of strength, as though you had been designed after the fairest young bull ever sacrificed to Zeus. All the laws of Lycurgus, as well as his concept of the love of youths, have become clear to me through the feelings you have awakened in me. Come to me! Listen, I want to tell you something. I have become fond of Altenstein, I have been entrusted with the drawing up of several edicts and I no longer doubt that I can reasonably expect to pass the test. I can work out a differential and write a poem; are not these the two summits of human capability? They will surely employ me, and soon, and with a salary: come to Anspach with me and let us enjoy the sweets of friendship. Let me have gained something from all these battles that makes my life at least bearable. You shared what you had with me in Leipzig, or you wanted to, which comes to the same thing; accept as much from me! I shall never marry—be wife to me, and children, and grandchildren! Go no farther along the road that you have walked. Don't throw yourself at the feet of destiny, it is mean-spirited and will trample you. Let one sacrifice be enough. Preserve the ruins of your soul, that they may forever remind us with pleasure of the romantic part of our lives. And if one day you are called to the battlefield to fight for your country, then go, your worth will be recognized if needs must be. Accept my suggestion. If you do not, I will feel that no one in the world loves me. I should like to say more, but it won't do in a letter. Diverse matters in person.

   Heinrich v. Kleist

---

HEINRICH VON KLEIST TO RÜHLE VON LILIENSTERN

*Königsberg*
*1806*

If I hesitated unnecessarily in answering until now, my friend, you would nonetheless pick up your pen so as to bind the unravelling garland of our friendship and, moreover, to add a new blossom to it; but this time you let it go, and as for you, it seems, it could fall apart forever. Well, it isn't important, my good Rühle, and I kiss you. This garland was well wound in the beginning and without further effort the binding will last as long as the flowers. If in your heart of hearts you change as little as I do, one day, if we see one another again, we can say "good day" and "did you sleep well?" and continue our last year's conversations as though they had taken place the day before. I have received the last part of your love and life story. My darling boy, love as long as you live, but do not love the sun as the Moor loves it, and turn black. When it rises or sets, glance up at it, and let it shine on you the rest of the time through your good deeds and fortify yourself for them and forget it. I cannot yet get the thought out of my head that there is still something we have to do together. Who would want to be happy in this world of ours! I might almost say "You ought to be ashamed of yourself if that is what you wish. What myopia, you noble creature, to strive for anything, here, where everything ends in death." We meet, we love one another through the springtimes of three years, and we shun one another for an eternity. And what is worth striving for, if not love! Oh, there must be something besides love, happiness, fame and X Y or Z, something that even our souls don't dream of. . . .

   H. K.

# ▼ THE CORNELIAN ▼

[Lord Byron & John Edleston]

The English Romantic poet George Gordon, Lord Byron (1788–1824) took up residence at Trinity College, Cambridge, in October 1805, and established an intimate friendship with John Edleston, a choirboy at Trinity Chapel, which lasted until he left Cambridge in June 1807. As a pledge of their love, Edleston in 1806 gave Byron a cornelian brooch pin in the shape of a heart, to which Byron refers in his poem "The Adieu" (about their parting) and the series of poems in which Edleston is disguised under the feminine name "Thyrza" (several of which were suppressed after their initial publication). Byron asked his other boyhood friend Edward Noel Long: "pray, keep the subject of my *'Cornelian'* a Secret."

Thomas Moore, Byron's friend and first biographer, who allowed Byron's memoir to be destroyed and who excised the homosexual passages from the surviving journals and letters, called Edleston Byron's "adopted brother"—a tag that does not adequately account for the passion of the poetry:

> Ours too the glance none saw beside;
>> The smile none else might understand;
> The whisper'd thought of hearts allied,
>> The pressure of the thrilling hand;
> The kiss so guiltless and refin'd
>> That Love each warmer wish forbore;
> Those eyes proclaim'd so pure a mind,
>> Ev'n passion blush'd to plead for more.

Byron left England with some urgency in 1809, probably because some affair threatened to come to light. Byron's confidant John Cam Hobhouse recorded in his diary on June 6, 1810: "messenger arrived from England—bringing a letter from [Francis] Hodgson to B[yron]—tales spread—the *Edleston* accused of indecency." Byron may once have struggled against his sexual inclinations, but his experiences in Greece and Turkey confirmed his far-ranging sexual appetite. In 1810 Byron had already acquired a new companion, the teenager Nicolo Giraud, whom he made his principal beneficiary in his will.

Byron returned to England—which he loathed because of its cant and puritanism—after the death of his mother in 1811, only to learn from Edleston's sister that his boyhood love had died in May that year. It was a greater shock than the death of his mother—indeed, Edleston was only twenty-one when he was felled by consumption—and prompted at least seven moving elegies, including "To Thyrza," "Away, away, ye notes of woe!" "One struggle more, and I am free," "And thou are dead, as young and fair,'' ''If sometimes in the haunts of men,'' ''On a Cornelian Heart Which Was Broken,'' and a Latin elegy newly discovered and published in 1974, the only poem that uses the masculine gender, ''Te, te, care puer! (Thee, beloved boy),'' with Edleston's name written three times at the top.

In 1812 Lady Caroline Lamb, mentally unbalanced, insulted Byron by sending him an envelope containing some of her pubic hair together with the inscription ''next to Thyrza Dearest.'' Byron had given the cornelian heart to Elizabeth Pigot, perhaps just before he left England in 1809, but in October 1811 he requested that it be returned to him as a memorial.

> Thou bitter pledge! thou mournful token!
> Though painful, welcome to my breast!
> Still, still preserve that love unbroken,
> Or break the heart to which thou'rt press'd.

The selections begin with a short note written in cypher characters just before Byron left Cambridge on June 27, 1807, and translated by Leslie Marchand with the help of an alphabetical key found in his papers.

---

LORD BYRON TO JOHN EDLESTON

*May, 1807*

D-R-T [Dearest?]—
Why not? With this kiss make me yours again forever.
    Byron

---

LORD BYRON TO ELIZABETH BRIDGET PIGOT

*Cambridge*
*June 30th, 1807*

. . . I am almost superannuated here. My old friends (with the exception of a very few) all departed, and I am preparing to follow them, but remain till Monday to be present at 3 *Oratorios*, 2 *Concerts*, a *Fair*, and a *Ball*. I find I am not only *thinner* but *taller* by an inch since my last visit. I was obliged to tell every body my *name*, nobody having the least recollection of *visage*, or person. Even the hero of *my Cornelian* (who is now sitting *vis-à-vis*, reading a volume of my *Poetics*) passed me in Trinity walks without recognising me in the least, and was thunderstruck at the alteration which had taken place in my countenance, &c., &c. Some say I look *better*, others *worse*, but all agree I am *thinner*,—more I do not require. . . .

I quit Cambridge with little regret, because our *set* are *vanished*, and my *musical protégé* before mentioned has left the choir, and is stationed in a mercantile house of considerable eminence in the metropolis. You may have heard me observe he is exactly to an hour two years younger than myself. I found him grown considerably, and as you will suppose, very glad to see his former *Patron*. He is nearly my height, very *thin*, very fair complexion, dark eyes, and light locks. My opinion of his mind you already know;—I hope I shall never have reason to change it. Every body here conceives me to be an *invalid*. The University at present is very gay from the fêtes of divers kinds. I supped out last night, but eat (or ate) nothing, sipped a bottle of claret, went to bed at two, and rose at eight. I have commenced early rising, and find it agrees with me. The Masters and the Fellows are all very *polite* but look a little *askance*—don't much admire *lampoons*—truth always disagreeable.

---

LORD BYRON TO ELIZABETH BRIDGET PIGOT

*Trin. Coll. Camb.*
*July 5th, 1807*

Since my last letter I have determined to reside *another year* at Granta, as my rooms, etc. etc. are finished in great style, several old friends come up again, and many new acquaintances made; consequently my inclination leads me forward, and I shall return to college in October if still *alive*. My life here has been one continued routine of dissipation—out at different places every day, engaged to more dinners, etc. etc. than my *stay* would permit me to fulfil. At this moment I write with a bottle of claret in my *head* and *tears* in my *eyes*; for I have just parted with my *"Cornelian,"* who spent the evening with me. As it was our last interview, I postponed my engagement to devote the hours of the *Sabbath* to friendship:—Edleston and I have separated for the present, and my mind is a chaos of hope and sorrow. To-morrow I set out for London: you will address your answer to "Gordon's Hotel, Albemarle Street," where I *sojourn* during my visit to the metropolis.

I rejoice to hear you are interested in my *protégé*; he has been my *almost constant* associate since October, 1805, when I entered Trinity College. His *voice* first attracted my attention, his *countenance* fixed it, and his *manners* attached me to him for ever. He departs for a mercantile house in town in October, and we shall probably not meet till the expiration of my minority, when I shall leave to his decision either entering as a *partner* through my interest, or residing with me altogether. Of course he would in his present frame of mind prefer the *latter*, but he may alter his opinion previous to that period;—however, he shall have his choice. I certainly love him more than any human being, and neither time nor distance have had the least effect on my (in general) changeable disposition. In short we shall put *Lady E. Butler* and *Miss Ponsonby** to the blush, *Pylades* and

---

*Byron is referring to the famous lesbian "Ladies of Llangollen,"—Lady Eleanor Butler (1739-1829), daughter of the Earl of Ormonde, and Sarah Ponsonby (1755-1831), who lived together in Wales in domestic bliss for more than fifty years; the other references are to Orestes, lover of Pylades, and son of Agamemnon of the House of Atreus in ancient Greece. Nisus, Trojan hero in Virgil's *Aeneid*, was the older lover of the young and brash Euryalus, and died avenging his lover.

*Orestes* out of countenance, and want nothing but a catastrophe like *Nisus* and *Euryalus* to give *Jonathan* and *David* the "go by." He certainly is perhaps more attached to *me* than even I am in return. During the whole of my residence at Cambridge we met every day, summer and winter, without passing *one* tiresome moment, and separated each time with increasing reluctance. I hope you will one day see us together. He is the only being I esteem, though I *like* many. . . . My *protégé* breakfasts with me; parting spoils my appetite—excepting from Southwell [i.e. leaving England altogether].

---

LORD BYRON TO FRANCIS HODGSON

*Newstead Abbey*
*October 10th, 1811*

I heard of a death the other day that shocked me more than any of the preceding, of one whom I once loved more than I ever loved a living thing, & one who I believe loved me to the last, yet I had not a tear left for an event which five years ago would have bowed me to the dust; still it sits heavy on my heart & calls back what I wish to forget, in many a feverish dream.

# ▼ BEST OF BLESSINGS ▼

[REV. JOHN CHURCH & NED]

John Church (*ca.* 1780–*ca.* 1825) was a foundling, an infant who could barely toddle when he was laid at the steps of the Church of St. John's in Clerkenwell, London, sometime between 1782–84. He began his career as a Dissenting minister in Banbury, Oxford, but in 1808 he was accused of having sodomitical relations with several devout young men in his congregation. He was reviled in the streets, and there were fears the Meeting House would be burned down. He fled to Birmingham, from where he wrote apologizing to the elders: "I have done most foolishly—I have acted most imprudently . . . the boys tell a simple plain story, and you do right to believe them in what they say; and I own that I have been too imprudent, but I am not conscious of having done the actual crime; if any thing of that nature has been of which they speak, it must have been without my knowledge, when I was asleep, and supposing I was in my own bed with my wife."

By 1809 he was in south London, serving as the regular conventicle preacher at the Obelisk Chapel, St. George's Fields, where he became immensely popular. Church was an active member of the gay community—or madge culls, as they called themselves. In 1809 he performed the funeral services for Richard Oakden, a bank clerk who was hanged at Tyburn for sodomy, and in 1810 he was officiating in the Marrying Room of The White Swan in Vere Street, the most famous of the early nineteenth-century gay brothels. The regulars at The Swan included a coal merchant named Kitty Cambric, Miss Selina a police constable, Black-eyed Leonora the Drummer of the Guards, Pretty Harriet the butcher, and James Cook the heterosexual landlord with whom Rev. Church unwisely fell in love.

The "gay parson" married many male couples, at ceremonies accompanied by "bridesmaids" in drag. Mock birth ceremonies were also performed at The Swan, where no doubt Rev. Church baptised the wooden dolls that were produced. But his duties were short-lived, for The Swan flourished for only six months before it was raided, and many members of the Vere Street Coterie were pilloried and imprisoned, and two were hanged. Church himself escaped detection until 1813, when an anti-gay newspaper campaign was mounted against him. Even his wife was beaten up, and threats were made to burn down the public house she kept.

Church's notoriety caused his flock to double in size, and increased earnings enabled him to build his own church. He managed to evade prosecution until 1816, when he was sentenced to two years' imprisonment for attempted buggery. He was regarded as a martyr by the women in his congregation, who regularly supplied him in prison with fine food and drink. He took the opportunity to write his autobiography, wherein he called himself "A Child of Peculiar Providence," and he preached to an assembly

Rev. John Church (*ca.* 1780–1825), known as the gay parson for the homosexual weddings he performed in early 19th century London (almost two centuries before the Hawaii Supreme Court decision). Frontispiece to his autobiography, *The Foundling*; or, *The Child of Providence* (1823).

of one thousand supporters upon his release.

He remained a popular preacher for the next five years, but seems to have succumbed to drink, and possibly died around 1825. (For a full biography, see Rictor Norton, *Mother Clap's Molly House* (1992), 199–211.) The following letters were written to the young attendant named Edward (Ned) at the Obelisk Chapel, with whom he was in love. One of the many scandals involving Church was brewing at the time, and his enemies had succeeded in persuading Ned to testify that Church had made advances to him, though the case did not go to court.

---

REV. JOHN CHURCH TO MR. EDWARD B—

*3 March 1809*

Dear Ned,

May the best of blessings be yours in life and in death, while the sweet sensations of real genuine disinterested friendship rules every power of our mind body and soul[.] I can only say I wish you was as much captivated with sincere friendship as I am but we all know our own feelings best— Friendship those best of names, affection [w]hose sweetest power like some powerful charm that overcomes the mind—I could write much on this subject but I dare not trust you with what I could say much as I esteem you— You would consider it as unmanly and quite effeminate, and having already proved what human nature is I must conceal even those emotions of love which I feel[.] I wish I had the honor of being loved by you as much and in as great a degree as I do you, Sometimes the painful thought of a separation overpowers me, many are now trying at it but last night I told the persons that called on me that let them insinuate what they would I would never sacrifice my dear Ned to the shrine of any other friend upon earth— and that them who did not like him should have none of my company at all[.] I find dear Ned many are using all their power to part us but I hope it will prove in vain on your side, the effect that all this has upon me is to make me love you ten times more than ever, I wish opposition may have the same effect upon you in this particular but I fear not, however I am confident if you love me now or at any other time my heart will ever be set upon you nor can I ever forget you till death. Your leaving of me will break my heart, bring down my poor mind with sorrow to the Grave and wring from my eyes the briny tears, while my busy meddling memory will call to remembrance the few pleasant hours we spent together, I picture to my imagination the affecting scene the painful thought, I must close the affecting subject 'tis more than my feelings are able to bear—My heart is full, my mind is sunk I shall be better when I have vented out my grief Stand fast my dearest Ned to me I shall to you whether you do to me or no, and may we be pardoned, justified, and brought more to the knowledge of Christ. O help me to sing—

When thou my righteous Judge shall come
To fetch thy ransom'd people home,
    May I among them stand,
Let such a worthless worm as I,
That sometimes am afraid to die,
    Be found at thy right hand.

I love to meet amongst them now,
Before thy gracious feet to bow,
    Tho' vilest of them all;
But can I bear the piercing thought,
What if my name should be left out,
    When thou for them should call.

Learn these two verses by heart and then I will write two more, as they are expressions of [my] mind['s] fears sensations and desires—I must close, I long to see your dear face again, I long for Sunday morning till then God bless you.

I remain unalterably thy dear thy loving friend,
    J. Church

---

*ca. 12 March 1809*

Dear Sir,

Is this thy kindness to thy once professed much loved friend, surely I never, never did deserve such cruel treatment at your hands; why not speak to me last night in James-street when you heard me call, Stop! stop! Ned! do, pray do; but cruel, cruel Ned, deaf to all intreaties—O why was I permitted to pass the door of Mr. Gibbons when you and West were coming out Why was I permitted to tramp up and down the New Cut after you; I only wanted to speak one bitter heart breaking painful distressing word, farewell; I only wanted to pour my sorrows into your bosom, to shake hands with you once more, but I was denied this indulgence. I never, never thought you would deceive me—O what an unhappy man am I; the thing that I most feared is come upon me, no excuse can justify such apparent duplicity; O my distress is great indeed. O my God! what shall I do? O Christ! O God! support me in this trying hour, what a night am I passing through, I cannot sleep, tis near three o'clock; alas! sleep is departed, how great my grief, how bitter my sorrows, the loss of my character is nothing to the loss of one dearer to me than any thing else. O let me give vent to tears, but I am too too much distressed to cry O that I could. I feel this like a dagger; never, never can I forgive the unhappy instrument of my distress in Charlotte-street[.] Why did my dear friend Edward deceive me! O how my mind was eased on Wednesday night; alas, how distressed on Thursday. I have lost my only bosom friend, dearest dearest friend, bosom from bosom torn, how horrid. Ah, dear Suffolk court, never surely can I see you again. How the Phillistines will triumph; there, so would we have it; how Ebeir, Calvin, Thompson, Edwards, Bridgman, all will rejoice, and I have lost my friend, my all in this world, except the other part of myself, my wife and poor babes; never did I expect this from my dear E— B—, O for a calm mind, that I might sleep till day light; but no, this I fear will be denied me. How can I bear the piercing thought, parted; a dreadful word, worst of sensations, the only indulgence, the only confident, the only faithful, the only kind and indulgent sympathising friend, to lose you. O what a stroke; O what a cut, what shall I do for matter for Sunday; O that I could get someone to preach for me; how can I lift up my head. O Sir, if you have a grain of affection left for me, do, do intreat of God to support me; this is a worse affliction than the loss of my character nine months ago. A man cannot lose his character twice. O I did think you knew better; I did think I had found one in you that I could not find elsewhere; but no, the first object presented to you seen suddenly, gained your mind, gained your affections; and I, poor unhappy distressed I, am left to deplore your loss. O for submission, but I am distressed; woe is me. O that I had never, never known you, then I should never feel what I do; but I thank you for your company hitherto, I have enjoyed it four months exactly, but this is over for ever. miserable as I am, I wish you well for ever, for ever. I write in the bitterness of my soul which I feel. May you never be cursed with the feelings I possess as long as you live. What a day I have before me; I cannot go out of my house till Sunday morning. How can I conceal my grief from my dear wife? how shall I hide it? what shall I say? I am miserable, nor can I surmount the shock at all. I have no friend to pour out my sorrows to now, I wish I had; I am sorry you are so easily duped by any to answer their purposes, my paper is full, my heart is worse; God help me; Lord God support me! what shall I do, dear God! O Lord! have mercy on me, I must close; this comes from your ever loving, but distressed

    J. Church

# ▼ WRITHING BEDFELLOWS ▼

[THOMAS WITHERS & JAMES HAMMOND]

When the following letters were written, twenty-two-year-old Thomas Jefferson Withers (1803–1866) was studying law at South Carolina College. He married in 1833 and was to become a journalist, lawyer, and judge of the South Carolina Court of Appeals until his death in 1866. James H. Hammond, aged nineteen at the time of the letters, was to become one of the prominent men in the antebellum South, serving as governor, congressman and senator for South Carolina, and active supporter of the pro-slavery argument and considered to be the likely heir to Vice President John C. Calhoun. He was a lusty young man, as indicated by the letters, and rumours of an incident in 1843 involving his brother-in-law's four teenage daughters eventually forced him into political retirement.

Male bonding was pronounced in the Old South but no letters of a remotely comparable nature—camp and sexy—have been discovered for this period in American history. The letters are liable to a wide range of interpretation, but they do suggest that homosexual experience between men could be nonchalant and unexceptional. The letters were re-discovered in 1978 by the American gay scholar Martin Duberman, who has written of his battle to get permission to publish them—the South Caroliniana Library suggesting, for example, that the text be published without any indication of the names of the correspondents—and how he was finally compelled to publish them in opposition to the guardians of the American heritage.

---

THOMAS JEFFERSON WITHERS TO
JAMES H. HAMMOND                          *Columbia, South Carolina*
                                                      *May 15, 1826*

Dear Jim:

I got your Letter this morning about 8 o'clock, from the hands of the Bearer . . . I was sick as the Devil, when the Gentleman entered the Room, and have been so during most of the day. About 1 o'clock I swallowed a huge mass of Epsom Salts—and it will not be hard to imagine that I have been at dirty work since. I feel partially relieved—enough to write a hasty dull letter.

I feel some inclination to learn whether you yet sleep in your Shirttail, and whether you yet have the extravagant delight of poking and punching a writhing Bedfellow with your long fleshen pole—the exquisite touches of which I have often had the honor of feeling? Let me say unto thee that unless thou changest former habits in this particular, thou wilt be represented by every future Chum as a nuisance. And, I pronounce it, with good reason too. Sir, you roughen the downy Slumbers of your Bedfellow—by such hostile—furious lunges as you are in the habit of making at him—when he is least prepared for defence against the crushing force of a Battering Ram. Without reformation my imagination depicts some awful results for which you will be held accountable—and therefore it is, that I earnestly recommend it. Indeed it is encouraging an assault and battery propensity, which needs correction—& uncorrected threatens devastation, horror & bloodshed, etc. . . .

> With great respect I am the old
> > Stud,
> > > Jeff

---

*September 24, 1826*

My dear Friend,

. . . Your excellent Letter of 13 June [untraced] arrived . . . a few weeks since. . . . Here, where anything like a systematic course of thought, or of reading, is quite out of the question—such system leaves no vacant, idle moments of painful vacuity, which invites a whole Kennel of treacherous passions to prey upon one's vitals . . . the renovation of spirit which follows the appearance of a *friend's* Letter—the diagram of his soul—is like a grateful shower from the cooling fountains of Heaven to reanimate drooping Nature. Whilst your letters are Transcripts of real—existing feeling, and are on that account peculiarly welcome—they at the same time betray too much *honesty* of purpose not to strike an harmonious chord in my mind. I have only to regret that, honesty of intention and even assiduity in excition [execution?] are far from being the uniform agents of our destiney [*sic*] here—However it must, at best, be only an a priori argument for us to settle the condemnation of the world, before we come in actual contact with it. This task is peculiarly appropriate to the acrimony of old age —and perhaps we had as well defer it, under the hope that we may reach a point, when 'twill be all that we can do—

I fancy, Jim, that your *elongated protuberance*—your fleshen pole— your [two Latin words; indecipherable]—has captured complete mastery over you—and I really believe, that you are charging over the pine barrens of your locality, braying, like an ass, at every she-male you can discover. I am afraid that you are thus prostituting the "image of God" and suggest that if you thus blasphemously essay to put on the form of a Jack—in this stead of that noble image—you will share the fate of Nebuchadnazzer of old. I should lament to hear of you feeding upon the dross of the pasture and alarming the country with your vociferations. The day of miracles may not be past, and the flaming excess of your lustful appetite may drag down the vengeance of supernal power.—And you'll "be damn-d if you don't marry"?—and felt a disposition to set down and gravely detail me the reasons of early marriage. But two favourable ones strike me now—the first is, that Time may grasp love so furiously as totally [?] to disfigure his Phiz. The second is, that, like George McDuffie [a politician], he may have the hap-hazzard of a broken backbone befal him, which will relieve him from the performance of affectual family-duty—& throw over the brow of his wife, should he chance to get one, a most foreboding gloom—As to the first, you will find many a modest good girl subject to the same inconvenience—and as to the second, it will only superinduce such domestic whirlwinds, as will call into frequent exercise rhetorical displays of impassioned Eloquence, accompanied by appropriate and perfect specimens of those gestures which Nature and feeling suggest. To get children, it is true, fulfills a department of social & natural duty—but to let them starve, or subject them to the alarming hazard of it, violates another of a most important character. This is the dilemma to which I reduce you—choose this day which you will do.

# ▼ A FAIRY TALE ▼

[HANS CHRISTIAN ANDERSEN & THE
HEREDITARY GRAND-DUKE OF SAXE-WEIMAR-EISENACH]

The life of the Danish writer Hans Christian Andersen (1805–75) resembles that of his most famous fairy tale, "The Story of the Little Mermaid." In letters written to his beloved young friend Edvard Collin in 1835–36 Andersen said "Our friendship is like 'The Mysteries,' it should not be analyzed," and "I long for you as though you were a beautiful Calabrian girl."

In the fairy tale, written when Collin decided to get married, Andersen displays himself as the sexual outsider who lost his prince to another. Andersen's most recent biographer, Elias Bredsdorff, in 1993 used diaries to argue that Andersen never had sexual intercourse but was a compulsive masturbator; Bredsdorff is uneasy with the notion of "homosexual emotions" and therefore declines to label his subject gay. Kinsey, according to his associate W. B. Pomeroy, suspected Andersen was gay, and was shown by a scholar in Copenhagen an immense pile of data and papers on Andersen: "seeing the original manuscripts which the scholar possessed, Kinsey could say unequivocally that they were straight-out homosexual stories"; like the mute Little Mermaid, "Andersen could not tell the world of his own homosexual love for the people of the world, but the original manuscripts showed his feelings clearly."

The following letters cover Andersen's later "homosexual emotional" relationship with Karl Alexander, Hereditary Grand-Duke of Saxe-Weimar-Eisenach (1818–1901), whom he met at the theatre in Weimar, and with whom he spent three weeks at Ettersburg in 1844. He then made a European tour, and in Rome, Paris and London was received with great approbation by the press, the public, and other great men of letters and the nobility. But even after an intervening war and eight years of separation, he still treasured the bright memory of his fairy-tale summer in Ettersburg. Andersen spent his annual summer holidays with the Duke from 1854 through 1857, and they continued to correspond until Andersen's death.

---

HANS CHRISTIAN ANDERSEN TO THE HEREDITARY
GRAND-DUKE OF SAXE-WEIMAR-EISENACH                    *Copenhagen*
                                                  *26th October 1844*

My Noble Hereditary Grand-Duke,—

Your Highness can easily imagine my happiness on receipt of your warm and affectionate letter; it was as if we were again together as at Ettersburg at the sad moment of parting. You pressed my hand, and said you would be a kind and sincere friend. Your Royal Highness has gained in me a poet's soul—a human heart the more. Your letter now lies among my most sacred treasures. . . .

*Copenhagen*
*3rd October 1847*

I am home again in the old street, in the old house. The same people are passing to and fro, the carts are rolling along,—everything is going on in the old track; I myself am making the usual visits, attending the theatre, and sitting alone once more in my own room, as if nothing had happened; and yet my head and heart are so full. It is with me as after a great ball, the music still sounding in my ears, my thoughts like dashing waves. I can find no rest. I have been at home now for eight days already, and yet have done nothing at all, not even written letters—this is the first one—and now I hope with this inauguration of the pen, that, from today forth, a great deal will be written, and the new novel will burst into bloom. . . .

My stay in Holland, England, and Scotland floats before me like a phantasy woven of joy and sunshine, and at the close come the beautiful days at Ettersburg, with our reunion, our life together there, and our parting. Yes, yes, my noble friend, I love you as a man can only love the noblest and best. This time I felt that you were still more ardent, more affectionate to me. Every little *trait* is preserved in my heart. On that cool evening, when you took your cloak and threw it around me, it warmed not only my body, but made my heart glow still more ardently.

Many of the exalted family are now at sylvan Ettersburg; your Royal sister is there,—recall me to her gracious remembrance, also to your exalted parents; and may I hope that your Royal Highness will present my most respectful thanks and greeting to the excellent Hereditary Grand-Duchess.

Our morning chats at the coffee-table were charming. The wreath, made by the clever, amiable young ladies, I have hung over Thorwaldsen's statue [the Danish sculptor famous for his male nudes]. The colour is still in every leaf, and sun is shining on it at this moment, the flowers are as fresh as the memories.

All my dear friends at Copenhagen I have found well. My dear Collin, who has now become "Excellency," and whom I love as a father, seems strong and well as ever; may he long remain so. It is beautiful autumn weather, and that also raises my spirits. . . .

The poems and the dramatic pieces are soon coming. I am rejoicing that your Royal Highness will hear these pulsations of my heart. . . .

And now may you be happy.

H. C. Andersen

---

*Copenhagen*
*4th May 1848*

How thoughtful of you to write me. I received the letter somewhat late, but, if it had not come at all, I should have known that I was not forgotten.

The agitations which are passing through the lands I feel to my finger tips. Denmark, my native country, and Germany, where there are so many whom I love, are standing opposite to each other in enmity! Your Royal Highness will be able to feel how all that pains me! I believe so firmly in the nobility of all men, and feel certain that if they only understood each other, everything would blossom in peace. Yet I did not wish to speak of politics, they stand far from me like a strange, distant cloud; but now they have spread over all Europe, and their sharp mist penetrates every member, and one breathes nothing but politics. . . .

When shall we meet, my noble friend? Perhaps never more! And as I think this, all the dear memories of every hour of our life together, the cordiality of our meetings flash through my mind, and my heart melts.

Thanks for your noble friendship! When this greeting reaches your hands, may you feel in it the pulsations of my heart. God grant that a better state of things may soon come about.

H. C. Andersen

---

*Trollhatte in Sweden*
*18th August 1849*

From the extreme north, on the boundary of Lapland, I have just reached here. I left Denmark in the spring, where I was useless in the struggle for victory, and have travelled through Sweden, have been up at Dalkarlien where no thunder of cannon resounds. Happy, politically-defined Sweden, with its secure boundaries! Three years ago I dreamt of undertaking the journey to Stockholm with you, but what a change has now come over everything! I travelled alone, but you were in my thoughts—yes, I may say daily in my thoughts—with melancholy and sadness. Oh, you scarcely know how highly I rate you, how firmly you have grown into my heart! I have only rightly understood that this summer. I have received no answer to my last letter which I wrote to you in the spring. I afterwards heard that a contingent of Weimar troops had marched to the north, and finally I read that your Royal Highness had yourself gone to the seat of war. I understood the circumstances, and sorrowed deeply on account of them, but could write no more. But now the proclamations of peace are ringing in my ears, I may follow the wishes of my heart and send this letter to my friend. In the far north of Sweden I received the news so late, and am only now listening to the sound of the joy-bells. I can see you again, and look into your honest, affectionate eyes. . . .

# ▼ PIECES OF GOD ▼

[HERMAN MELVILLE & NATHANIEL HAWTHORNE]

The relations between Herman Melville (1819–91) and his wife were never very good; the first novel published after his wedding, *Mardi* (1849), is a celebration of the intimate friendship of two men, and equates marriage with suicide. When his son Stanwix was born, Melville on the birth certificate accidentally identified the mother as his own mother—this was when he was writing his novel *Pierre*, which is explicitly devoted to themes of incest.

Melville's wide-ranging sea adventures made him familiar with homosexuality at first hand. His maiden voyage as a cabin boy from New York to Liverpool in 1837, when he was seventeen, was the basis of his novel *Redburn* in which we find gay elements in the characters of Jackson and Bolton. During a voyage to the South Seas in 1841–42, Melville jumped ship in the Marquesas Islands with his friend Richard Tobias Greene, and drew upon this experience in his first novel *Typee*, which also has homosexual undertones. In his novel *Omoo*, drawing upon his experience of "bosom friends" in Tahiti, he specifically refers to the "unnatural crimes" of the Tahitian Prince Pomaree II.

His experience as a seaman in 1843 was fictionalized in *White Jacket*, in which ships are called "wooden-walled Gomorrahs of the deep." The hero of the novel is based upon Jack Chase, the Captain of the Maintop with whom Melville served, and to whom he dedicated *Billy Budd* shortly before his death. This latter novel describes a triangular love relationship between the stern father-figure Captain Vere, the innately evil Claggart, and Billy Budd, "a fine specimen of the genus homo, who in the nude might have posed for a statue of young Adam before the fall." The "Handsome Sailor" is the archetypal desired object. Claggart's envy and antipathy are a result of repression: "sometimes [his] melancholy expression would have in it a touch of soft yearning, as if Claggart could even have loved Billy but for fate and ban." Captain Vere similarly suppresses his own love in favour of the rules of society. The novel is a paradigm of closet homosexuality.

In the opening pages of Melville's greatest novel, *Moby Dick* (1851), the narrator Ishmael and the cannibal Queequeg go to bed together, and symbolically marry and even give birth. The bed in which they sleep at the Spouter Inn is the landlord's marriage bed; Ishmael plays the role of the terrified coy maiden, waiting in bed while the bridegroom gets undressed: "This accomplished, however, he turned round—when, good heaven, what a sight!" Queequeg springs under the covers with his tomahawk (!) and Ishmael "shrieks." There is some "kicking about" and Queequeg begins "feeling" Ishmael. Next morning Ishmael awakes with "Queequeg's arm thrown over me in the most loving and affectionate manner. You had almost thought I had been his wife.''

Melville emphasizes the point by referring again to "his bridegroom clasp" and "hugging a fellow male in that matrimonial sort of style." And they even bear offspring, rather more quickly than heterosexuals: "Throwing aside the quilt, there lay the tomahawk sleeping by the savage's side, as if it were a hatchet-faced baby."

An imagination informed by large symbolic relevance also marked Melville's relationship with his fellow author Nathaniel Hawthorne (1804–64), for whom he felt a powerful love that excluded consideration of both their wives. When he met Hawthorne, his neighbor in Massachusetts, he immediately fell for him, as yin for yang: "A man of a deep and noble nature had seized me in this seclusion. . . . The soft ravishments of the man spun me round about in a web of dreams. . . . But already I feel that Hawthorne had dropped germinous seeds into my soul. He expands and deepens down, the more I contemplate him; and further and further shoots his strong New-England roots into the hot soil in my Southern soul."

---

HERMAN MELVILLE TO NATHANIEL HAWTHORNE

*Pittsfield*
*[1? June 1851]*

My Dear Hawthorne,

. . . In a week or so, I go to New York, to bury myself in a third-story room, and work and slave on my "Whale" while it is driving through the press. . . . It is a rainy morning; so I am indoors, and all work suspended. I feel cheerfully disposed, and therefore I write a little bluely. Would the Gin were here! If ever, my dear Hawthorne, in the eternal times that are to come, you and I shall sit down in Paradise, in some little shady corner by ourselves; and if we shall by any means be able to smuggle a basket of champagne there (I won't believe in a Temperance Heaven), and if we shall then cross our celestial legs in the celestial grass that is forever tropical, and strike our glasses and our heads together, till both musically ring in concert,—then, O my dear fellow-mortal, how shall we pleasantly discourse of all the things manifold which now so distress us,—when all the earth shall be but reminiscence, yea, its final dissolution an antiquity. Then shall songs be composed as when wars are over; humorous, comic songs,—"Oh, when I lied in that queer little hole called the world," or, "Oh, when I toiled and sweated below," or, "Oh, when I knocked and was knocked in the fight"—yes, let us look forward to such things. Let us swear that, though now we sweat, yet it is because of the dry heat which is indispensable to the nourishment of the vine which is to bear the grapes that are to give us the champagne hereafter. . . .

*Pittsfield, Monday afternoon*
*[17? November 1851]*

. . . Your letter [praising *Moby Dick*] was handed me last night on the road going to Mr. Morewood's, and I read it there. Had I been at home, I would have sat down at once and answered it. In my divine magnanimities are spontaneous and instantaneous—catch them while you can. The world goes round, and the other side comes up. So now I can't write what I felt. But I felt pantheistic then—your heart beat in my ribs and mine in yours, and both in God's. A sense of unspeakable security is in me this moment, on account of your having understood the book. I have written a wicked book, and feel spotless as the lamb. . . .

Whence come you, Hawthorne? By what right do you drink from my flagon of life? And when I put it to my lips—lo, they are yours and not mine. I feel that the Godhead is broken up like the bread at the Supper, and that we are the pieces. Hence this infinite fraternity of feeling. Now, sympathizing with the paper, my angel turns over another page. You did not care a penny for the book. But, now and then as you read, you understood the pervading thought that impelled the book—and that you praised. Was it not so? You were archangel enough to despise the imperfect body, and embrace the soul. Once you hugged the ugly Socrates because you saw the flame in the mouth, and heard the rushing of the demon,—the familiar,—and recognized the sound; for you have heard it in your own solitudes. . . .

If the world was entirely made up of Magians, I'll tell you what I should do. I should have a paper-mill established at one end of the house, and so have an endless riband of foolscap rolling in upon my desk; and upon that endless riband I should write a thousand—a million—billion thoughts, all under the form of a letter to you. The divine magnet is on you, and my magnet responds. Which is the biggest? A foolish question—they are *One*.

H.

# ▼ THE LOVE OF COMRADES ▼

[WALT WHITMAN & FRED VAUGHAN & LEWIS BROWN & PETER DOYLE]

Walt Whitman's (1819-91) volume of poetry *Leaves of Grass*, enlarged and refined from 1855 to 1892, foresees the bright promise of America being fulfilled in the love of comrades, which he called "adhesiveness" in opposition to "amativeness" or heterosexual love. For celebrating a reality which included sex, he was branded as an obscene writer throughout his lifetime, though hailed as a prophet by young men, in Europe as well as America, who felt that a new world was dawning.

Whitman's first homosexual experience probably occurred during a visit to New Orleans in 1848, described in "Once I pass'd Through A Populous City" (the discovery of the original hand-written manuscript in 1925 shows that he changed "he" to "she" before publishing the poem). In his pioneering book *Calamus Lovers: Walt Whitman's Working Class Camerados* (San Francisco: Gay Sunshine Press, 1987) Professor Charley Shively argues convincingly that the gay Calamus cluster of poems in the 1860 edition of *Leaves of Grass* were inspired by a sexual relationship Whitman was having with teenager Fred Vaughan. They shared a house together between 1856 and 1859 and stayed in touch in later years (1870s–80s). "Whitman's relationship to Fred Vaughan," writes Shively, "was that of teacher, mentor and lover."

Whitman "came out" poetically in the *Calamus* cluster of poems: "I will therefore let flame from me the burning fires that were threatening to consume me, / I will lift what has too long kept down those smouldering fires. / I will give them complete abandonment, / I will write the evangel-poem of comrades and of love." He was taken aback by the public reaction, and spent most of his remaining years changing pronouns, suppressing passages, and deleting whole poems from later editions.

When John Addington Symonds in 1890 wrote a letter demanding to know whether or not adhesiveness involved homosexuality, Whitman flew into a panic and claimed to have sired six illegitimate children—none of which has been traced by industrious American scholars. Because Whitman is part of the canon of American literature taught in the classrooms, there is still much resistance to labelling him gay, despite evidence such as the fairly well documented story that he fellated a fourteen-year-old lad who grew up to become a lawyer in Chicago (see Martin Duberman, "Walt Whitman's Anomaly," *About Time: Exploring the Gay Past* (Meridian, 1986, rev. 1991), pp. 106–20). See also Charley Shively's perceptive essays on Whitman's gay relationships in *Calamus Lovers* and *Drum Beats* (San Francisco: Gay Sunshine Press, 1987, 1989).

Edward Carpenter, who visited Whitman in 1877 and is said to have slept with him (testimony from Gavin Arthur, who slept with Carpenter; see

Walt Whitman and Peter Doyle, 1869; drawing by H. D. Young from a photograph taken by Rice. Reproduced as frontispiece to *Calamus: A Series of Letters Written during the Years 1868–1880 by Walt Whitman to a Young Friend* (1897).

Gavin Arthur, "The Gay Succession," *Gay Roots* (1991), pp. 323-25), explained why Whitman could not openly declare himself: "He knew that the moment he said such a thing he would have the whole American Press at his heels, snarling and slandering, and distorting his words in every possible way." Whitman's best-known comrade was the street car conductor Peter Doyle (ca. 1848-1907), whom he met in Washington in 1866 when the Irish immigrant recently paroled from the Confederate Army was eighteen, to whom he wrote many letters beginning "Dear Pete, dear son, my darling boy, my young & loving brother."

Doyle was interviewed in 1877 and described their very first meeting, during a storm when Whitman was his only passenger: "We were familiar at once—I put my hand on his knee—we understood. He did not get out at the end of the trip—in fact went all the way back with me." The number of Doyle's streetcar was "14," which Whitman used as a secret cypher in his private journal, in which he records that he (Whitman) picked up and "slept with" literally dozens of other young men. The two lovers regularly took long walks in the moonlight along the Potomac river, and saw each other at least once a week—if not more often—for the next seven years, then less often after Whitman suffered a paralysis and had to move to Camden, New Jersey.

The following selections begin before he met Doyle, with letters to and from Lewy Brown, whose left leg was amputated five inches below the knee on January 5, 1864. Whitman did what he could to comfort him, and slept on the adjoining cot for the next two nights. Their correspondence illustrates the less well appreciated aspect of comradeship experienced by many young soldiers during the American Civil War. Whitman served as a nurse throughout these years and for some years afterwards, distributing oranges and tobacco to the boys in the hospital wards, dressing their wounds, writing letters to their families and friends, and daily attending the sick and the dying.

He was a man of tremendous health and personal magnetism, and the soldiers never forgot his healing powers, the source of which was adhesiveness: "The men feel such love more than anything else. I have met very few persons who realize the importance of humoring the yearnings for love and friendship of these American young men, prostrated by sickness and wounds. To many of the wounded and sick, especially the youngsters, there is something in personal love, caresses, and the magnetic flood of sympathy and friendship, that does, in its way, more good than all the medicine in the world. Many will think this mere sentimentalism, but I know it is the most solid of all facts."

FRED VAUGHAN TO WALT WHITMAN

*New York*
*March 27, 1860*

Walt, I received your kind letter the day after you mailed it, and immediately wrote you again. But finding some trouble in procuring a stamp, I sent it down to Frank Moran to have him mail it for me. It appears Frank was taken ill that day, and oblidged to go home; and has not been out of the house since. I did not find it out until today.—But of course my letter to you was not mailed, and now I have once more to reply to yours.—

I am glad you like Boston Walt, you know I have said much to you in praise both of the city and its people.—It is true the first is quite *crooked*, but it is generally clean, and the latter, though a little too straight-laced for such free thinkers as you and I are, a very hospitable, friendly lot of folks.—You tell me Mr. Emmerson (one m to many I guess?) came to see you and was very kind.—I heard him lecture in Fr. Chapins church on Friday evening last, on the subject of *manners*, and though very much pleased with the *matter*, I did not at all like his delivery. It appeared to me to be strained, and there was a certain hesitation in his speech and occasional repetition of words that did not affect the hearer very well.—

But, Walt, when I looked upon the man, & thought that it was but a very few days before that he had been so kind and attentive to you, I assure you I did not think much of his *bad delivery*, but on the contrary, my heat warmed towards him very much. I think he has *that* in him which makes men capable of strong friendships.—This theme he also touched on, and said that a man whose heart was filled with a warm, ever enduring *not to be shaken by anything* Friendship was one to be set on one side apart from other men, and almost to be worshipped as a saint.—There Walt, how do you like that? What do you think of them setting you & myself, and one or two others we know up in some public place, with an immense placard on our breast, reading *Sincere Friends*!!! Good doctrine that but I think the theory preferable to the practice.—I am glad very glad Walt to hear you are succeeding so well with your book.—I hope you will not forget the promise you made of sending me on some of the first proof sheets you have.—I am quite anxious to see them.—

There is nothing new here, Walt. Everything remains about he same. I suppose of course you see the New York papers every day. Our streets are just about as dirty as ever, but the dirt is not allowed to remain long in one place, this March wind picks it up and scatters it with a perfect looseness in your eyes, ears, mouth, and nose. It penetrates to the house, covering the floor, the furniture and even the beds in a manner not at all agreeable to persons who have any idea of cleanliness.—Monuments erected in mud to the honour of the street inspector have to be regularily wet down, or like riches, and birds they take to themselves wings and fly away.—I have an idea that "There is a better time coming" But so far have been unable to find any one who could satisfactorily *fix the date*. Robert is drinking tea, Mrs Cooper is moving around the room as usual ready to wait upon Bob even before he needs it. They both join me in wishes for the best success to you, and Mrs Cooper says if you will make love to her you had better do so personally the next time you call, as she cannot put much faith in a profession made in a letter to an outside party.

Write me a good long letter Walt, as I am anxious to hear from you.
Yours,
Fred.

---

LEWIS K. BROWN TO WALT WHITMAN

*Elkton, Maryland*
*20 July 1863*

My Dear Freind Walter.

It is with mutch pleasure that I take my pen in hand to inform you that I am well and that my leg is mending verry fast  I left Washington on the 2nd on the 6½ O clock train but It was the rong train and I had to get of at Haver de gras and stay all night on the Boat or els go on to Wilmington and so I got of and stayed on the boat and as good luck would have it I met 3 men on the boat that I knowed and they maid me verry comfortable that night and then I left the next morning and got home in the evening and I gave Mother a verry agreeable Supprise I was verry tired the next day but I feel well now. I think that I will soon get well hear for I have everything that I want we have a splendid garden and we have a good many cherries in fact every thing, the nice grain fields around the house and every thing looks so well. I have had a good many of my young friends to see me. I have got your picture and I am a going to have it fraimed the first time I get whear I can have it don. I expect to go on a visit up to my GranFathers in about 4 weeks and I think that I will have a nice time up thear. I only wish that you were hear  I am sure that you would enjoy it for it is so nice or it appears so to me [w]ho has been pennd up in the Hospital for 10 months. My Father and Mother are well and send their respects to you for Mother says whoeve[r] did me a faivor or was a friend to me was one to her and you have bin a friend in nead and that is a friend in*dead*. I expect that you still visit the Hospital if so give my respects to the boys  I have nothing more to write at present so I will have to close hoping verry soon to hear from you so good by and God bless you from your affectionet friend

Lewis K Brown

WALT WHITMAN TO LEWIS K. BROWN

*Washington, D.C.*
*1 August 1863*

Both your letters have been received, Lewy—the second one came this morning & was welcome as any thing from you will always be, & the sight of your face welcomer than all, my darling—I see you write in good spirits, & appear to have first-rate times—Lew, you must not go around too much, nor eat & drink too promiscuous, but be careful & moderate, & not let the kindness of friends carry you away, lest you break down again, dear son—

. . . .—You speak of being here in Washington again about the last of August—O Lewy, how glad I should be to see you, to have you with me—I have thought if it could be so that you, & one other person & myself could be where we could work & love together, & have each other's society, we three, I should like it so much—but it is probably a dream—

. . . .—Dear son, you must write me whenever you can—take opportunity when you have nothing to do, & write me a good long letter—your letters & your love for me are very precious to me, for I appreciate it all, Lew, & give you the like in return.

---

LEWIS K. BROWN TO WALT WHITMAN

*Maryland*
*10 August 1863*

My Dear Friend Walter,

Your very kind and long looked for letter of Aug 1st came to hand on the 6th & I was verry glad to hear from you but was verry sorry to hear that you wer so sick & I think that it would be much better for your health if you would give your self that furlou but I think that the boys about the Hospital could ill spare you, if you are as good to them as you wer to me. I shal never for get you for your kindness to me while I was a suffering so mutch, and if you do not get your reward in this world you will in Heaven. . . .

---

WALT WHITMAN TO LEWIS K. BROWN

*Washington, D.C.*
*15 August 1863*

. . . Lew, you speak in your letter how you would like to see me—well, my darling, I wonder if there is not somebody who would be gratified to see you, & always will be wherever he is—Dear comrade, I was highly pleased at your telling me in your letter about your folks' place, the house & land & all the items—you say I must excuse you for writing so much foolishness —nothing of the kind—My darling boy, when you write to me, you must write without ceremony, I like to hear every little thing about yourself &

your affairs—you need never care how you write to me, Lewy, if you will only—I never think about literary perfection in letters either, it is the *man* & the *feeling*— . . .

---

ALONZO S. BUSH TO WALT WHITMAN

*Glymont, Maryland*
*22 December 1863*

Friend Walt,

Sir I am happy to announce the arrival of Your Kind and verry wellcom Epistel and I can assure you that the contents ware persued with all the pleasure immaginable. I am glad to Know that you are once more in the hotbed City of Washington So that you can go often and See that Friend of ours at Armory Square, L[ewis] K. B[rown]. The fellow that went down on your BK,* both So often with me. I wished that I could See him this evening and go in the Ward Master's Room and have Some fun for he is a gay boy. I am very Sorry indeed to here that after laying So long that he is about to loose his leg, it is to bad, but I Suppose that the Lord will must be done and We must submit. Walter I Suppose that you had a nice time while at Home. I am glad to report that I enjoyed my Self finely and had a gay time. Generaly I am now paying up for the good times I had at Armory Square & at Home. . . .

Johny Strain my companion wishes to be remembred to all  I am sorry to inform you that He met with another misfortune after he got Here he was thrown from his Horse and had his arm broken but is getting along very well at presant. My Love & best Wishes to all I will close Hoping to Here from you soon.

I remain your True Friend,
Alonzo Bush

---

WALT WHITMAN TO PETER DOYLE

*New York*
*Friday, 25 Sept., 1868*

Dear Boy,

I received your second letter yesterday—it is a real comfort to me to get such letters from you, dear friend. Every word does me good. . . . There is nothing new or special to write about to-day, still I thought I would send you a few lines for Sunday. I put down off hand and write all about myself and my doings, etc., because I suppose that will be really what my dear comrade wants most to hear while we are separated. . . . I think of you very often, dearest comrade, and with more calmness than when I was there. I find it first rate to think of you, Pete, and to know that you are there all right and that I shall return and we will be together again. I don't know what I should do if I hadn't you to think of and look forward to. . . .

---

*In *Calamus Lovers* Charley Shively tentatively identifies "BK" as "buck," which in regional dialect can mean as a noun "cock" and as a verb "fuck."

*New York*
*Oct. 2, 1868*

Dear Boy and Comrade,

  You say it is a pleasure to get my letters—well boy, it is a real pleasure to me to write to you. . . . Dear Pete, with all my kind friends here and invitations, etc., though I love them all and gratefully reciprocate their kindness, I finally turn to you and think of you there. Well, I guess I have written enough for this time. Dear Pete, I will now bid you good-bye for the present. Take care of yourself and God bless you, my loving comrade. I will write again soon.

---

WALT WHITMAN TO PETER DOYLE

*Brooklyn, N. Y.*
*Saturday evening, Aug. 21 [1869]*

Dear Pete,

  I have been very sick the last three days—I don't know what to call it—it makes me prostrated and deadly weak, and little use of my limbs. I have thought of you, my darling boy, very much of the time. I have not been out of the house since the first day after my arrival . . . And now dear Pete for yourself. How is it with you, dearest boy—and is there anything different with the face? [Doyle had an obstinate skin disease, tinea sycosis, and an eruption on his face which the army doctor that Whitman took him to said had to be lanced and cauterized. This depressed him so much that Whitman thought he was contemplating suicide.] Dear Pete, you must forgive me for being so cold the last day and evening. I was unspeakably shocked and repelled from you by that talk and proposition of yours— you know what—there by the fountain. It seemed indeed to me, (for I will talk out plain to you, dearest comrade) that the one I loved, and who had always been so manly and sensible, was gone, and a fool and intentional murderer stood in his place. I spoke so sternly and cutting. (Though I see now that my words might have appeared to have a certain other meaning, which I didn't dream of—insulting to you, never for one moment in my thoughts.) But will say no more of this—for I know such thoughts must have come when you was not yourself, but in a moment of derangement, —and have passed away like a bad dream.

  Dearest boy, I have not a doubt but you will get well, and entirely well [he did]—and we will one day look back on these drawbacks and sufferings as things long past. The extreme cases of that malady, (as I told you before) are persons that have very deeply diseased blood, probably with syphilis in it, inherited from parentage, and confirmed by themselves— so they have no foundation to build on. You are of healthy stock, with a sound constitution and good blood—and I know it is impossible for it to continue long. My darling, if you are not well when I come back I will get a good room or two in some quiet place, (or out of Washington, perhaps in Baltimore), and we will live together and devote ourselves altogether to the job of curing you, and rooting the cursed thing out entirely, and making you stronger and healthier than ever. I have had this in my mind before but never broached it to you. I could go on with my work in the Attorney General's office just the same—and we would see that your mother should have a small sum every week to keep the pot a-boiling at home.

Dear comrade, I think of you very often. My love for you is indestructible, and since that night and morning has returned more than before.

Dear Pete, dear son, my darling boy, my young and loving brother, don't let the devil put such thoughts in your mind again—wickedness unspeakable—death and disgrace here, and hell's agonies hereafter—Then what would it be afterward to the mother? What to *me*?—Pete, I send you some money by Adam's Express—you use it, dearest son, and when it is gone you shall have some more, for I have plenty. I will write again before long—give my love to Johnny Lee, my dear darling boy. I love him truly—(let him read these three last lines)—Dear Pete, *remember*—

     Walt

---

*Brooklyn*
*Saturday afternoon, July 30 [1870]*

Dear Pete,

Well here I am home again with my mother, writing to you from Brooklyn once more. We parted there, you know, at the corner of 7th St. Tuesday night. Pete there was something in that hour from 10 to 11 o'clock (parting though it was) that has left me pleasure and comfort for good—I never dreamed that you made so much of having me with you, nor that you could feel so downcast at losing me. I foolishly thought it was all on the other side. But all I will say further on the subject is, I now see clearly, that was all wrong. . . .

Love to you, dear Pete—and I won't be so long again writing to my darling boy.

     Walt

---

*Brooklyn*
*Wednesday night, Aug. 3, [1870]*

Dear Pete,

Dear son, I received your second letter to-day. . . . Dear son, I can almost see you drowsing and nodding since last Sunday, going home late—especially as we wait there at 7th St. and I am telling you something deep about the heavenly bodies—and in the midst of it I look around and find you fast asleep, and your head on my shoulder like a chunk of wood—an awful compliment to my lecturing powers. . . . Good night, Pete—Good night, my darling son—here is a kiss for you, dear boy—on the paper here—a good long one. . . . *10 o'clock at night*—As this is lying here on my table to be sent off to-morrow, I will imagine you with your arm around my neck saying Good night, Walt—and me—Good night, Pete.

Ludwig II (1845–1886), king of Bavaria from 1864 to 1886 of the thousand year old Royal House of Wittelsbach. Photo of *ca.* 1864 when he became king at the age of 19.

# ▼ GRAND OPERA ▼

[RICHARD WAGNER & KING LUDWIG II]
*Translated from German by Edward Carpenter*

Richard Wagner's great opera cycles might not exist were it not for the support of his patron Ludwig II, King of Bavaria (1845–86). His enormous fairy-tale castles, Teutonic, neo-gothic and oriental versions of Versailles which virtually bankrupted the country, were the grand opera sets made flesh. He endeavoured to be an absolute monarch at the dawn of the modern republican world, when such goals were impossible. But having failed in the political and domestic realm, he made his dream reality in art and music. No expense was spared for the staging of Wagner's operas, which were often performed with Ludwig the sole member of the audience, and in return Wagner gave him his genius and his love. Wagner acknowledged that "Without him I am as nothing! Even in loving him he was my first teacher. O my King! You are divine!" They exchanged some 600 letters, and it is hard to say who was more enthusiastic, at least at the beginning.

Wagner: "What bliss enfolds me! A wonderful dream has become a reality! . . . I am in the Gralsburg, in Parsifal's sublime and loving care. . . . I am in your angelic arms! We are near to one another." Or Ludwig: "My only beloved Friend! My saviour! My god! . . . Ah, *now* I am happy, for I know that my Only One draws near. Stay, oh stay! adored one for whom alone I live, with whom I die." Their relationship was almost certainly physical, though not necessarily "genital." Wagner at one time held homoerotic ideals, and wrote that "from genuine delight in the beauty of the most perfect human body—that of the male—arose that spirit of comradeship which pervades and shapes the whole economy of the Spartan State. . . . The higher element of that love of man to man . . . not only included a purely spiritual bond of friendship, but this spiritual friendship was the blossom and the crown of the physical friendship. The latter sprang directly from delight in the beauty, aye in the material bodily beauty of the beloved comrade."

Ludwig refused to get married, even for state reasons, and wanted to give up the throne to live with and for Wagner. But it was not to be, for Wagner loved women as well as music and power. Ludwig's physical satisfactions were achieved primarily with his equerry for twenty years, Richard Hornig, and later with the young Hungarian actor Joseph Kainz. The first time Ludwig saw Kainz on stage, during the interval he sent him a pair of ivory opera glasses; several nights later he gave him a diamond and sapphire ring and a gold chain from which hung a swan, symbol of the Dream King. Unable to give substance to his dreams on the political stage, Ludwig refused to meet his ministers and gradually became a recluse; always at odds with his family, they managed to keep him virtually imprisoned at his hunting box Schloss Berg, where he apparently held orgies with the troopers under his command.

A secret committee of the Bavarian Parliament heard testimony of the king's weakness for muscular country lads. In June 1886 they had him declared insane, and shortly afterwards he was found drowned together with his psychiatric attendant. No one today seriously believes this was either an accident or suicide. (The translation of the letters is by Edward Carpenter, who included these selections in the enlarged 1929 edition of his pioneering gay anthology *Ioläus*.)

---

RICHARD WAGNER TO MME. ELIZA WILLE

*9th Sept., 1864*

It is true that I have my young king who genuinely adores me. You cannot form an idea of our relations. I recall one of the dreams of my youth. I once dreamed that Shakespeare was alive: that I really saw and spoke to him: I can never forget the impression that dream made on me. Then I would have wished to see Beethoven, though he was already dead. Something of the same kind must pass in the mind of this lovable man when with me. He says he can hardly believe that he really possesses me. None can read without astonishment, without enchantment, the letters he writes to me.

---

LUDWIG II TO RICHARD WAGNER

*15th May, 1865*

Dear Friend,

O I see clearly that your sufferings are deep-rooted! You tell me, beloved friend, that you have looked deep into the hearts of men, and seen there the villainy and corruption that dwells within. Yes, I believe you, and I can well understand that moments come to you of disgust with the human race; yet always will we remember (will we not, beloved?) that there are yet many noble and good people, for whom it is a real pleasure to live and work. And yet you say you are no use for this world!—I pray you, do not despair, your true friend conjures you; have Courage: "Love helps us to bear and suffer all things, love brings at last the victor's crown!" Love recognizes, even in the most corrupt, the germ of good; she alone overcomes all!—Live on, darling of my soul. I recall your own words to you. To learn to forget is a noble work!—Let us be careful to hide the faults of others; it was for all men indeed that the Saviour died and suffered. And now, what a pity that "Tristan" can not be presented today; will it perhaps tomorrow? Is there any chance?

 Unto death your faithful friend,
  Ludwig

LUDWIG II TO RICHARD WAGNER

*Purschling*
*4th Aug., 1865*

My one, my much-loved Friend,—

You express to me your sorrow that, as it seems to you, each one of our last meetings has only brought pain and anxiety to me.—Must I then remind my loved one of Brynhilda's words?—Not only in gladness and enjoyment, but in suffering also Love makes man blest. . . . When does my friend think of coming to the "Hill-Top," to the woodland's aromatic breezes? —Should a stay in that particular spot not altogether suit, why, I beg my dear one to choose any of my other mountain-cabins for his residence.—What is mine is his! Perhaps we may meet on the way between the Wood and the World, as my friend expressed it! . . . To thee I am wholly devoted; for thee, for thee only to live!

Unto death your own, your faithful
Ludwig

---

RICHARD WAGNER TO HIS BROTHER-IN-LAW

*10th Sept., 1865*

I hope now for a long period to gain strength again by quiet work. This is made possible for me by the love of an unimaginably beautiful and thoughtful being: it seems that it *had* to be even so greatly gifted a man and one so destined for me, as this young King of Bavaria. What he is to me no one can imagine. My guardian! In his love I completely rest and fortify myself towards the completion of my task.

---

LUDWIG II TO RICHARD WAGNER

*Hohenschwangau*
*2nd Nov., 1865*

My one Friend, my ardently beloved!

This afternoon, at 3.30, I returned from a glorious tour in Switzerland! How this land delighted me!—There I found your dear letter; deepest warmest thanks for the same. With new and burning enthusiasm has it filled me; I see that the beloved marches boldly and confidently forward, towards our great and eternal goal.

All hindrances I will victoriously overcome like a hero. I am entirely at thy disposal; let me now dutifully prove it.—Yes, we must meet and speak together. I will banish all evil clouds; Love has strength for all. You are the star that shines upon my life, and the sight of you ever wonderfully strengthens me.—Ardently I long for you, O my presiding Saint, to whom I pray! I should be immensely pleased to see my friend here in about a week; oh, we have plenty to say! If only I could quite banish from me the curse of which you speak, and send it back to the deeps of night from whence it sprang!—How I love, how I love you, my one, my highest good! . . .

My enthusiasm and love for you are boundless. Once more I swear you faith till death!

Ever, ever your devoted
Ludwig

# ▼ SO LIKE AN ANGEL ▼

[BROTHER AUGUSTINE & SAMUEL HASE]

In 1864 in Norwich, Norfolk (England), Samuel Hase, a fifteen-year-old boy apprenticed to a printer, became attracted to the order of Anglican Benedictine monks to whose monastery on Elk Hill he delivered print orders. He was a good singer, a member of the choir of St. Saviour's Church, and soon he was attending services at the monastery and singing in its choir. The Superior, Father Ignatius, was said by another boy to be "sweet" on Samuel, and often gave him gifts of fruit and asked him to take tea with him after the services.

One day in September the boy took home a hymn book presented to him by Father Ignatius, and showed it to his widowed stepmother. She promptly returned it with an indignant note, and subsequently met with the Superior and refused her consent for her stepson to enter the order. Samuel (who had lied to Ignatius about obtaining his stepmother's approval) nevertheless continued to serve as a singing boy at the monastery, sometimes slept there, wore the gown and hood, and became baptized. He even asked his master to cancel his indenture so he could devote himself entirely to the monks, but the printer refused. His stepmother, a Protestant antipapist, one day intercepted a letter sent to him from Brother Augustine, the second-in-command at the monastery, which is printed below. She sent the letter to the *Norfolk News*, which had been conducting a campaign against popery aimed specifically against the monastery at Elk Hill, and they published it. As a result, Brother Augustine fled the monastery and disappeared.

Father Ignatius wrote to the paper from Newcastle (he was on a northern tour to collect money for his mission) that it was a very foolish letter and Augustine had been expelled for violating the order's rule against secret communications; before leaving on his trip he had begged Augustine not to spoil the boy, but nothing untoward ever took place in the monastery and they were not ashamed of inviting young people to join their order.

The *Norfolk News* continued its attack, asserting that the letter revealed that the sham monks (for they were not really Roman Catholics, but very "high" Anglicans) were kidnapping and mesmerizing the sons of Protestant families: "The system is essentially unnatural, and nothing can come of it but mischief, disorder, and monstrosities, either ridiculous or frightful. . . . these Monasteries are for the most part cages for unclean birds."

Every issue of the *Norfolk News* through December continued the attack on these "mad" and "unnatural" monks. In October Ignatius (real name Joseph Leycester Lyne, of Brighton, 1837–1908) spoke at the Bristol Church Congress and was shouted down; he argued that collegiate churches should be established in all large towns to reach the masses, that they should follow the Rule of St. Benedict, and that it was contrary to nature for their priests to be married and shackled to a family. He appeared at this meeting in full Benedictine garb, and the following speaker derided him as a "startling apparition." Later that month the Norwich Young Men's Church of England Association called for Ignatius to be expelled from the church.

A year later Brother Stanislaus tried to overthrow Ignatius's authority, but failed, and fled with a boy from its associated Guild of St. William. In 1868 ex-Brother Stanislaus spoke at Protestant meetings, revealing the scandalous "semi-Popish and improper practices" established by Ignatius; at a meeting in London two lads charged Brother Augustine with homosexual practices. In 1869 another boy alleged that he (the boy) had lived at the monastery in a sexual relationship with Stanislaus, with the encouragement of Ignatius. The continuing scandals are part of the history of the Anglo-Catholic brotherhoods that attracted gay men in the mid-nineteenth century, and also part of the history of homophobia and anti-Catholic hysteria in Protestant Britain. The letter that stirred it all up is really nothing worse than a very touching love letter, not utterly different from letters exchanged between monks eight centuries earlier.

---

BROTHER AUGUSTINE TO SAMUEL HASE

*[Elk Hill Monastery]*
*Feast Sancti Crucis, 1864*

My Darling Child—

I want you to promise me that during the Superior's absence you will strive as much as possible to keep from doing wrong, and that you will daily pray for God's grace and help to fulfil the same.

You will not be allowed to be here much, if at all, as I rather expected you would, so that I am obliged to write that which I should have preferred saying to you in person, but oh! my dearest one! you will *never* realize how much I really love you, and how wretched I feel all day without seeing you. My love for you is *so* deep, *so* tender, that I cannot bear even to be separated from you, and when I *do* see you I have such a heavy weight at my heart, and you seem *so* careless and light-hearted and *so* taken up with others, and all this makes me worse.

Then the Superior, who is always having fresh favourites and likings, seems so dreadfully afraid even of one's looking at you, that I am perfectly obliged to look calm and indifferent when my heart is literally burning for you.

*This* love I NEVER felt for a living creature beside yourself, it seems to consume me, and it is quite a comfort to write it down to you.

Sometimes I think you know your power over me, you give me *such* searching looks, and what do you meet with in return? What but the most *earnest, burning*, tender look of love, as pure as that of angels.

Were I and you in the world [rather than a religious order] I would lavish every care, every affection upon you that money or time could procure, every wish should be gratified if possible.

Sometimes on Sundays you have sat in your cassock and cotta looking so like an angel I could have worshiped you.

I *have* striven to collect my thoughts to the solemn service on which I was engaged, but no! you happen to look my way whilst I am at the lectern, and then I grow quite confused and my breath even seems to fail, and I wonder if you have ever seen it and guessed the cause.

Morning, noon, and night, nothing haunts me but *your* sweet *darling* face; in my very dreams I see it; in a word, I am infatuated and wretched and wish sometimes I had never seen you. I feel I could clasp you in my arms and never unfold them whilst I looked into the depths of those sweet eyes.

It is very weak, perhaps wicked, to write like this, but I scarcely know what I am doing, and feel forced to write and tell you all this.

Suppose I were to go away from here (as they want me at home) when my noviciate is up in February, I feel that leaving you would make me intensely miserable and perhaps break my heart. I know you will only laugh at me.

Is there anyone here loves you like this? No! I am sure of it. Why do you avoid me, or content yourself with a passing glance?

What I am now going to say must be a secret to *everyone* if you don't wish me to be troubled. I want you one day (I will tell you the time) to go to [the photographer] Mason's, St. Giles', to have your portrait taken. Dear mama shall send the postage stamps to you so that it will not be with any money from here.

I will manage your having a cotta and cassock without anyone's knowing here what you want it for.

Burn *this*. I would not have anyone know anything about it for the world, and if you have the slightest respect for me you will do so. I do not ask it out of love, for I know and feel you have none for me, and this, indeed, is the reason of my misery. Good bye, dear, sweet child, and my prayers shall ever be for your peace and happiness.

Your affectionate brother in Xt.,

†Augustine, O.S.B.

Joseph ("Posh") Fletcher (*ca.* 1838–*post* 1907), the rough-hewn Suffolk fisherman who captured the heart of poet/translator Edward Fitzgerald.

# ▼ HERRING MERCHANTS ▼

[EDWARD FITZGERALD & JOSEPH FLETCHER]

The English poet and translator Edward Fitzgerald (1809–83) led a split life: as the friendly local man known as "old Fitz" who socialized with simple fisher folk, and as the literary man, translator of the *Rubaiyat of Omar Khayyam*, who corresponded with Thackeray, Tennyson, and Carlyle: neither group had any knowledge of the other. His first beloved was William Kenworthy Browne, with whom he spent most of his summers from 1832, when Browne was sixteen. Browne married in 1844, and died in a riding accident in 1859.

After Browne's death Fitzgerald moved to Lowestoft in Suffolk, where he walked along the beach at night, as he told Browne's widow, "longing for some fellow to accost me who might give me some promise of filling up a very vacant place in my heart." That fellow turned out to be Joseph Fletcher, called "Posh," an east coast fisherman whom he met in 1865, when Posh was twenty-seven and Fitzgerald was fifty-six. Fitzgerald was cruising in the area of Harwich and Felixstowe in his fifteen-ton schooner, originally named the *Shamrock* but known as the *Scandal*.

Posh was proprietor of a longshore punt or beach lugger, fishing for cod, haddock, shrimp, rather than deep sea fishing in a proper lugger. He immediately became Fitzgerald's protégé aboard the *Scandal*, and in the following year became a proper herring merchant with Fitzgerald as his partner. A year after that, Fitzgerald paid for a new boat to be built, which was named the *Meum and Tuum* (Mine and Yours), known all along the coast as the *Mum Tum*, "a queer name for a boat." Fitzgerald was "infatuated with the breezy stalwart comeliness" of his captain, but himself always went to sea in a silk top hat, with a lady's fur boa wrapped around his neck. Posh had wife and children, and Fitzgerald spent nearly every evening smoking his pipe in their cottage, or drinking with Posh at the inn.

There was a quarrel between them in autumn 1869 because of Posh's habitual drunkenness; Posh asserted his independence by buying another boat without consulting his partner, which led to another squall. Their partnership broke up in 1870; arrangements were made for Posh to become full owner of the *Meum and Tuum*, and Fitzgerald in his will directed his heirs not to call in the principal of the mortgage to which Posh was indebted to him. As a memento of their relationship, Fitzgerald commissioned Samuel Laurence to paint a portrait of Posh, whom he described as "a Gentleman of Nature's grandest Type," and sent him a photo of Posh sitting on a chair, in his jersey, holding an oar, a big but handsome man (the photo survives but the portrait is untraced).

Fitzgerald wrote to Laurence "I am sure the Man is fit to be King of a Kingdom as well as of a Lugger. . . . Made in the mould of what Humanity should be, Body and Soul, a poor Fisherman. The proud Fellow had better have kept me for a Partner in some of his responsibilities. But no; he must rule alone, as is right he should too." They occasionally wrote and saw one another again for several years. There was a further rift in 1873 when Fitzgerald, genuinely concerned for his friend's health, tried to force him to become teetotal.

In these last years when they met Fitzgerald would grab hold of Posh's blue woollen jersey and pinch him, and say "Oh dear, oh dear, Posh! To think it should have come to this." Fitzgerald was also married, but he and his wife quickly separated, and lived apart. Posh was interviewed in 1907 (when he said "He was a master rum un, was my old guv'nor!"), and told a wonderful story of how one day he and Fitzgerald were walking along when they saw Mrs. Fitzgerald walking towards them. As they came up to one another, Fitzgerald and his wife both removed their gloves and reached out in a formal greeting—but Posh could swear that their hands just hovered above one another and that their fingers *never actually touched.*

---

EDWARD FITZGERALD TO JOSEPH FLETCHER

*Markethill, Woodbridge*
*Saturday [Spring 1866]*

My good Fellow,

When I came in from my Boat yesterday I found your Hamper of Fish. Mr. Manby has his conger Eel: I gave the Codling to a young Gentleman in his ninetieth year: the Plaice we have eaten here—very good—and the Skaite I have just sent in my Boat to Newson. I should have gone down myself, but that it set in for rain; but, at the same time, I did not wish to let the Fish miss his mark. . . .

I had your letter about nets and Dan. You must not pretend you can't write as good a Letter as a man needs to write, or to read. I suppose the Nets were cheap if good; and I should be sorry you had not bought more, but that, when you have got a Fleet for alongshore fishing, then you will forsake them for some Lugger; and then I shall have to find another Posh to dabble about, and smoke a pipe, with. . . .

---

*Markethill Woodbridge*
*Thursday [ca. January 1867]*

My dear Poshy,

My Lawyer can easily manage the Assignment of the Lugger to me, leaving the Agreement as it is between you and Fuller [the builder]. But you must send the Agreement here for him to see.

As we shall provide that the Lugger when built shall belong to me; so we will provide that, in case of my dying *before* she is built, you may come on my executors for any money due.

I think you will believe that I shall propose, and agree to, nothing which is not for your good. For surely I should not have meddled with it at all, but for that one purpose.

And now, Poshy, I mean to read you a short Sermon, which you can keep till Sunday to read. You know I told you of *one* danger—and I do think the only one—you are liable to—*Drink*.

I do not the least think you are *given* to it: but you have, and will have, so many friends who will press you to it: perhaps *I* myself have been one. And when you keep so long without *food; could* you do so, Posh, without a Drink—of some [of] your bad Beer too—now and then? And then, does not the Drink—and of bad Stuff—take away Appetite for the time? And will, if continued, so spoil the stomach that it will not bear anything *but* Drink. And this evil comes upon us gradually, without our knowing how it grows. That is why I warn you, Posh. If I am wrong in thinking you want my warning, you must forgive me, believing that I should not warn at all if I were not much interested in your welfare. I know that you do your best to keep out at sea, and watch on shore, for anything that will bring home something for Wife and Family. But do not do so at any such risk as I talk of.

I say, I tell you all this for your sake: and something for my own also— not as regards the Lugger—but because, thinking you, as I do, so good a Fellow, and being glad of your Company; and taking *Pleasure* in seeing you prosper; I should now be sorely vext if you went away from what I believe you to be. Only, whether you do well or ill, *show me all aboveboard*, as I really think you have done; and do not let a poor old, solitary, and sad Man (as I really am, in spite of my Jokes), do not, I say, let me waste my Anxiety in vain.

I thought I had done with new Likings: and I had a more easy Life perhaps on that account: *now* I shall often think of you with uneasiness, for the very reason that I have so much Liking and Interest for you.

There—the Sermon is done, Posh. You *know* I am not against Good Beer while at Work: nor a cheerful Glass after work: only do not let it spoil the stomach, or the Head.

Your's truly,
E. FG.

---

*Woodbridge*
*Friday [June 1867]*

My dear Poshy,

I am only back To-day from London where I had to go for two days; and I am very glad to be back. For the Weather was wretched: the Streets all Slush: and I all alone wandering about in it. So as I was sitting at Night, in a great Room where a Crowd of People were eating Supper, and Singing going on, I thought to myself—Well, Posh might as well be here; and then I should see what a Face he would make at all this—This Thought really came into my mind. . . .

Well, here is a letter, you see, my little small Captain, in answer to yours, which I was glad to see, for as I do not forget you, as I have told you, so I am glad that you should sometime remember the Old Governor and Herring-merchant

Edward FitzGerald

---

EDWARD FITZGERALD TO S. LAURENCE

*Woodbridge*
*January 20, 1870*

. . . I should certainly like a large Oil-sketch like Thackeray's, done in your most hasty, and worst, style, to hang up with Thackeray and Tennyson, with whom he shares a certain Grandeur of Soul and Body. As you guess, the colouring is (when the Man is all well) the finest Saxon type: with that complexion which Montaigne calls "vif, Mâle, et flamboyant"; blue eyes; and strictly auburn hair, that any woman might sigh to possess. He says it is coming off, as it sometimes does from those who are constantly wearing the close, hot Sou-'westers. We must see what can be done about a Sketch.

# ▼ FANNY AND STELLA ▼

[ERNEST BOULTON, FREDERICK PARK, LOUIS HURT,
JOHN FISKE & LORD ARTHUR PELHAM CLINTON]

On April 28, 1870 Lady Stella Clinton and Miss Fanny Winifred Park—
otherwise known as Ernest Boulton, age twenty-two, and Frederick William Park, a twenty-three-year-old law student—attended a performance
at the Strand Theatre, London, in full evening frocks. The police had been
keeping an eye on this pair since 1869, and they were arrested, together with
another man, while two more of their associates escaped. All of the men
lived at separate addresses, but they kept a house on Wakefield Street, off
Regent Square, where they would dress up before going out of an evening,
and where they stayed with friends for a day or two at a time. The police
made an inventory: sixteen dresses in satin or silk with suitable lace trimmings, a dozen petticoats, ten cloaks and jackets, half a dozen bodices,
several bonnets and hats, twenty chignons, and a variety of stays, drawers,
stockings, boots, curling-irons, gloves, boxes of violet powder and bloom
of roses. Their landlady described their dresses as "very extreme."

Boulton was very good looking, effeminate, and musical, with a wonderful soprano voice, and he and Park played female parts in amateur
theatricals in legit theatres, country houses and elsewhere. Earlier that
month Fanny and Stella, as "sisters," attended the Oxford and Cambridge
boat race, dressed as women. They also frequented the theatres and Burlington Arcade dressed as men, but wearing make-up, winking at respectable gentlemen, which initially attracted the attention of the police.

Their apartments were searched, and letters from John Safford Fiske
were found. Fiske's apartment in Edinburgh was searched, and behind the
fire grate in his bedroom police found an album of photographs of Boulton in female attire. Fiske had received enough advance warning to destroy
Boulton's letters. Fiske was an American citizen who had lived in Edinburgh for two and a half years. He was a friend of Louis Charles Hurt, a
young Post Office surveyor, a boyhood friend of Boulton. From October
1868 through April 1869 Boulton lived with Hurt in Edinburgh, and this
is how Fiske met and fell in love with Boulton, to whom he wrote romantic letters after Boulton returned to London.

Boulton and Park were initially arrested for appearing in public in
women's clothes, a misdemeanour, but after a police surgeon examined
them they were charged with conspiracy to commit a felony (i.e. sodomy).
Their initial appearance in the dock was startling; Boulton, with wig and
plaited chignon, wore a cherry-coloured silk evening dress, trimmed with
white lace, and bracelets on his bare arms, while Park, his flaxen hair in
curls, wore a dark green satin dress, low necked, trimmed with black lace,
and a black lace shawl, and a pair of white kid gloves. The court was be-

157

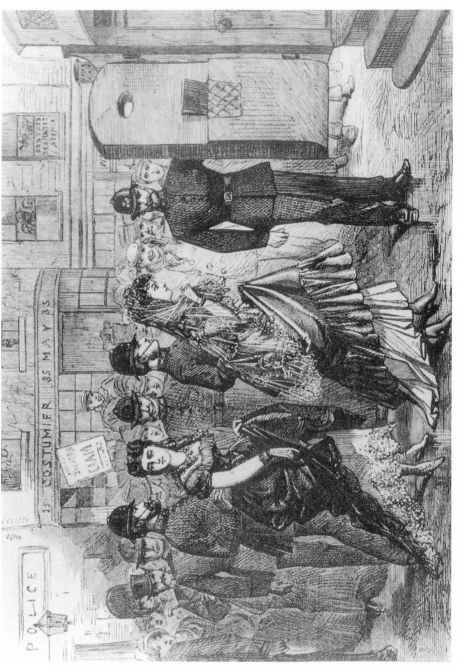

The arrest of Ernest Boulton and Frederick William Park in full drag, April 1870. From *The Day's Doings*.

sieged by an enormous crowd through the committal proceedings, and the trial—appropriately called The Queen v. Boulton and Others (Boulton, Park, Fiske, Hurt, and two others in absentia)—continued throughout most of May the following year.

One person connected with the case was Lord Arthur Pelham Clinton, MP, third son of the Fifth Duke of Newcastle. Boulton told others "I am Lady Clinton, Lord Arthur's wife," and showed the wedding ring on his finger. Lord Arthur lodged near him, paid for Stella's hairdresser who came every morning, and had ordered from the stationers a seal engraved "Stella" and even visiting cards printed "Lady Arthur Clinton." There are theatre posters of Lord Arthur and Boulton performing together in the play *A Morning Call* in which Lord Arthur played Sir Edward Arnold and Boulton played Mrs. Chillington, and in *Love and Rain*, in which Lord Arthur played Captain Charles Lumley and Boulton played Lady Jane Desmond, a Young Widow.

Lord Arthur's name was on the original indictment, but he died on June 18, 1870, age thirty, before the case came to court, reportedly from scarlet fever exacerbated by anxiety (but in fact suicide). One full day during the trial was spent reading out more than a thousand letters by the defendants, most of which still exist in the Public Record Office, Hurt to Boulton, Hurt to Fiske, Hurt to Lord Arthur, Fiske to Boulton, Willie Somerville (a City clerk, who had absconded) to Boulton, Park to Lord Arthur. But conviction of conspiracy to commit a felony could not be sustained without proof of the actual commission of the felony; even the prosecution came to feel that all the evidence merely pointed to disgraceful behaviour. It has been argued that the jury either did not comprehend the existence of the gay subculture (they certainly missed the meaning of the gay slang in the letters), or that they wilfully blinded themselves to the subversive facts of life. All the defendants were acquitted, to loud cheers and cries of Bravo! from the gallery.

---

ERNEST BOULTON TO LORD ARTHUR PELHAM CLINTON

*4th December 1868*

My dear Arthur,—

I am just off to Chelmsford with Fanny [Park]. We stay until Monday. Not sent me any money, wretch!

—Stella Clinton

---

*[Several days later]*

My dear Arthur,—

We were very drunk last night, and consequently I forgot to write. . . . And now, dear, I must shut up, and remain affectionately yours,

—Stella

*[Several days later]*

My dear Arthur,—

I have waited for two hours for you, and do not like to be treated with such rudeness. . . . I shall not return to-night—not at all, if I am to be treated with such rudeness. . . . I am consoling myself in your absence by getting screwed. . . . Mamma sends her kind regards, and will be glad to see you on Sunday.

---

FREDERICK WILLIAM PARK TO LORD ARTHUR PELHAM CLINTON

*Duke Street*
*Nov. 21 [1869?]*

My dearest Arthur,—

How very kind of you to think of me on my birthday! I had no idea that you would do so. It was very good of you to write, and I am really very grateful for it. I require no remembrances of my sister's husband, as the many kindnesses he has bestowed upon me will make me remember him for many a year, and the birthday present he is so kind as to promise me will only be one addition to the heap of little favours I already treasure up. So many thanks for it, dear old man. I cannot echo your wish that I should live to be a hundred, though I should like to live to a green old age. Green, did I say?? Oh, *ciel!* the amount of paint that will be required to hide the very unbecoming tint. My "caw fish undertakings" are not at present meeting with the success which they deserve. Whatever I do seems to get me into hot water somewhere. But, *n'importe.* What's the odds as long as you're happy?

Believe me, your affectionate sister-in-law,
Fanny Winifred Park

---

*[no date]*

My dearest Arthur,—

You really must excuse me from interfering in matrimonial squabbles (for I am sure the present is no more than that); and though I am as you say Stella's *confidante* in most things, that which you wish to know she keeps locked up in her own breast. My own opinion on the subject varies fifty times a day when I see you together. She may sometimes treat you brusquely; but on the other hand see how she stands up for your dignity of position (in the matter of Ellis's parts, for instance), so that I really cannot form an opinion on the subject. As to all the things she said to you the other night, she may have been tight and did not know all she was saying; so that by the time you get my answer you will both be laughing over the whole affair, as Stella and I did when we quarrelled and fought down here—don't you remember, when I slapped her face? My address is the same, as I do not move out of this street. I have enclosed a note to you in the one I wrote Stella last night. Good-bye, dear.

—Ever yours,

Fan

---

*Duke Street,*
*Friday*

My dearest Arthur,—

I think I would rather you came in the middle of the week, as I fancy I am engaged on the Saturday (15th) in London, though I am not certain yet. If you came on Wednesday and stayed until Saturday morning (if you could endure me so long), we could all go up together—that is if I go. But please yourselves. I am always at home and a fixture. I shall be glad to see you both at any time. Is the handle of my umbrella mended yet? If so, I wish you would kindly send it me, as the weather has turned so showery that I can't go out without a dread of my back hair coming out of curl. Let me hear from you at any time; I am always glad to do so.

Ever your affectionate,

Fanny

---

LOUIS CHARLES HURT TO ERNEST BOULTON

*Lochalsh, Inverness, and Wick*
*April 1870*

I have told my mother that you are coming, but have not yet had time to receive her answer. I thought it well to tell her that you were very effeminate, but I hope you will do your best to appear as manly as you can—at any rate in the face. I therefore beg of you to let your moustache grow at once. . . . even if in town, I would not go to [the Derby] with you in drag. . . . I am sorry to hear of your going about in drag so much. I know the moustache has no chance while this sort of thing goes on. You have now less than a month to grow . . . Of course I won't pay any drag bills, except the one in Edinburgh. I should like you to have a little more principle than I fear you have as to paying debts.

---

JOHN SAFFORD FISKE TO ERNEST BOULTON

*Edinburgh, 136 George Street*
*18th April 1870*

My darling Ernie,—

I am looking for Louis [Hurt] tonight, and wishing as I do a hundred times each day that you were to be here. I have eleven photographs of you (and expecting more tomorrow) which I look at over and over again. I have four little notes which I have sealed up in a packet. I have a heart full of love and longing; and my photographs, my four little notes, and my memory are all that I have of you. When are you going to give me more? When are you going to write a dozen lines of four words each to say that all the world is over head and ears in love with you, and that you are so tired of adoration and compliments that you turn to your humdrum friend as a relief? Will it be tomorrow or will it be next week? Believe me, darling, a word of remembrance from you can never come amiss, only the sooner it comes the better. "Hope deferred"—you know the saying. Adventures do turn up, even in Edinburgh. Perhaps you would envy me for five whole minutes if I were to tell you of one that I've had since you left; but I will keep it for your own ear when very likely you try after the same happiness. I shall not write you a long note, darling, at least not tonight, perhaps never again, if you don't write to say that I may. I hear Robbie Sinclair [a clerk in the Edinburgh Register Office] is coming here; his smiling face with the clear grey eyes and vivid roses. I wonder if Louis will like him. I hope not—at least not too much. I am getting very fond of Louis, and as I am fond of Robbie too, I don't want them to take too violently to each other. But what are these fancies and likings to the devotion with which I am yours always, *jusqu' á la mort,*

John S. Fiske

*À un ange qu'on nommé Ernie Boulton, Londres.*

---

*Office, Edinburgh*
*April 20, 1870*

My darling Ernie,—

I had a letter last night from Louis which was charming in every respect except the information it bore that he is to be kept a week or so longer in the North. He tells me you are living in drag. What a wonderful child it is! I have three minds to come to London and see your magnificence with my own eyes. Would you welcome me? Probably it is better I should stay at home and dream of you. But the thought of you—Lais and Antinous in one—is ravishing. Let me ask your advice. A young lady, whose family are friends of mine, is coming here. She is a charmingly-dressed beautiful fool with £30,000 a year. I have reason to believe that if I go in for her I can marry her. You know I never should care for her; but is the bait tempting enough for me to make this further sacrifice to respectability? Of course, after we were married I could do pretty much as I pleased. People don't mind what one does on £30,000 a year, and the lady wouldn't much mind, as she hasn't brains enough to trouble herself about much beyond her dresses, her carriage, etc. What shall I do? You see I keep on writing to you, and expect some day an answer to some of my letters. In any case, with all the love in my heart, I am yours,

John S. Fiske

# ▼ THE SUMMER OF LIFE ▼

[Sir Edmund Gosse & William Hamo Thornycroft]

Sir Edmund Gosse (1849–1928) was the archetypal British man of letters: assistant librarian at the British Museum, translator at the Board of Trade, librarian at the House of Lords, contributor of several biographies for the English Men of Letters series, poet and influential literary critic, friend of Swinburne, Robert Louis Stevenson, Henry James, and many of the leading literary figures of his day. His relationship with his father is beautifully documented (sometimes not entirely truthfully) in his famous biography *Father and Son*.

The love of friends was the ruling passion of his life. In 1870 he wrote to his school friend John Blaikie, "How I long to know all about you! You are seldom from my thoughts. I think the time has already come, of which you spoke, when you said that one day our love would be so magnified that it would seem as though we had not loved at all." They wrote poetry to one another and their friendship continued for several years. But the great love of his life was the handsome young sculptor William Hamo Thornycroft, whom Gosse had met long before his marriage to Nellie Epps in 1875. Although Gosse took great pleasure in his wife and children, the relationship with Thornycroft, six months younger than he, filled an equally strong need. They went on many expeditions together in search of a pastoral Arcadia.

In May 1879 Gosse was standing on Richmond Bridge when he suddenly saw Hamo skim past in his father's boat the *Waterlily*: "It was the queerest sensation and, if the battlements of the bridge had been lower, I don't know but what I might have thrown myself into the river and committed suicide out of sheer companionableness." In June he and Hamo, Hamo's father and two other men cruised up the Thames in the *Waterlily*, bathing together naked in the warm evenings. An almost mystical union between the two men took place while they swam at Goring creek on June 19, which he mentioned to his wife: "We are lying now in a delicious quiet creek full of the scented rush—the calamus." He must have been familiar with the homoerotic symbolism attached to this plant by Walt Whitman, to whom he had sent his first volume of poems in 1873. He wrote a poem which he trusted Hamo would "be able to read between the lines," full of longing for the past:

> Already that flushed moment grows
> So dark, so distant; . . .
> But we can never hope to share
> Again that rapture fond and rare,
> Unless you turn immortal there . . .

163

Gosse obviously failed to seize the day, and several years later acknowledged that he was "so much haunted all the time . . . with a memory of that sedgey creek at the back of Goring, with the silence and the sunshine, and that mood of unbelief, the Pilgrim at the very gates of Happiness, turning back with tears to renounce Hope for ever." For several years Gosse and Thornycroft spent their holidays together, in Scotland, Paris, Switzerland, and the north of England, climbing mountains or swimming naked in the black lakes "wherein we believed that the sword Excalibur might at any moment be brandished, dreaming all our dreams of poetry and art. The spirit of youth was dancing in our veins."

In 1883 Thornycroft became engaged to be married, and the dream came to an end. In July 1883 Gosse wrote to thank Thornycroft "for these four wonderful years, the summer of life, which I have spent in a sort of morning-glory walking by your side." They nevertheless remained friends for the rest of Gosse's life; in 1885 Gosse wrote from America; "My dear Hamo, by the banks of the Susquehanna and the waters of the Squittersquash, I love you as much as I ever did by the sedged brooks of Thames's tributaries." Before and after the period of 1879–83, when his relationship with Thornycroft brought relief, Gosse was subject to fits of more or less severe depression, almost certainly caused by sexual repression.

When Lytton Strachey was asked if Gosse was a homosexual, he replied "No, but he's Hamo-sexual." Gosse's friend John Addington Symonds, the art historian and father of gay history, had acquired photographs of many of Thornycroft's nude male statues, including the famous *Teucer* (a Thracian archer, exhibited at the Royal Academy in 1881), and collected photographs of nude youths by Wilhelm von Gloeden and Guglielmo Plüschow. He exchanged packets of these photographs with Gosse, who kept stealing glances at one all through the funeral service held for Browning at Westminster Abbey.

Gosse wrote sympathetically to Symonds about how to persuade society to reform the laws against homosexuality, but sent him a poem suggesting that he himself had "tamed the chimaera." Gosse presumably destroyed the letters Thornycroft had written to him, just as he destroyed letters received from Blaikie with whom he was intimate prior to his developing passion for Thornycroft—and just as he threw on a bonfire all of Symonds's letters and diaries and papers that had been bequeathed to him (saving only Symonds's memoir, with the injunction that it not be opened for fifty years). Symonds's granddaughter Janet Vaughan was nauseated by the "smug gloating delight" with which Gosse informed her what he had done to preserve Symonds's good name. Similarly he had carefully suppressed an important part of his own life for the sake of middle class respectability.

SIR EDMUND GOSSE TO WILLIAM HAMO THORNYCROFT
*Board of Trade, S. W.*
*18.12.79*

My dear Hamo,—

Were you not rather tired on Saturday? I ached in every bone, and lay in bed till 12 next day. After getting off my skates, I came and stood above you at the head of the lake. It was too dark for me to distinguish any one but you: I stayed there watching you talking and meditatively pirouetting on the ice till I made up my mind to go. I hope you saw the splendid bar of crimson in the west, behind the trees.

You have been busy this week, I expect. I have been doing a great deal since I saw you. I shall have—I hope, rather an important poem to read you when we meet next in any quietude. For the moment, I send you a sonnet, fantastic and very unintelligible, I daresay, to most people. . . .

Think ever kindly of
Thine
Edmund W. G.

To H. T.

When by the fire we sit with hand in hand,
    My spirit seems to watch beside your knee,
Alert and eager, at your least command,
    To do your bidding over land and sea.
You sigh—and, of that dubious message fain,
    I scour the world to bring you what you lack,
Till from some island of the spicy main
    The pressure of your fingers calls me back;
You smile—and I, who love to be your slave,
    Post round the orb at your fantastic will,
Though, while my fancy skims the laughing wave
    My hand lies happy in your hand, and still;
Nor more from fortune or from life would crave
    Than that dear silent service to fulfil.

---

*29, Delamere Terrace*
*31.12.79*

My dear Hamo,—

I have been as busy as possible all the evening with proofs, letters, etc., and now having cleaned up everything, and made clear decks, I mean to spend the last half hour of 1879 with you. I have a pleasant fancy that you are at this very moment writing to me, but I daresay that is only superstition. . . .

Reviewing 1879, I see that it has been the most prosperous and the happiest in my life. I have gained several valuable acquaintances; I have published two important books; a son has been born to me; but above all these things I put the fact that *you* have come up out of the rank of a common friend into the first place of all, as something better than a brother. You are the inestimable treasure for which I was waiting nearly thirty years, and which, God knows, I long ago thought would never come at all. . . .

Will you dine here at 6 next Monday? Do. If you positively cannot, tell me a day soon that I may come and spend an evening with you, when *you have no company*. But I hope you will come on Monday.

If I write any longer, it will be 1880. My last thoughts in this year and my first thoughts in next year will be of you.

May you enjoy every desirable and happy wish of your heart through 1880, may your work grow steadily better and better, and if you must have any troubles may they only be such as you can share with

    Thy

      Edmund W. G.

---

*29, Delamere Terrace*
*Friday night. 16.1.80*

My dear Hamo,—

Will you dine here next Monday at 6? If you can't, fix any day you like next week. . . .

I have a great longing to talk to you, and nothing to say. What a foolish person, you will say—but I have long given up trying to make you think me anything else. . . .

I have such a bad rheumatism in my right arm that I cannot write without pain, and I have had to write for three hours this evening. So altogether my horizon is rather leaden, and the only sunlight I find just at present is when I absorb myself in the thoughts of you, grand and serious, face to face with your goddess [a statue of Artemis which he was sculpting], putting on her robes for her, like Apollo when he winds the body of the Dawn in fleecy raiment of clouds. You are Apollo to me: how glumpy and wretched was I when I began this note, and already your far-reaching beams have pierced my darkness. But you must expect to find me excessively dull and spiritless on Monday . . .

I can't believe that anything pleasant will ever happen to me again. Why can't fortune let us alone, when we want so little, just a nest of domestic quietude in which to brood over our two blue eggs, Friendship and Art, till they hatch two fledgeling immortalities?

This is mere jabbering; but I write on because I am too tired to leave off, and because the only thing that would really quiet me would be to drop my head into the paws of some feline creature—a jaguar for instance—and sleep a dreamless sleep. . . .

*29, Delamere Terrace*
*Saturday [early 1880]*

Dear Dr. Hamo,—

The patient was troubled yesterday with a very large sore lip and a general feeling of brains having been well-shaken [by a fall while ice-skating]. But otherwise he did great credit to his physician; and is better still today.

No more ice this season, I am afraid. You agree with me, I hope, in spite of the tumbles, that Thursday was by far the best of the good days we have had on the ice. The glow of the sun as we sat on the bench, how it thrilled us. . . . Few people know how moving a sunshiny day in mid-winter is; it sets all the summer veins pulsing, welling up blood from the heart in the great throb of the arteries, till the whole body is in a sort of melting ravishment, ready to take in every hint of colour and perfume and bodily touch. I could say many curious things about that bask we had in the sun on Thursday; but I saw in your eyes that you were thinking them too, so I will not waste my speech.

Do you not perceive that, like the bees, we are storing a great deal of the honey of memory for our old age? Strange, that people don't do this more; but I suspect few people live quite so much at their own finger-tips as we do. . . . I could not help thinking as we skated about what a poor thing all the matters I used to boast myself of—I mean mere acquirement of knowledge and book-learning—are in comparison with living one's life while one is young. It seems to me much more worth doing to be able to ride a colt across a rough piece of country than to be able to read a page of Thucydides. Ten years ago it would have seemed blank idiocy to me to have said that, but now the long months and months I have spent in stuffing the inside of my sheet of brown paper seem to me almost wasted. I think I could be quite happy to go with you to some place in the Back Woods, where we could make a clearing, build ourselves a hut, grow our own food and go off with our rifles into the forest when we wanted a change of employment. Do you know that you are a great wizard? I am very oddly bewitched; I scarcely know myself. . . .

Your

E. W. G.

Edward Carpenter (1844–1929) in middle age.

# ▼ TO DO A LITTLE GOOD ▼

### [EDWARD CARPENTER & GEORGE MERRILL]

Edward Carpenter (1844–1929) was at the forefront of British romantic socialism, whose philosophy was inspired by Whitman but had a clear political agenda and active "engagement" to radically reform social institutions. He practiced what he preached, giving away most of his money and earning a subsistence living as a sandal-maker as well as lecturer and journalist. His book of poetry *Towards Democracy*, consciously modelled upon Whitman's Calamus poems, is a forthright celebration of gay love:

> O child of Uranus, wanderer down all times,
> Yet outcast and misunderstood of men—
> I see thee where for centuries thou hast walked,
> Yet outcast, slandered, pointed at by the mob.
> The day draws nigh when from these mists of ages
> Thy form in glory clad shall reappear.

The personal liberation ("exfoliation") in the poetry was matched by numerous articles and books on politics, religion, anthropology and sexology, covering subjects ranging from prisons, vivisection, nudism and mysticism, to "homogenic love," feminism, socialism, communalism and the Labour movement—the thrust of them all is brilliantly summed up in the title of *Civilisation: Its Cause and Cure*. Virtually none of Carpenter's personal letters have been traced, but it is appropriate to include a few of the surviving letters from his "band of friends" to show the effect he had upon his followers, for he was considered to be almost a healer.

George Hukin was a razor-grinder, who met Carpenter while organizing a political campaign for the Sheffield Socialist Society. George Merrill (1870–1928) was an uneducated odd-job man from the slums whom Carpenter picked up in a railway car in 1896. Merrill's letters printed below are probably the first he ever sent to Carpenter, which explains why they were cherished and still survive. Soon he was the resident market-gardener, cook and housekeeper at Carpenter's small farm at Millthorpe near Sheffield. They lived together quite openly as a gay couple for the next thirty years. Merrill once chased away a clergyman who came to the door to give him a tract: "Keep your tract," said Merrill, "I don't want it. Can't you see we're in heaven here—We don't want any better than this, so go away."

Carpenter's philosophy of brotherhood was no abstract concept; he had occasional affairs with some of the intellectuals and gay writers who came on pilgrimage to Millthorpe, and Merrill had occasional flings with hired hands and the local farm boys. Merrill served as a model for the gamekeeper in E. M. Forster's gay novel *Maurice*, which Forster acknowledged was a direct result of a visit to Carpenter, when Merrill "touched my backside—gently and just above the buttocks. I believe he touched most people's. . . . It seemed to go straight through the small of my back into my ideas, without involving my thoughts. If it really did this, it would have acted in accordance with Carpenter's yogified mysticism, and would prove that at that precise moment I had conceived."

---

GEORGE HUKIN TO EDWARD CARPENTER

*26 Sept. 1886*

Dear Edward,

 . . . it is so good of you to love me so. I dont think I ever felt so happy in my life as I have felt lately. And I'm sure I love you more than any other friend I have in the world.

---

*21 May 1887*

. . . yes, Ted, it did help me a great deal that talk we had in bed that Monday morning—oh how often I wanted to tell you about it—ever since that first night I slept with you at Millthorpe. You dont know how miserable I have felt all day long just because I wanted to tell you, and yet somehow I was afraid to. But I shall not be afraid to tell you anything in future if only you will let me, Ted.

---

GEORGE MERRILL TO EDWARD CARPENTER

*26 Sept. 1896*

I'm so sorry for . . . the impediment in my speech. I think I should be able to do a little good for the social cause if I could converse better, but never mind it may wear away when I get to you and read for you. I do feel it very much at times. I thought about you all last night dear . . .

 love from your affectionate Sonny X.

---

*8 Nov. 1896*

Dear Ted,

 . . . I shall be glad to see thy dear face again as I have such longings to kiss those sweet lips of thine. I will wait till I hear from you, first. So I must close dear heart as I am feeling a little low and lonesome. I'm always with thee every night in spirit,

 fondest love from your dear Boy G XXX.

# ▼ PATHETIC SYMPHONY ▼

[Piotr Ilyich Tchaikovsky & Bob Davïdov]
*Translated from Russian by Galina von Meck*

Gay men have taken to their hearts the music of Piotr Ilyich Tchaikovsky (1840–93) because it is perceived to contain all the longing and despair of homosexual angst in a homophobic world. Although Tchaikovsky was one of the great musical thinkers, it is for the melodic lyricism and suffering so audible in his work, rather than its complexity or brilliance, that he will be remembered. His homosexuality was denied by Soviet musicologists until fairly recently, and much material still remains to be retrieved from Russian archives and published in English.

Tchaikovsky's lovers included Alexey Apukhtin in his music student days 1867–70; the wealthy Vladimir Shilovsky, whom he also met at the Moscow Conservatory, during 1868–72; Alexei Sofronov his valet from 1872 to the end of his life; his pupil Eduard Zak, who killed himself in 1873 (he inspired the *Romeo and Juliet Fantasy Overture*); Joseph Kotek in the mid-1870s; his nephew Vladimir Davïdov (second son of his sister Alexandra) in the 1880s–90s, to whom he dedicated the *Symphonie Pathétique* (1893); the young pianist Vassily Sapelnikov who went with him on a tour to Germany, France and England; as well as brief affairs recorded in his cryptographic diary (e.g. on March 22, 1889 he records that a "Negro came in to me," to his hotel room in Paris).

Tchaikovsky's brother Modest was also gay, and lived relatively openly with his boyfriend Nikolai ("Kolia") Hermanovich Konradi (1868–1923), a deaf and dumb boy whom Modest tutored and with whom he lived for about seventeen years from 1876. Tchaikovsky was uneasy about his homosexuality, but he was tormented more by *homophobia* than by his sexual nature. During a mid-life crisis at the age of thirty-six, Piotr wrote to Modest "I think that for both of us our dispositions are the greatest and most insuperable obstacle to happiness, and we must fight our natures to the best of our ability. . . . Surely you realize how painful it is for me to know that people pity and forgive me when in truth I am not guilty of anything. How appalling to think that those who love me are sometimes ashamed of me. In short, I seek marriage or some sort of public involvement with a woman so as to shut the mouths of assorted contemptible creatures whose opinions mean nothing to me, but who are in a position to cause distress to those near to me."

Tchaikovsky married in 1877, frankly told his wife he did not love her but would be her devoted friend, and not surprisingly the marriage ended disastrously after a few months, which brought Tchaikovsky close to a nervous breakdown and helped him accept his unchangeable sexual nature. Vladimir Lvovich Davïdov (1871/2–1906)—nicknamed "Bob"—became

Russian composer Peter Ilyich Tchaikovsky (1840–1893) with his nephew "Bob" Davïdov in 1892.

his lover from the late 1880s. Tchaikovsky was always homesick during his musical tours abroad—he hated the loneliness of large cities—and he always longed to get back home to be with his beloved nephew—"my idol"—whom he made his heir. His letter to Bob from a hotel room in London in May 1893 shows this correspondence to have been his lifeline: "I am writing to you with a voluptuous pleasure. The thought that this paper is going to be in your hands fills me with joy and brings tears to my eyes."

Later that year "Kolia" chucked out Modest, and there were plans to set up an apartment in St. Petersburg where Modest, Piotr and Bob would live together. But it was not to be, for in November 1893, less than a month after the premiere of the *Symphonie Pathétique*, Tchaikovsky was in effect murdered. It was reported that he died from cholera, caused by drinking an unboiled glass of water, but in the 1920s one of the doctors who attended him, Vasily Bertenson, admitted that Tchaikovsky had poisoned himself.

Alexandra Orlova, a Soviet musical scholar who emigrated to the USA in 1979, revealed that Duke Stenbok-Fermor had written a letter addressed to Tsar Alexander III complaining of the attentions the composer was paying the Duke's young nephew; this letter was handed to the civil servant Nikolay Jacobi, of the St. Petersburg School of Jurisprudence. Exposure would have meant public disgrace not only for Tchaikovsky, but for his fellow former students of this school. Instead of passing on the letter, Jacobi assembled a court of honor of the old boys of the school and summoned Tchaikovsky to his apartment. After the meeting which lasted five hours Tchaikovsky ran unsteadily from the room, very white and agitated, according to Jacobi's wife, who told Alexander Voitov (the school historian, who told Orlova), that Jacobi told her that the court of honor had required Tchaikovsky to kill himself and he had promised to comply with their demand.

The granddaughter of the sister of the wife of Tchaikovsky's eldest brother Nikolay, after reading Orlova's account, confirmed the truth of the story in 1987. In 1993 various experts debated the story on a BBC broadcast, and the most persuasive arguments were those supporting the view that Tchaikovsky had been ordered to do the decent thing, and that the symptoms of arsenic poisoning helped the authorities disguise the death as a case of cholera.

Tchaikovsky's sixth and last symphony, the *Pathétique*, provokes as much speculation as his death. It is profoundly enigmatic yet profoundly self-revealing: a longing to reveal something, a sense of tragic destiny, a struggle for happiness defeated by implacable "fate," i.e. oppression, a union of defiance and despair with which many gay men have identified at least until the 1970s. Tchaikovsky decided not to leave a detailed programmatic explanation of his darkest work: "Let them guess!" he told Modest. The last movement, the Adagio Lamentoso, is prophetic not only

of Tchaikovsky's own death, but also that of its dedicatee, for Bob Davïdov, who became curator of the Tchaikovsky Museum at his uncle's
home in Klin, killed himself at the age of thirty-five.

---

PIOTR ILYICH TCHAIKOVSKY TO VLADIMIR LVOVICH DAVÏDOV

*New York*
*2 May 1891*

Things have gone so far that it is quite impossible to write letters. Not a
free moment, and I scarcely manage to write my diary. I made a trip to
Niagara. As soon as I returned I had to visit one Mayer at his country house
and pay some visits in the few free hours I had left. Then I was invited out
to lunch. Altogether I have been frightfully busy, and I am completely
numb with exhaustion. Tonight I have to be at a big dinner, and then leave
at midnight for Baltimore; tomorrow a rehearsal and concert there, the day
after that Washington, then Philadelphia, then two days here, where all my
time is already booked, and at last, on the morning of the 21st, I leave. Oh
God! Will I ever come to that happy moment!!!

In about a week after you receive this letter I will be with you!!! This
seems an unattainable, impossible happiness! I try to think of it as little as
possible, to have enough strength to stand up to the last insufferable days.
But in spite of all I feel that I shall remember America with love. Everybody has been wonderfully kind.

Here are a few newspaper cuttings. Shall bring many more with me. I
think that you will all much prefer reading my diary than getting only short
news from my letters.

I embrace you all.
P. Tchaikovsky
In only one week!!!

---

*Paris*
*12–24 January 1892*

I feel an awful fool. Here I have another two weeks without anything to
help me kill time. I thought this would be easier in Paris than anywhere else
but, except for the first day, I have been bored. Since yesterday I do not
know what to think up to be free of the worry and boredom that come
from idleness. . . . Am still keeping my incognito. . . .

I often think of you and see you in my dreams, usually looking sad and
depressed. This has added a feeling of compassion to my love for you and
makes me love you even more. Oh God! How I want to see you this very
minute. Write me a letter from College during some boring lecture and send
it to this address (14, Rue Richepanse). It will still reach me as I am stay-

ing here for nearly two weeks.

I embrace you with mad tenderness.

Yours

P. Tchaikovsky

---

*Klin*
*12 August 1892*

My dear Golubchik!

I have just received your letter, and was terribly pleased to hear that you are in a happy state of mind. Could it be that one of my letters to you has been lost? I did not write very often but I did write. With all my soul I long to join you, and think about it all the time. But what can I do? There are more and more complications and more work every day. . . .

So all I can say is that it is impossible for me to leave before I have finished all my business in Moscow.

I embrace you to suffocation!!!

P. T.

---

*Moscow*
*14 August 1892*

I have just received the Paris photographs from Yurgenson and have told him to send four of them to you. I was so glad to see what a good likeness they were that I nearly started crying in the presence of Yurgenson. All this proof correction had completely destroyed all other feelings and thoughts and it had to be this little incident which made me feel again how strong my love for you is. . . . Oh God! How I want to see you.

I embrace you.

P. Tchaikovsky

---

*Berlin*
*16–28 December 1892*

I am still sitting in Berlin. I haven't got enough energy to leave—especially as there is no hurry. These last days I have been considering and reflecting on matters of great importance. I looked perfectly objectively through my new symphony and was glad that I had neither orchestrated it or launched it; it makes a quite unfavourable impression. . . . What must I do? Forget about composing? Too difficult to say. So here I am, thinking, and thinking, and thinking, and not knowing what to decide. Whatever happens these last three days were unhappy ones.

I am however, quite well, and have at last decided to leave for Basle tomorrow. You wonder why I am writing about all this to you? Just an irresistible longing to chat with you. . . . The weather is quite warm. I can picture you sitting in your room, scented nearly to suffocation, working at your college exercises. How I would love to be in that dear room! Give my love to everybody.

    I embrace you.

        P. Tchaikovsky

If only I could give way to my secret desire, I would leave everything and go home.

---

*Klin*
*11 February 1893*

If you do not want to write, at least spit on a piece of paper, put it in an envelope, and send it to me. You are not taking any notice of me at all. God forgive you—all I wanted was a few words from you.

I am going to Moscow tonight. The concert will be on the 14th. On the 15th I shall be going to Nijny-Novgorod for about three days and from there straight to Petersburg. About the end of the second week in Lent, therefore, I shall be with you.

I want to tell you about the excellent state of mind I'm in so far as my works are concerned. You know that I destroyed the symphony I had composed and partly orchestrated in the autumn. And a good thing too! There was nothing of interest in it—an empty play of sounds, without inspiration. Now, on my journey, the idea of a new symphony came to me, this time one with a programme, but a programme that will be a riddle for everyone. Let them try and solve it. The work will be entitled *A Programme Symphony* (No. 6) *Symphonie à Programme* (No. 6), *Eine Programmsinfonie* (Nr. 6) [Modest suggested the title finally adopted, *Symphonie Pathétique*]. The programme of this symphony is completely saturated with myself and quite often during my journey I cried profusely. Having returned I have settled down to write the sketches and the work is going so intensely, so fast, that the first movement was ready in less than four days, and the others have taken shape in my head. Half of the third movement is also done. There will still be much that is new in the form of this work and the finale is not to be a loud *allegro*, but the slowest *adagio*. You cannot imagine my feelings of bliss now that I am convinced that the time has not gone forever, and that I can still work. Of course, I may be wrong, but I do not think so. Please, do not tell anyone, except Modest.

I purposely address the letter to the College, so that no one shall read it. Does all this really interest you? It sometimes seems to me that you are not interested at all and that you have no real sympathy for me. Good-bye, my dear. . . .

    Yours

        P Tchaikovsky

*Klin*
*3 [or 2] August 1893*

In my last letter to Modest I complain that you don't want to know me, and now he is silent too, and all links with your crowd are completely broken. . . .

What makes me sad is that you take so little interest in me. Could it be that you are positively a hard egotist? However, forgive me, I won't pester you again. The symphony which I was going to dedicate to you (not so sure that I shall now) is getting on. I am very pleased with the music but not entirely satisfied with the instrumentation. It does not come out as I hoped it would. It will be quite conventional and no surprise if this symphony is abused and unappreciated—that has happened before. But I definitely find it my very best, and in particular the most sincere of all my compositions. I love it as I have never loved any of my musical children.

. . . At the end of August I shall have to go abroad for a week. If I were sure that you would still be in Verbovka in September I would love to come at the beginning of the month. But I know nothing about you.

I embrace you with all my love.

P. Tchaikovsky

Oscar Wilde (1854–1900), left, and Lord Alfred Douglas (''Bosie'') (1870–1945). Photo of *ca.*
1893 at Oxford. Courtesy Clark Library, Los Angeles.

# ▼ AN ILL-FATED FRIENDSHIP ▼

[OSCAR WILDE & LORD ALFRED DOUGLAS]

In November 1993 an unpublished letter from Oscar Wilde (1854–1900) to one of his lovers, the wealthy twenty-year-old Phillip Griffiths, together with a signed photograph was auctioned by Christies in London for £18,700. In the letter, written in 1894, Wilde asked Griffiths to send him a photograph "which I will keep as a memory of a charming meeting, and golden hours passed together. You have a beautiful nature made to love all beautiful things, and I hope we shall see each other soon. Your friend Oscar Wilde." Wilde enclosed a photograph of himself inscribed to Griffiths with the message "The secret of life is Art." The secret of Wilde's sex-life is also art: Wilde idealized his affairs with upper-class youths in terms of pastoral mythology, and romanticized his affairs with lower-class rough trade as "feasting with panthers." But it was in fact his aristocratic lover Lord Alfred Douglas (1870–1945) who was the real panther.

The first letter selected below is the "infamous" letter which Wilde sent to "Bosie" which fell into the hands of a homosexual pimp and was used to blackmail Wilde, and which eventually contributed to his conviction on charges of "gross indecency," and two years' imprisonment. Wilde received an ovation when he defended the "Love that dare not speak its name" in court, as "that deep, spiritual affection that is as pure as it is perfect. It dictates and pervades great works of art like those of Shakespeare and Michelangelo, and those two letters of mine, such as they are. . . . It is beautiful, it is fine, it is the noblest form of affection. There is nothing unnatural about it. It is intellectual, and it repeatedly exists between an elder and a younger man, when the elder man has intellect, and the younger man has all the joy, hope and glamour of life before him. That it should be so the world does not understand. The world mocks at it and sometimes puts one in the pillory for it." But this impassioned defence crumbled over the succeeding days as the prosecution produced its evidence from a string of hustlers, reducing visions of crystalline beauty to stains on hotel bed sheets.

The last selection contains excerpts from the long letter—called "De Profundis," from the depths—which Wilde wrote to Bosie from prison. Bosie destroyed it unread, but Wilde's most faithful lover Robert Ross had kept a copy. These two letters thus document the beginning and end of an affair that went horribly wrong. Wilde has been not quite accurately cast in the role of gay martyr to the hypocrisy and sex-repression of Victorian society; it would be truer to say that he was willingly victimized. Douglas used Wilde as a pawn in his argument with his father the Marquess of Queensberry, whom he loathed. When Queensberry publicly accused Wilde of being a sodomite, Douglas urged Wilde to foolishly sue for libel. When

179

the trial began, Douglas fled abroad, and offered little help when the libel was dismissed and Wilde was subsequently tried for homosexual relations with various male prostitutes. He abandoned Wilde during his bitter imprisonment, but took up with him again in France after his release. In later life Douglas converted to Roman Catholicism, though recalling Oscar affectionately at the end of his long life.

OSCAR WILDE TO LORD ALFRED DOUGLAS

*January 1893*
*Babbacombe Cliff*

My own Boy,

Your sonnet is quite lovely, and it is a marvel that those rose-red lips of yours should have been made no less for the music of song than for the madness of kisses. Your slim gilt soul walks between passion and poetry. I know Hyacinthus, whom Apollo loved so madly, was you in Greek days.

Why are you alone in London, and when do you go to Salisbury? Do go there to cool your hands in the grey twilight of Gothic things, and come here whenever you like. It is a lovely place—it only lacks you; but go to Salisbury first.

Always, with undying love,

Yours,

Oscar

*Savoy Hotel, London*
*[March 1893]*

Dearest of all Boys,

Your letter was delightful, red and yellow wine to me; but I am sad and out of sorts. Bosie, you must not make scenes with me. They kill me, they wreck the loveliness of life. I cannot see you, so Greek and gracious, distorted with passion. I cannot listen to your curved lips saying hideous things to me. I would sooner be blackmailed by every renter in London than have you bitter, unjust, hating. I must see you soon. You are the divine thing I want, the thing of grace and beauty; but I don't know how to do it. Shall I come to Salisbury? My bill here is £49 for a week. I have also got a new sitting-room over the Thames. Why are you not here, my dear, my wonderful boy? I fear I must leave; no money, no credit, and a heart of lead.

Your own Oscar

*Early 1897*
*H.M. Prison, Reading*

Dear Bosie,

After long and fruitless waiting I have determined to write to you myself, as much for your sake as for mine, as I would not like to think that I had passed through two long years of imprisonment without ever having received a single line from you, or any news or message even, except such as gave me pain.

Our ill-fated and most lamentable friendship has ended in ruin and public infamy for me, yet the memory of our ancient affection is often with me, and the thought that loathing, bitterness and contempt should for ever take that place in my heart once held by love is very sad to me: and you yourself will, I think, feel in your heart that to write to me as I lie in the loneliness of prison-life is better than to publish my letters without my permission or to dedicate poems to me unasked, though the world will know nothing of whatever words of grief or passion, of remorse or indifference you may choose to send as your answer or your appeal. . . .

But most of all I blame myself for the entire ethical degradation I allowed you to bring on me. The basis of character is will-power, and my will-power became absolutely subject to yours. It sounds a grotesque thing to say, but it is none the less true. Those incessant scenes that seemed to be almost physically necessary to you, and in which your mind and body grew distorted and you became a thing as terrible to look at as to listen to: that dreadful mania you inherit from your father, the mania for writing revolting and loathsome letters: your entire lack of any control over your emotions as displayed in your long resentful moods of sullen silence, no less than in the sudden fits of almost epileptic rage: all these things in reference to which one of my letters to you, left by you lying about at the Savoy or some other hotel and so produced in Court by your father's Counsel, contained an entreaty not devoid of pathos, had you at that time been able to recognise pathos either in its elements or its expression:—these, I say, were the origin and causes of my fatal yielding to you in your daily increasing demands. You wore one out. It was the triumph of the smaller over the bigger nature. It was the case of that tyranny of the weak over the strong which somewhere in one of my plays I describe as being "the only tyranny that lasts."

And it was inevitable. In every relation of life with others one has to find some *moyen de vivre*. In your case, one had either to give up to you or to give you up. There was no alternative. Through deep if misplaced affection for you: through great pity for your defects of temper and temperament: through my own proverbial good-nature and Celtic laziness: through an artistic aversion to coarse scenes and ugly words: through that incapacity to bear resentment of any kind which at that time characterised me: through my dislike of seeing life made bitter and uncomely by what to me, with my eyes really fixed on other things, seemed to be mere trifles too petty for more than a moment's thought or interest—through these reasons, simple as they may sound, I gave up to you always. As a natural result, your claims, your efforts at domination, your exactions grew more and more unreasonable. Your meanest motive, your lowest appetite, your most common passion, became to you laws by which the lives of others were to be guided always, and to which, if necessary, they were to be without scruple sacrificed. Knowing that by making a scene you could always have your way, it was but natural that you should proceed, almost unconsciously I have no doubt, to every excess of vulgar violence. At the end you did not know to what goal you were hurrying, or with what aim in view. Having made your own of my genius, my will-power, and my fortune, you required, in the blindness of an inexhaustible greed, my entire existence. You took it. At the one supremely and tragically critical moment of all my life, just before my lamentable step of beginning my absurd action, on the one side there was your father attacking me with hideous card left at my club, on the other side there was you attacking me with no less loathsome letters. The letter I received from you on the morning of the day I let you take me down to the Police Court to apply for the ridiculous warrant for your father's arrest was one of the worst you ever wrote, and for the most shameful reason. Between you both I lost my head. My judgment forsook me. Terror took its place. I saw no possible escape, I may say frankly, from either of you. Blindly I staggered as an ox into the shambles. I had made a gigantic psychological error. I had always thought that my giving up to you in small things meant nothing: that when a great moment arrived I could reassert my will-power in its natural superiority. It was not so. At the great moment my will-power completely failed me. In life there is really no small or great thing. All things are of equal value and of equal size. . . .

You send me a very nice poem, of the undergraduate school of verse, for my approval: I reply by a letter of fantastic literary conceits [reproduced above]: I compare you to Hylas, or Hyacinth, Jonquil or Narcisse, or someone whom the great god of Poetry favoured, and honoured with his love. The letter is like a passage from one of Shakespeare's sonnets, transposed to a minor key. It can only be understood by those who have read the *Symposium* of Plato, or caught the spirit of a certain grave mood made beautiful for us in Greek marbles. It was, let me say frankly, the sort of letter I would, in a happy if wilful moment, have written to any graceful young man of either University who had sent me a poem of his own making, certain that he would have sufficient wit or culture to interpret rightly its fantastic phrases. Look at the history of that letter! It passes from you into the hands of a loathsome companion: from him to a gang of blackmailers: copies of it are sent about London to my friends, and to the manager of the theatre where my work is being performed: every construction but the right one is put on it: Society is thrilled with the absurd rumours that I have had to pay a huge sum of money for having written an infamous letter to you: this forms the basis of your father's worst attack: I produce the original letter myself in Court to show what it really is: it is denounced by your father's Counsel as a revolting and insidious attempt to corrupt Innocence: ultimately it forms part of a criminal charge: the Crown takes it up: The Judge sums up on it with little learning and much morality: I go to prison for it at last. That is the result of writing you a charming letter. . . .

There is, I know, one answer to all that I have said to you, and that is that you loved me: that all through those two and a half years during which the Fates were weaving into one scarlet pattern the threads of our divided lives you really loved me. Yes: I know you did. No matter what your conduct to me was I always felt that at heart you really did love me. Though I saw quite clearly that my position in the world of Art, the interest my personality had always excited, my money, the luxury in which I lived, the thousand and one things that went to make up a life so charmingly, and so wonderfully improbable as mine was, were, each and all of them, elements that fascinated you and made you cling to me; yet besides all this there was something more, some strange attraction for you: you loved me far better than you loved anybody else. But you, like myself, have had a terrible tragedy in your life, though one of an entirely opposite character to mine. Do you want to learn what it was? It was this. In you Hate was always stronger than Love. Your hatred of your father was of such stature that it entirely outstripped, o'erthrew, and overshadowed your love of me. There was no struggle between them at all, or but little; of such dimensions was your Hatred and of such monstrous growth. You did not realise that there is no room for both passions in the same soul. They cannot live together in that fair carven house. Love is fed by the imagination, by which we become wiser than we know, better than we feel, nobler than we are: by which we can see Life as a whole: by which, and by which alone, we can understand others in their real as in their ideal relations. Only what is fine, and finely conceived, can feed Love. But anything will feed Hate. There was not a glass of champagne you drank, not a rich dish you ate of in all those years, that did not feed your Hate and make it fat. So to gratify it, you gambled with my life, as you gambled with my money, carelessly, recklessly, indifferent to the consequence. If you lost, the loss would not, you fancied, be yours. If you won, yours you knew would be the exultation, and the advantages of victory. . . .

You see that I have to write your life to you, and you have to realise it. We have known each other now for more than four years. Half of the time we have been together: the other half I have had to spend in prison as the result of our friendship. Where you will receive this letter, if indeed it ever reaches you, I don't know. Rome, Naples, Paris, Venice, some beautiful city on sea or river, I have no doubt, holds you. You are surrounded, if not with all the useless luxury you had with me, at any rate with everything that is pleasurable to eye, ear, and taste. Life is quite lovely to you. And yet, if you are wise, and wish to find Life much lovelier still and in a different manner you will let the reading of this terrible letter—for such I know it is—prove to you as important a crisis and turning-point of your life as the writing of it is to me. Your pale face used to flush easily with wine or pleasure. If, as you read what is here written, it from time to time becomes scorched, as though by a furnace-blast, with shame, it will be all the better for you. The supreme vice is shallowness. Whatever is realised is right. . . .

You came to me to learn the Pleasure of Life and the Pleasure of Art. Perhaps I am chosen to teach you something much more wonderful, the meaning of Sorrow, and its beauty.

Your affectionate friend
Oscar Wilde

# ▼ TREMENDOUS INTIMACY ▼

[HENRY JAMES & HENDRIK ANDERSEN]

The inner life of Henry James (1843–1916) is as difficult to penetrate as the secret history of the characters in his convoluted novels. To be certain about his homosexuality is to be certain about the existence of the ghost Peter Quint in *The Turn of the Screw*. The full truth probably matches the admission of the narrator of *The Sacred Fount*: "It would have been almost as embarrassing to have had to tell them how little experience I had had in fact as to have had to tell them how much I had had in fancy."

James's letters to Hugh Walpole typically begin "dearest, dearest, darlingest Hugh," but when the young novelist offered the Master his body, James is said to have recoiled with "I can't, I can't, I *can't*." But later in life he probably became less hesitant, and biographers suggest that he may have had a sexual affair with the bisexual William Morton Fullerton, to whom he wrote in September 1900 "You are dazzling, my dear Fullerton; you are beautiful; you are more than tactful, you are tenderly, magically *tactile*."

James tried to ensure that his biographers would have only an inscrutable mystery to deal with. In 1910 he was one of two people allowed, by the widow of Byron's grandson, to examine the Byron papers so as to corroborate the accusation of incest against the poet. Several days after finishing this task and learning its salutary lesson, James destroyed his own archive of forty years of letters, manuscripts and notebooks. He continued regularly with such bonfires until his death, and told his executor "My sole wish is to frustrate as utterly as possible the post-mortem exploiter . . . [and] to declare my utter and absolute abhorrence of any attempted biography or the giving to the world . . . of any part or parts of my private correspondence." But of course he could destroy only the letters he received, and many people kept the letters he sent them (some 7,000 letters recovered so far!).

One of these recipients was the young sculptor Hendrik Christian Andersen (1872–1940), remotely related to Hans Christian Andersen (elsewhere represented in this anthology), who emigrated with his family from Norway and grew up in Newport, Rhode Island. James met him in Rome in 1899, where he had established his studio, and purchased his bust of the young Conte Alberto Bevilacqua, which he placed upon his chimney-piece in the dining room of his home in Rye, Sussex. The selections that follow come from the beginning of their relationship, but its intensity continued unabated for many years. It was undoubtedly a tactile relationship: "Every word of you is as soothing as a caress of your hand, and the sense of the whole as sweet to me as being able to lay my own upon *you*" (August 10, 1904). James and "Carrissimo Enrico Mio" visited Newport, Rhode

Island together in 1905, and later they were briefly together both in Rye and Rome.

In 1906 James had misgivings about a vast monument full of naked bodies on which Andersen was working, of which he sent James photographs. James felt unable to see "where this colossal multiplication of divinely naked and intimately associated gentlemen and ladies, flaunting their bellies and bottoms and their other private affairs, in the face of day, is going, on any *American* possibility, to land you." Andersen's women looked like his men, lacking only the distinguishing particular, as James observed. In the 1910s James became embarrassed by his friend's pursuit of immensity and his megalomaniac plans for a World City peopled by his colossal nude statues and fountains. Andersen had succumbed aesthetically to the rise of Italian fascism, completely antithetical to James's love of human scale and individualism, and their correspondence ceased in 1913.

Hendrik was devastated by the early death of his older brother Andreas, who was probably his lover; Andreas has painted a languidly post-coital homoerotic self-portrait, with Hendrik lying naked in bed with a sheet pushed down below his waist and bulging above his genitals, one arm behind his head, the other stretched out to pet a cat, while Andreas sits naked on the edge of the bed, about to draw on a pair of socks. Andersen's letters do not survive, and there is little hard evidence to support Leon Edel's view that Andersen was an opportunist interested solely in how James could advance his career. Andersen later wanted to publish James's letters to him as a testimonial of their friendship, but James's nephew refused permission during his lifetime.

---

Henry James to Hendrik C. Andersen

*Lamb House, Rye*
*July 27th 1899*

My dear Boy!

I am very glad to hear from you of the safe arrival of my missive and of the good news of your escape from Rome being well in sight. I think of you with the liveliest sympathy and I have, even, when I do so, almost a bad conscience about my own happy exemptions (though it *can* roast a little here too); my little green garden where shade and breeze and grass keep their freshness and where a particular chair awaits you under a certain wide-spreading old mulberry-tree. I shall make you very welcome here when your right day comes. May nothing occur to delay or otherwise damage it. Only let me know as soon as you can before you *do* approach—that I may advise you properly about your best train from London, etc. And don't expect to find me "lovely" or anything but very homely and humble. My little old house is *in* a small—a very small—country-town and is on a very limited scale indeed. But it serves my turn and will serve yours. I've struck

Hendrik Christian Andersen (1872–1940) (left), a young sculptor who had an intense affair with novelist Henry James (1843–1916). Photo taken in Rome, 1907.

up a tremendous intimacy with dear little Conte Alberto, and we literally can't live without each other. He is the first object my eyes greet in the morning, and the last at night. But I'm afraid I said some thing (accidentally) that misguided you in leading you to suppose I have written in a journal about.him. I haven't. What I meant was that sooner or later a great many persons will see, and be struck with him, *here*. *Pazienza*—and for God's sake keep yourself well. Good-bye—*à bientôt*. If you see the Elliotts [Maude and John Elliott, the sculptor at whose studio in Rome James met Andersen] please tell them I have a very affectionate memory of them and wrote to them in fact after the vile earth-shock. As you don't mention that I gather it didn't shatter you, nor anything that is yours. Bravo for all the big things you feel stirring within you.

Yours very heartily
Henry James

---

*Lamb House, Rye, Sussex*
*September 7th 1899*

My dearest little Hans: without prejudice to your magnificent stature! Your note of this morning is exactly what I had been hoping for, and it gives me the liveliest pleasure. I hereby "ask" you, with all my heart. *Do*, unfailingly and delightfully, come back next summer and let me put you up for as long as you can possibly stay. There, mind you—it's an engagement. I was absurdly sorry to lose you when, that afternoon of last month, we walked sadly to the innocent and kindly little station together and our common fate growled out the harsh false note of whirling you, untimely away. Since then I have *missed* you out of all proportion to the three meagre little days (for it seems strange they were only *that*) that we had together. I have never (and I've done it three or four times) passed the little corner where we came up Udimore hill (from Winchelsea) in the eventide on our bicycles, without thinking ever so tenderly of our charming spin homeward in the twilight and feeling again the strange perversity it made of that sort of thing being so soon *over*. Never mind—we *shall* have more, lots more, of that sort of thing! If things go well with me I'm by no means without hope of having been able, meanwhile, to take the studio [a studio in Watchbell street] so in hand that I shall be ready to put you into it comfortably for a little artistic habitation. Rye, alas, is not sculpturesque, nor of a sculpturesque inspiration—but what's good for the man is, in the long run, good for the artist—and we shall be good for each other; and the studio good for both of us. May the terrific U.S.A be meanwhile not a brute to you. I feel in you a *confidence*, dear Boy—which to show is a joy to me. My hopes and desires and sympathies right heartily and most firmly, go with you. So keep up *your* heart, and tell me, as it shapes itself, your (inevitably,

I imagine, more or less weird) American story. May, at any rate, *tutta quella gente* be good to you.

Yours, my dear Hans, right constantly
Henry James

---

*Lamb House, Rye*
*4 May 1901*

My dearest Boy Hendrik.

What an arch-Brute you must, for a long time past, have thought me! But I am not really half the monster I appear. Let me at least attenuate my ugly failure to thank you for certain valued and most interesting photographs. I spent the whole blessed winter—December to April—in London (save a week at Christmas), and returned here to take up my abode again but three or four weeks ago. It was only *then* that I found, amid a pile of postal matter unforwarded (as my servants, when I am away, have instructions only to forward *letters*), your tight little roll of views of your Lincoln. It had lain on my hall-table ever since it arrived (though I don't quite know when that had been); and my first impulse was [to] sit down and "acknowledge" it without a day's delay. Unfortunately—with arrears here, of many sorts, to be attended to after a long absence, the day's delay perversely imposed itself—and on the morrow my brother and his wife, whom you saw in Rome, arrived for a long stay, with their daughter in addition. They are with me still, and their presence accounts for many neglects—as each day, after work and immediate letters etc.—I have to give them much of my time. But here, my dear boy, I am at last, and I hold out to you, in remorse, remedy, regret, a pair of tightly-grasping, closely-drawing hands.

. . . [The photographs] show me how big a stride with it you have made in this short time and how stoutly you must have sweated over it; but I won't conceal from you that there are things about it that worry me a little. . . . A *seated* Lincoln in itself shocks me a little—he was for us all, then, standing up very tall: though I perfectly recognise that that was a condition you may have *had*, absolutely, to accept. . . . It's in general a *softer*, smaller giant than we used to see—to see represented and to hear described. I do think he wants facially more light-and-shade, and more breaking-up, under his accursed clothing, more bone, more mass. . . . But forgive this groping criticism; far from your thing itself, I worry and fidget for the love of your glory and your gain; and I send you my blessing on your stiff problem and your, I am sure, whatever mistake one may make about it, far from superficial solution.—I hope you have had a winter void of any such botherations as to poison (in any degree) your work or trouble your brave serenity or disturb your youthful personal bloom; a winter of health, in short, and confidence and comfort. It has been a joy to me to be with any one who had lately seen you—and I wish that, without more delay, I could do the sweet same! There is much I want to say to you—but it's half past midnight, and I wax long-winded. So I bid you good night with my affectionate blessing. I count on seeing you here this summer. Give me some fresh assurance of the prospect. I have had a charming letter from Mrs. Elliott, very happy over her Jack's finally-placed Boston show. *Meno male!*

Yours, my dear Hans, always and ever
Henry James

---

*Lamb House, Rye*
*September 13th 1901*

Dear, dear Hendrik!

Yes, your letter has been a joy, as I wired you this noon; I had rather dolefully begun to give you up, and I am now only sorry so many days must elapse before I see you. Don't, dearest boy, for heaven's sake, make them any more numerous than you need. Subject to that caution, I bow to your necessities, and can easily see that, for a week in London, you must have much to do. But make it, oh, make it, your advent, not a day later than Saturday 21st, will you not? I count on you intensely and immensely for *that* afternoon, when the 4.28 from Charing Cross, thoroughly handy for you, will (changing at Ashford) bring you here by 6.40, and I shall, at the station take very personal possession of you. . . . I am alone now—have been so this fortnight, and hope pretty confidently to be so while you are with me. You shall therefore have the best berth—such as that is—in the house: trust me for it. Put through your London jobs and mind your London ways: write me once more before you come, and come the first moment you can; and above all think of me as impatiently and tenderly yours.

Henry James

---

*105 Pall Mall S.W.*
*February 9th 1902*

My dear, dear, dearest Hendrik.

Your news [of the death of your brother Andreas] fills me with horror and pity, and how can I express the tenderness with which it makes me think of you and the aching wish to be near you and put my arms round you? My heart fairly bleeds and breaks at the vision of you *alone*, in your wicked and indifferent old far-off Rome, with the haunting, blighting, unbearable sorrow. The sense that I can't *help* you, see you, talk to you, touch you, hold you close and long, or do anything to make you rest on me, and feel my participation—this torments me, dearest boy, makes me ache for you, and for myself; makes me gnash my teeth and groan at the bitterness of things. I can only take refuge in hoping you are *not* utterly alone, that some human tenderness of *some* sort, some kindly voice and hand *are* near you that may make a little the difference. What a dismal winter you must have had, with this staggering blow at the climax! I don't of course know *what* fragment of friendship there may be to draw near to you, and in my uncertainty my image of you is of the darkest, and my pity, as I say, feels so helpless. I wish I could go to Rome and put my hands on you (oh, how lovingly I should lay them!) but that alas, is odiously impossible. (Not, moreover, that apart from *you*, I should so much as like to be there now.) I find myself thrown back on anxiously and doubtless vainly, wondering if there may not, after a while, [be] some possibility of your coming to England, of the current of your trouble inevitably carrying you here—so that I might take consoling, soothing, infinitely close and tender and affectionately-healing *possession* of you. This is the one thought that relieves me about you a little—and I wish you might fix your eyes on it for the idea, just of the possibility. I am in town for a few weeks but I return to Rye April 1st, and sooner or later to *have* you there and do for you, to put my arm round you and *make* you lean on me as on a brother and a lover, and keep you on and on, slowly comforted or at least relieved of the first bitterness of pain—this I try to imagine as thinkable, attainable, not wholly out of the question. There I am, at any rate, and there is my house and my garden and my table and my studio—such as it is!—and your room, and your welcome, and your place everywhere—and I press them upon you, oh so earnestly, dearest boy, if isolation and grief and the worries you are overdone with become intolerable to you. There they are, I say—to fall upon, to rest upon, to find whatever possible shade of oblivion in. I will *nurse* you through your dark passage. I wish I could do something *more*—something straighter and nearer and more immediate but such as it is please let it sink into you. Let all my tenderness, dearest boy, do *that*. . . .

---

*Lamb House, Rye*
*February 28th 1902*

Dearest, dearest Boy, more tenderly embraced than I can say!—How woefully you must have wondered at my apparently horrid and heartless silence since your last so beautiful, noble, exquisite letter! *But*, dearest Boy, I've been dismally *ill*—as I was even when I wrote to you from town; and it's only within a day or two that free utterance has—to this poor extent—become possible to me. *Don't waste any pity*, any words, on me now, for it's, at last, blissfully over, I'm convalescent, on firm grounds, safe, gaining daily. . . . So I've pulled through—and am out—and surprisingly soon—of a very deep dark hole. *In* my deep hole, how I thought yearningly, helplessly, dearest Boy, of *you* as your last letter gives you to me and as I take you, to my heart. . . . And now I am tired and spent. I only, for goodnight, for five minutes, take you to my heart. And I'm better, better, better, dearest Boy; don't think of my having been ill. Think only of my love and that I am yours always and ever
Henry James

# ▼ THE LAST CHORD ▼

[F. HOLLAND DAY & NARDO]

Fred Holland Day (1864–1933) was the first American photographer to promote the idea of photography as an art form. A wealthy and eccentric aesthete, he retrieved many boys from the Boston slums. His most famous protégé and discovery was the mystical poet Kahlil Gibran, a thirteen-year-old immigrant whom he took under his wings. Many of Day's photographs illustrate Christian homoeroticism: he was his own model for "The Seven Last Words of Christ" (1898), a shocking series of portraits of himself as Christ wearing the crown of thorns, and a notorious series of full frontal nude portraits of himself hanging on the cross, with Athletic Model Guild type "Roman soldiers" standing guard in loin cloths.

Many other photographs were in the pagan idyllic mode—grainy prints of naked boys playing flutes. A young Italian lad from Chelsea (called "Nardo") posed nude with lyre for a series of Apollonian photographs by Day during the summer of 1907. The photographs were republished in 1981 and bear ample testimony to the model's beauty. Day supported him in art school, and introduced him to employers, and tried to find another patron for him in the world of commercial art. Nardo wrote many letters to Day implying that he wanted more money, and he even asked him for a "loan" of $500 when he decided to pursue a rich girl in New York. This provoked an exasperated reply from Day, but he continued to support the potential blackmailer for several more years.

As late as 1912 the vain model asked Day to send him another set of the famous photos, especially "the figure with the lyer standing beside the big rock and the last cord that was striking and then no more do you know which one I mean the last breath." His mind was not quite so ideal as his body, though an improvement in the style of his letters at least demonstrates that the money Day paid for his English lessons was not altogether wasted.

---

NARDO TO F. HOLLAND DAY

*January 7, 1907*

My dearest Mr. Day—
  You are making me Happy every single Day of the week. I feel as if I had a lot of powre when you mak me feel Happy do not thing for one moment becouse I do not say anything to you you might thing I forget you. . . . Often time I thing that you are to kind to me My dearest Mr. Day—But I am sure that the day will come when you shall fell so happy for what you have done for me . . . for I thing there is nothing like F. H. Day in this while while [wide wide] world for wherever you go I shall for wherever you

step I shall step I will fowlow you through Hell if it is nessissery I mean it so Help me god this is the trut and nothing but the trut.

    N

---

F. HOLLAND DAY TO NARDO

*February 17, 1909*

I am enclosing the loan you ask, but I want you to know that I do so out of no sort of sympathy with your distress, brought on as it is by certain disregard of the good advice you have long had and your stubborn determination to do as you please without hindrance.

---

NARDO TO F. HOLLAND DAY

*August 8, 1909*

Many a time I think of you during the day the joyfull and happy times we had together. My life then was one joy of happness, and allways cheerful full of love life and ambition. I will never forget the day we were out to Brockton, how happy I was, I thought the world was mine. When both of us walking in through the woods together ame in ame [arm in arm] and the beautiful birds that were singing sweet melodies . . . What paradise it was! Tell me dear Mr. Day, do you not remember the happy time we had there? . . . I will leave you in piece I will go far away where know body will know where I am. That is just as soon as I get enough money of my own.

Frederick William Rolfe (1860–1913), "Baron Corvo" (far left), his friend John Holden aged 21 (center), and Leon Schwartz (student, aged 15) in Holywell, North Wales 1896 (where Corvo was living at the time).

# ▼ THE VENICE LETTERS ▼

[FREDERICK WILLIAM ROLFE, AMADEO & PIERO]

Frederick William Rolfe (1860–1913), self-styled Baron Corvo, was expelled from a Roman Catholic seminary in 1887 only nine months after entering it. He left England for Italy, where he discovered the source of his inspiration and future work, in the Alban Hills and a young peasant named Toto. His "Stories Toto Told Me" were published in the notorious *Yellow Book* in 1895. But he never earned much from writing, and always struggled to make ends meet as a tutor, painter, photographer, and journalist. His most famous novel is *Hadrian the Seventh* (1904), in which he imagines himself as the Pope, which D. H. Lawrence called "the book of a man demon, not a mere *poseur*." His Venetian novel *The Desire and Pursuit of the Whole*, which he finished during the course of the letters printed here, is based upon his motto "He who desires must pursue his desire though the whole world obstructs him."

Corvo remained in Venice after a holiday in 1908 rather than return to England and the struggle to earn money by writing. Thrown out of his hotel when it was apparent the arrears would never be cleared up, he lived as a tramp in borrowed shelter, and even briefly as a freelance gondolier. "But I am not humbled, nor will be. Better by far to wear ruin as a diadem." He quarrelled with all his friends in England, who dropped him one by one, and with the English colony in Venice. He was befriended by Charles Masson Fox (1866–1935), an Anglican clergyman and timber merchant from Falmouth, Cornwall, while on holiday in Venice.

Fox gave him so much money that Rolfe set himself up in a Renaissance palazzo on the Grand Canal, with his bedroom hung in scarlet brocade. He had a private boat manned by four gondoliers, in which he reclined in the stern on a leopard skin—John Cowper Powys recalled in his autobiography that this "floating equipage . . . resembled the barge of Cleopatra." But all the money was squandered within a year, and the following letters are a remarkable record of his relationship with his benefactor.

Rolfe and Fox were never lovers—they both preferred boys—and the correspondence constitutes a kind of mutual masturbation. Corvo expected Fox to obtain a vicarious pleasure from learning how he spent his patron's money on handsome young stevedores: "I gave [poor dear Piero] five francs *from you* and took him to a trattoria and filled him with polenta and wine." The two men exchanged photographs of their boys, sometimes nude. The last few pathetic letters record the increasing number of rats (more than 61) Corvo has drowned in the slop bucket in his increasingly squalid lodgings, where he came down with bronchitis and pneumonia.

Rolfe wanted Fox, or someone secured through Fox, to become his "financial partner," to send him a regular monthly income and a large loan to pay off his debts, in expectation of being repaid from royalties on his unfinished books, which the patron would arrange to publish. In return, Corvo would pimp for Fox: "If this thing comes off and I get clear and some money in my pocket to play with I shall take a month's holiday and bring Peter and Carlo to England and live at an hotel at Falmouth where I can return your hospitality in a way which would enchant you." But their correspondence ended on August 21, 1910, Fox's charity having apparently ceased just as Rolfe predicted it would, and Rolfe, physically worn out by his poverty, died in 1913. Fox successfully brought an action for blackmail against a woman who threatened to reveal that he had seduced her son; he died a bachelor in 1935.

---

FREDERICK ROLFE, BARON CORVO TO
CHARLES MASSON FOX                    *[Late November 1909]*

To-day I have had adventures. . . . A Sicilian ship was lying alongside the quay and armies of lusty youths were dancing down long long planks with sacks on their shoulders which they delivered in a warehouse ashore. The air was filled with a cloud of fine white floury dust from the sacks which powdered the complexions of their carriers most deliciously and the fragrance of it was simply heavenly. As I stopped to look a minute one of the carriers attracted my notice. They were all half naked and sweating. I looked a second time as his face seemed familiar. He was running up a plank. And he also turned to look at me. Seeing my gaze he made me a sign for a cigarette. I grabbed at my pockets but hadn't got one; and shook my head. He ran on into the ship. I ran off to the nearest baccy shop and came back with a packet of cigs and a box of matches to wait at the foot of his plank. Presently he came down the plank dancing staggering under a sack. I watched him. Such a lovely figure, young, muscular, splendidly strong, big black eyes, rosy face, round black head, scented like an angel. As he came out again running (they are watched by guards all the time) I threw him my little offering. "Who are you?" *"Amadeo Amadei"* (lovely medi- aeval name). The next time, "What are you carrying?' *"Lily-flowers for soap-making."* The next time, "Where have I seen you?" *"Assistant gon- dolier one day with Piero last year"*—then*"Sir, Round Table—"* My dear F. I'm going to that ship again to-morrow morning. I want to know more. . . . I couldn't stay longer to-day because of the guards but I shall try to get Amadeo Amadei to some *trattoria* for his lunch. I have a faint remem- brance of his face, but only a faint one. It's as though he had grown up sud- denly. I expect he was some raggamuffin whom Peter scratched up once suddenly, and since then he has developed wonderfully. And of course, Peter has been talking. Well, all I can say is that if this is a real Knight of the Round Table and knows his way to Caerleon, you may depend on me to collect information, which I of course will verify *the first moment I am* *able.* Peter, Gildo, Carlo and the Greek (and I take it also Eduardo) are private practitioners: for none of them have let slip the password. But this florescent creature one would think is a professional. However there will be news tomorrow. Here I stop to leave a blank space to show through the envelope. N.B. *"Signore"* not *"Seniore"* which means "Elder." Do write. I have only you to speak to.

     R.

*November 28, 1909*

. . . I went off to the Quay of San Basegio on the Zattere to see the Knight of the Round Table [Amadeo Amadei]. It was getting dusk and I was just in time to see his lissome muscular figure come dancing down the long plank from the ship with his last sack of dried lily flowers silhouetted against the sunset. As he passed, I said, "Do me the pleasure to come and drink a little beaker of wine." "With the greatest possible respect to your valorous face," he answered, passing on. When he had delivered his load in the warehouse he came out and joined me. While he was working he had on a pair of thin flannel trousers tightly tucked into his socks, canvas slippers, and a thin sleeveless shirt open from neck to navel. Over this, his day's work done, he wore a voluminous cloak of some thick dark stuff and a broad-brimmed hat. He flung one end of the cloak over his shoulder like a toga. I describe his attire thus particularly, for reasons which will appear later on. "Take me," I said, "to a quiet wine shop where we can have much private conversation." We went through a few back alleys to a little quay in a blind canal off the Rio Malcontent where there was a very decent wineshop kept by an apparent somnambulist. I called for a litre of New Red (very fresh and heady) at 6d. We sat at the back of the shop among the barrels, our two chairs being together on one side of the only table there. The counter with its sleepy proprietor was between us and the door; and no one else was present.

I asked him to tell me about the Round Table; and took care that he drank two glasses to my one. Of course I fed him with cigarettes. He said there was formerly a house on the Fondamenta Osmarin: but, owing to the fear which struck all Italy last year, when Austria seized Herzegovina and suddenly placed 80,000 men on the frontier where Italy has only 6,000 (remember this frontier is not 30 miles away, and Venice I know was frightened out of her wits) then the Venetians took a hatred of all Germans and went and smashed the windows, calling the boys and men there "Eulenbergs" [referring to the notorious homosexual scandal involving the German prince of that name]. Wherefore the committee (*comitato*) of the club, for it was a private club of Signiori of the very gravest respectability, moved the club to a house which they purchased at Padova, about an hour and a half by steamer and train. He said that the club used to be open day and night; and ten boys were there always ready for use. The fee was 7 fr. payment for the room and what you pleased to the boy, but you had to pay the latter in the presence of the steward and never more than 5 fr. even though you stayed all day or all night, i.e. 5 fr. and 7 fr. for 12 hours. Beside the staff, any boy could bring a Signiore. And many did, chiefly school-boys at some of the public or technical schools who liked to make a little pocket-money. But now, unfortunately, these and other Venetian boys were out of employment; for at Padova there is a great University with about 1,300 students of all ages, besides many schools; and students were generally in want of money. . . . it was difficult for an honest lad—he is 16½—to find a way of employing his nights. During the day he works as a stevedore along the Zattere or in the harbour of Marittima earning 3.50 generally, of which he has to give 3 fr. to his father, also a stevedore and earning the same. His elder brother is doing military service. His cousin gondoles for a merchant, i.e. a grocer with whom he lives and sleeps. One younger brother of 12 earns 1.50 as a milkboy. Beside these three there are a mother and grandmother, five sisters and three small brothers to be kept out of the joint earnings of 8 fr. a day. Naturally he wants to earn money for himself.

He assured me that he knew incredible tricks for amusing his patrons. "First, Sior, see my person," he said. And the vivacious creature did all which follows in about 30 seconds of time. Not more. I have said that we were sitting side by side of the little table. Moving, every inch of him, as swiftly and smoothly as a cat, he stood up, casting a quick glance into the shop to make sure that no one noticed. Only the sleepy proprietor slept there. He rolled his coat into a pillow and put it on my end of the table, ripped open his trousers, stripped them down to his feet, and sat bare bottomed on the other end. He turned his shirt up right over his head, holding it in one hand, opened his arms wide and lay back along the little table with his shoulders on the pillow (so that his breast and belly and thighs formed one slightly slanting line unbroken by the arch of the ribs, as is the case with flat distention) and his beautiful throat and his rosy laughing face strained backward while his widely open arms were an invitation. He was just one brilliant rosy series of muscles, smooth as satin, breasts and belly and groin and closely folded thighs with (in the midst of the black blossom of exuberant robustitude) a yard like a rose-tipped lance. And—the fragrance of his healthy youth and of the lily flower's dust was intoxicating. He crossed his ankles, ground his thighs together with a gently rippling motion, writhed his groin and hips once or twice and stiffened into the most inviting mass of fresh meat conceivable, laughing in my face as he made his offering of lively flesh. And the next instant he was up, his trousers buttoned, his shirt tucked in and his cloak folded around him. The litre of wine was gone. I called for another. "Sior" he said, "half a litre this time, with permission." So we made it half. Would I not like to take him to Padova from Saturday till Monday? Indeed I would. Nothing better. But because I see that you, my Amadeo (i.e. Love God, quite a Puritan name), are a most discreet youth as well as a very capable one, I shall tell you my secret: for, in fact, you shall know that I am no longer a rich English but a poor, having been ruined by certain traitors and obliged to deny myself luxuries. To hear that gave him affliction and much dolour. But he wished to say that he was all and entirely at my disposal simply for affection; because, feeling sure that he had the ability to provide me with an infinity of diversions, each different and far more exciting than its predecessor, he asked me as a favour, as a very great favour, that I should afterwards recommend him to nobles who were my friends. And, without stopping, he went on to describe his little games.

He would let me lie on his belly, my yard in the warmth of his thighs, his body in my arms, his throat in my mouth, or his breast, his shoulders, his armpits to be bitten at my will, and I might lie there, still, so still, with his legs held in mine, my hands under his thighs to guide my yard when it swelled, as swell it should, swell, swell, stiff, till all of me throbbed and I thrust and thrust, striving to pierce his thighs, thrusting 242 times fiercely and more fiercely, thrusting with all of me—then—suddenly—a little opening of the fat of the thighs to let the strong yard through, panting and spitting with joy. Such indeed was his power of giving joy that he would urge me on, even then, to thrust more, fifty times more, even through, and a second time spit deeper joy before my yard should tire. He, if I wished it so, would spit simultaneously. Or, if I preferred, would lie on me while I was resting and spit four times in twenty-two minutes of the clock.

This for the beginning of the evening. Then we could rest in each other's arms to recover breath for a little kissing and fondling. And he knew how to wriggle just a little all the time, flesh to flesh, entirely naked for the diversion of Signiori. Kissing, he thoroughly understood in every part, especially a certain kind of kissing in his patron's armpit, whose body he held in his arms, clasping his legs with his legs—kissing of a fury inconceivable, admirable for excitation. Next, he was ready to be rammed behind, spreading his knees as wide as they would go, and as for bounding meanwhile, well, I ought to see it, for truly he could bound (opening himself) so well that he would have the whole yard thrust among his hot interiors, till he himself was stiffened with it and the spitting took place in his throat. And also, as to spitting in the throat, let his patron but lie on the bed, legs hanging over the end, and he above would lie on the body, breast to belly, arms in advance opening the thighs; and he would suck at his patron's yard with his mouth, but his own feet high on the bed head, his thighs also open, he would dangle his own yard to be sucked at will by his patron's lips till, both together at a signal, both might drink the juices of one another.

A little sleep, locked together, for an interval. Then, both being very hot, for the sake of coolness before sleeping for the night and to appease his patron's lust, he would extend himself across the bed, his legs hanging here and head and arms hanging there, his body and thighs ready to receive his patron. Let him mount. Let him ride. I stretched out with him to do with me what he will. And then a night of sleep in embrace. Who wakes first lies along and on the other, taking his fill of pleasure. Perhaps the patron wishes a little passage in the streets to take the air. We return and begin again. I shall always have new twists of my body for the Patron. We eat lunch. We spend the afternoon in bed. We eat dinner. Perhaps we see a kinematograph. Then another night, meeting together for diversion as before. In the morning early we wake and cling together before parting. And so to Venice. Sior, I pray you to try me. Only for affection (*pro affetto*) let me make you know what I can do. I said I couldn't afford it. Would I not then let him come to my palace. Any evening after five till six in the morning he was at the disposal of this Signiore. NO: I couldn't have him there; it was not convenient. Did he know of any place where we could go for an hour or so? It grieved him, but, No, not now. He had a patron, an artist, in Calle something on Zattere, also an English, who at 3.50 a day painted him naked on Wednesdays and used him for diversion then—but he could not take another patron there. I should think not, indeed. If I would go to Padova, he would pay his own fare. No. No. I was sorry. I was in despair. I would let him know when I could and then I most certainly would. Have some more wine. A thousand thanks but, no. Another cigarette. Twenty thousand thanks. So we came away.

He says that Peter and Zildo love each other and do everything to each other but to no one else, though he and Peter once had a whole summer night together on the lagoon in P's father's gondola. P. also is in much request among women but cannot spit more than twice a night. Whereas Amadeo has done it 8 times and vows that he could do 12 with a hot patron! Comments please.

    R.

---

*December 11, 1909*

I changed the [Money] Order quite easily at a money-changers *without signing it* and got 6.25 for it, i.e. 2½d. more than its face-value. How this came about I do not know; and it is needless to inquire. But oh, my dear, my dear, if you only knew that each loan of this kind stamps me down deeper and deeper and more loathsomely into the mire—relieves me for the moment, but is worse than useless for setting me free and on my feet! This is not ungracious. I am indeed most grateful for your kind feelings to me. You are absolutely the only person in this world to whom I can speak openly and friendly. Imagine then how I value your friendship—and how anxious I must be to deserve it and to maintain it. And, *just because I have the most ardent desire to keep your friendship, which comes to me at a time when I have no other friend,*—I implore you to read and ponder what follows as earnestly as you can. I'm certain that this state of things cannot continue. Why is it that I have had so many friends in the past, and now have lost them all? The reason is simple. They got tired. They liked me; and they pitied my penury; and they gave me little teaspoonsful of help. But friendship is only possible among equals. There must not be any money mixed up with it. And, by and bye, you also will get tired and bored and annoyed by the continual groans which I'm forced to emit, howling for a strong hand once for all to come along and haul me out of this damned bog and set me on my feet. . . . if you were an ordinary man, like C. or J. [Fox's wealthy American friend Cockerton, and the solicitor and editor Charles Kains Jackson], on seeing me shabby, miserable and poor, you would have done as they did and been civil and said good morning. That would have been natural. But, being one of ten thousand, you went a jolly sight further. The poverty and misery and shabbiness which were inauspicious enough to put them off, did not have that effect on you. But, it will, my dear, it will—unless we can change my inauspicious circumstances right soon. . . . Now I know you're not the kind of man who does good deeds for the sake of a reward. So I'm sure you won't misunderstand what I'm going to say next. You say that you look forward to next Autumn. . . . Peter will be in the *carabinieri* by next Autumn, Zorzi (the Greek in England), Amadeo and Zildo and Carlo much too big. [Fox preferred small boys.] But if I were free NOW, . . . I would have your place ready with suitable servants by next Autumn. And more—if I were free NOW, there wouldn't be any difficulty about putting my property in proper management and getting enough cash out of it to pay off the £260, and also, to bring Peter and Carlo to any place you liked in England for a month *whenever you pleased*. See that now. Think it over; and then strike out boldly. . . .

I'm glad you like my descriptions. Tell me, do they make you see, and feel, and give you pleasure, really? I particularly want to know: because writing is my trade, and I am always seeking to find out my faults and weaknesses so that I may improve them. Writing's a poor sort of job: but I want to get mine as perfect as I can. And it's only perfect when I succeed in exciting my reader, carrying him out of himself and his world, into my world and the things which I am describing. The newspaper critics (who are about as tedious a class of men as you can find anywhere) say that my writing is "extraordinarily vivid." But that's not good enough for me. It doesn't tell me what I want to know, viz. whether my writing makes my readers' imagination see and smell and hear and taste and feel what I describe. I'm afraid I made rather a failure of the Amadeo incident. But it was so utterly out of the common, even here—his quick hot chatter, all to the point, poured into my ear like a torrent—his feverish anxiety to give himself, every atom of himself inside and out, entirely away—his lightning-like exposure of his stock-in-trade, stripping in a flash, tossing his big, rosy, muscular nakedness backward—the wriggle, the stretching out of all, the instant of stiff waiting, the alluring grin—and then the quick recoil and covering up. What he would be like in use I tremble to imagine. The boiling passion of him was absolutely amazing. As far as I am concerned, I'm certain that a Saturday to Monday at Padua would simply be one long violent bout of naked wrestling and furious embracing so strengthening and invigorating to mind and body that I should be set up for a month. I'm not by any means a weak creature myself; and though I'm very slow to work up to a pitch, yet, when I am worked up I can behave quite terribly and not tire. And Amadeo is just ripe, just in his prime. I know that type so well. A year ago that day when he came to take the 3rd oar in my *pupparin*, he was a lanky uninteresting wafer. Since then, the work of dancing up and down planks with heavy sacks has filled him out, clothed him with most lovely pads of muscular sweet flesh, sweated his skin into rosy satin fineness and softness, made his black eyes and his strong white teeth and his mouth like blood glitter with health and vigour, and fired his passions to the heat of a seven times heated furnace. He'll be like this till Spring, say 3 months more. Then some great fat slow cow of a girl will just open herself wide, and lie quite still, and drain him dry. First, the rich bloom of him will go. Then he'll get hard and hairy. And, by July, he'll have a moustache, a hairy breast for his present great boyish bosom, brushes in his milky armpits, brooms on his splendid young thighs, and be just the ordinary stevedore to be found by scores on the quays. Oh Lord—and not to be able to devour his beauty so freely offered now! That's the sort he is. Do you know I'm convinced of this—there's a lot of lovely material utterly wasted and thrown away. Boys who *like* sporting with their own sex are rare. Oughtn't they therefore to be made welcome and carefully cultivated when they're found? And, isn't this a fact also? Given a boy, a fine strong healthy boy, who does actually enjoy the love of a male with all its naked joys, who burns for it, seeks it, flings himself gleefully into the ardent strivings of it with no reserve, with utter and entire abandon, offering himself a willing sacrifice or operating in turn with equal and greedy unreservedness, is it not a fact that such a one keeps his youthful freshness and vigour infinitely longer than the ordinary lad who futters the ordinary lass from puberty on? And isn't it also true that the passionate boy must have an outlet for his passion; and, if he (preferring the male) can't for whatever reason have what his nature prefers, doesn't he almost automatically sink into the arms of a female and instantly become "man-like." Look at Fausto. That Jew is a begetter of offspring. He certainly isn't a source of pleasure, pure pleasure, to his kind. He's young enough yet to be amusing, perhaps for ten minutes. But I defy anyone to regard him as a dainty morsel to devour, as a piece of sweet young flesh for the embracing of one's arms and thighs, as a lovely body panting with love to be hugged to one's own. And so I say with regard to all of the present set—unless they are used and cultivated *now*, they will flower at Easter, fruit at Midsummer, and be fallen by the Autumn. Of course there are others. But how to find them ready when wanted?—Now I must tell you about my typhoid boy and his brother. I think I mentioned the first to you, Betta-mio by name. I used to go and see him every day when he had typhoid (caught at Castelfranco) last August. We went a very long way *in words* on the road of love then. He was beautiful in bed, what I saw of him, which was not much, for his people were always present. But once we kissed hands. His father's a captain-engineer in the Navy. He lives with his mother (separated privately from the father on account of difference of tempera-ment, but not divorced) and two brothers of 13 and 11 (he is 16) in a poor but very respectable way. When he got better, he took a clerkship at 7 fr. a week; and I used to walk home with him at night. Of course I don't go to his mother's house ever. (He was ill at an uncle's house.) A bachelor can't go to a semi-divorced woman's house. Well: we were very friendly. He is dark, tall, slim, straight, very sweet-spoken, with engaging manners and a charming way of fondling one's arms. In fact he had just got to the point when he would have been delighted to be kissed on parting. Kissing would have become habitual. And, a boy like that, although he does go oc-casionally to a bordel, would only have been too glad to learn the safer sweeter way. Well, one day he didn't keep an appointment. After that, for various reasons, I made no attempt to see him for some days. First, because I am easily offended: next, because I was desperately poor, miserable, and unable to take the next step, to do what I wanted, in short to go with him to Burano for a night and a day, say Sat. to Mond. where we could have slept together. And for several weeks, until yesterday actually, we neither met nor had any communication. We had no quarrel. I simply made no movement to avoid him, nor to see him because I hadn't the means to see him naked. And he made no movement to see me, no doubt because he was shy. Then, yesterday he called me up on the telephone, would I meet him that evening as usual, said very shyly and hesitatingly. I said that I would write. This morning at 8 I was rushing out to hear a mass (I've been in bed since my last to you) when I ran bang into Bettamio. (He was exquisite.) He raised his hat and held out a nervous hand and began to explain. He had forgotten the appointment. "Why have you left me alone?" Silence. "I can't wait." So I rushed on. I have just written him this:—"I don't un-derstand why thou hast saluted me on the street this morning. Either thou wishest to have me for your friend, or thou dost not. If, in truth, thou wishest to have me for a friend, why hast thou deserted me all these weeks? The appointment was that I might see thee in uniform (he's a Volunteer). I was at the Bridge of St. Euphemia from 6.30 to 8.30 and thou didst not come. Several weeks of silence followed. Thou hast not sought me, in per-son, or by letter, to explain or to excuse thyself. And now, after long negligence, thou treatest me as though I had offended thee. Thou makest me tired. I have not offended thee; but by thee I am offended, me, a friend ready to give thee my all. If any trouble or ill fortune prevented thee, why hast thou hidden it from thy friend? Why hide anything at all of thine from him? Why dost thou not give me the frankness and the confidence and also the affection which I have given to thee, and which thou must give to me if thou wishest to have me for a friend. I have been ill in bed and am not able even now to come out at night to talk. Therefore, write, if thou desirest, from heart to heart.''

I think you'll agree that this is a pretty plain declaration which either will finish with him or will bring him to my arms. If the former, he is not worth worrying about. If the latter, Heaven send me means to *take him on the hop*. This will be from Sat. to Mon. next ensuing. I do hope it will come off; for I believe him capable of causing and enjoying ecstasies of pleasure. There is another reason also why I earnestly desire it: I have my eye on his brother (Gallieno or some such name) aged 13. When Bettamio was ill this youngster must needs have a day in bed in the same room too with a cold. He was quite naked and much too active to remain still, bounding about and scrambling across the room every now and then in an entrancing manner, manifesting fine and joyous thighs and a perfectly lovely little breast muscle extended to the shoulder. He is a lively creature with a sunny skin, hot eyes, chestnut locks, a big burning mouth; and likely by next Summer to be a bounding bouncing piece of virgin flesh well worth squeezing. I have an eye to the future you see. . . .

---

*January 27, 1910*

Now I'm going to make you sit up. . . . I told you that I had tipped Zildo and Carlo in your name. Two days after they wrote hideous picture postcards saying that they had been to see Cavalleria and Pagliacci at the Rossini Theatre and thanked you for the pleasure of your gracious gentility. Very well. That ends that.

Now about yesterday. It appeared to me that the time was come *to break out of all caution and prudence. So I did, as thoroughly as you please.* Peter met me as agreed on Fondamenta Nuove. I explained to him exactly how I stood as to money, and I offered to give him all I had left of yours for his needs, or else to take him out for a day's pleasure.

If you could have seen how he beamed on me! He instantly chose the last. "My pleasure is to be with my Padron," he said. Fancy a great big boy of seventeen being as sweet as that! And he took my bag—I had a satchel full of papers for the sake of looking business-like—and declared himself at my disposition. So we took the steamer to Burano where we lunched on beef steaks and cheese and wine, not at the inn you went to but another up the street. Lord, how he wolfed. It was a fiendish day—snow all night and the snow at Burano a good yard deep and still snowing. . . .

Then Piero and I went upstairs. I never saw anyone slip out of his clothes as he did—like a white flash—he must have unlaced his boots and undone all his buttons on the way up. Then he turned to me. He was scarlet all over, blushing with delight, his eyes glittered and his fingers twitched over my clothes with eagerness. As for his rod—lawks! As I came out of my guernsey he flung himself back on the bed, across the bed as he knows I like it, throat up, ankles crossed, thighs together and body expectant.

The clutch of us both was amazing. I never knew that I loved and was loved so passionately with so much of me by so much of another. We simply raged together. Not a speck of us did not play its part. And the end came simultaneously. Long abstinence had lost us our self-control. He couldn't, simply couldn't wait his turn, and we clung together panting and gushing torrents—torrents. Then we laughed and kissed, rolled over and cleaned up and got into bed to sleep, embraced. His breath was delicious. He pressed his beautiful breast and belly to mine and our arms and legs entwined together. So we took a nap.

I was wakened by a gentle voice "Sior, Sior, Sior, with permission!" And his rod was rigid and ready. I took him on me. "Slowly, and as hard as you like" I said. Oh what a time we had. He took me at my word splendidly and laboured with the sumptuous abandon of a true artist, straining his young body to his very utmost but holding himself in control prolonging the pleasure for the pure joy of it. As he writhed, I became excited in my turn and rolled him over to do with him; and close-locked we wrestled, how long I don't remember but I know that presently we were both gasping for breath and as rigid as ever. For a few minutes we lay side by side, hugging, laughing, devouring each other's lips and each trying to clip the other's thighs with his own. Then we began again, more fiercely than ever, and finished the matter. *"Oh, che bel divertimento!"* says Peter, squeezing me as we spouted—"Oh, what a beautiful diversion."

# ▼ THE BEGINNING ▼

[RUPERT BROOKE & DENHAM RUSSELL-SMITH]

Henry James met Rupert Brooke (1887–1915) in Cambridge in 1909, when Brooke acknowledged "I pulled my fresh, boyish stunt" and bewitched the novelist. James's last published writing, in response to Brooke's death in World War I, and shortly before his own, celebrated Brooke's "wondrous, heroic legend." Brooke's war poems were already famous even before he died at Skyros in April 1915, of an infection rather than in battle. Winston Churchill consolidated the icon: "Joyous, fearless, deeply instructed, with classic symmetry of mind and body, he was all that one would wish England's noblest sons to be in days when no sacrifice but the most precious is acceptable, and the most precious is that which is most freely proffered."

His war poetry was popularized precisely because its rosy images denied the realities of war, and ironically drew many young men to join up and go to their own deaths. He was widely celebrated as a golden-haired Apollo—his photograph at age twenty-five is the first modern icon of beauty—and was desired by everyone, male and female, who came within the Bloomsbury magic circle. The following letter describes the weekend of October 29, 1909 when he decided to lose his virginity, with a friend of the same age from Rugby school, Denham Russell-Smith (the more attractive younger brother of his closer friend Hugh Denham-Smith). But Brooke, as he later described himself, was one-half outright heterosexual, one-quarter outright homosexual and one-quarter sentimental homosexual (i.e., his idealized homoerotic longing for young men is a longing for his own youth at public school). In the same year that he bedded Russell-Smith, he was determined to marry Noel Oliver, who resisted his advances. By 1911 he was in a passionate relationship with Ka Cox, who herself was having an affair with Henry Lamb, the bisexual "wife" of Lytton Strachey, and he also had a brief fling with Arthur Hobhouse, former boyfriend of both Maynard Keynes and Lytton Strachey.

The first half of his *Poems*, published in 1911, are implicitly homosexual and explicitly neo-pagan. The Bloomsburyites prided themselves on their freedom from conventions, but Brooke felt trapped by the double standards of society, and could not live out his hidden desires without guilt. Sexual confusion drove him to a nervous breakdown in 1912 and six weeks of psychiatric care. It was during his convalescence that he wrote this letter to James Strachey, Lytton's brother, also gay, as a therapeutic exorcism of his sexual identity. He decided, in effect, that he was a golden boy with a rotten core, and he came to reject Bloomsbury out of shame, and to seek purification through death in war. He was commissioned in August 1914, and his "1914" sonnet sequence shows a desire for death as the only resolution to his inner conflict.

RUPERT BROOKE TO JAMES STRACHEY

*10 July 1912*

How things shelve back! History takes you to January 1912—Archaeology to the end of 1910—Anthropology to, perhaps, the autumn of 1909.—

The autumn of 1909! We had hugged & kissed & strained, Denham and I, on and off for years—ever since that quiet evening I rubbed him, in the dark, speechlessly, in the smaller of the two small dorms. An abortive affair, as I told you. But in the summer holidays of 1906 and 1907 he had often taken me out to the hammock, after dinner, to lie entwined there.—He had vaguely hoped, I fancy,—But I lay always thinking Charlie [Lascelles].

Denham was though, to my taste, attractive. So honestly and friendlily lascivious. Charm, not beauty, was his *forte*. He was not unlike Ka [Ka Cox, with whom Brooke had an affair], in the allurement of vitality and of physical magic—oh, but Ka has beauty too.—He was lustful, immoral, affectionate, and delightful. As romance faded in me, I began, all unacknowledgedly, to cherish a hope—But I was never in the slightest degree in love with him.

In the early autumn of 1909, then, I was glad to get him to come and stay with me, at the Orchard. I came back late that Saturday night. Nothing was formulated in my mind. I found him asleep in front of the fire, at 1.45. I took him up to his bed,—he was very like a child when he was sleepy—and lay down on it. We hugged, and my fingers wandered a little. His skin was always very smooth. I had, I remember, a vast erection. He dropped off to sleep in my arms. I stole away to my room; and lay in bed thinking —my head full of tiredness and my mouth of the taste of tea and whales, as usual. I decided, almost quite consciously, I *would* put the thing through the next night. You see, I didn't at all know how he would take it. But I wanted to have some fun, and, still more, to see what it was *like*, and to do away with the shame (as I thought it was) of being a virgin. At length, I thought, I shall know something of all that James and [Harry] Norton and Maynard [Keynes] and Lytton [Strachey] know and hold over me.

Of course, I *said* nothing.

Next evening, we talked long in front of the sitting room fire. My head was on his knees, after a bit. We discussed sodomy. He said he, finally, thought it *was* wrong . . . We got undressed there, as it was warm. Flesh is exciting, in firelight. You must remember that *openly* we were nothing to each other—less even than in 1906. About what one is with Bunny (who so resembles Denham). Oh, quite distant!

Again we went up to his room. He got into bed. I sat on it and talked. Then I lay on it. Then we put the light out and talked in the dark. I complained of the cold: and so got under the eiderdown. My brain was, I remember, almost all through, absolutely calm and indifferent, observing progress, and mapping out the next step. Of course, I planned the general scheme beforehand.

I was still cold. He wasn't. "Of course not, you're in bed!" "Well then, you get right in, too."—I made him ask me—oh! without difficulty! I got right in. Our arms were round each other. "An adventure!" I kept thinking: and was horribly detached.

We stirred and pressed. The tides seemed to wax. At the right moment I, as planned, said "come into my room, it's better there . . ." I suppose he knew what I meant. Anyhow he followed me. In the large bed it was cold; we clung together. Intentions became plain; but still nothing was said. I broke away a second, as the dance began, to slip my pyjamas. His was the woman's part throughout. I had to make him take his off—do it for him. Then it was purely body to body—my first, you know! I was still a little frightened of his, at any sudden step, bolting; and he, I suppose, was shy. We kissed very little, as far as I can remember, face to face. And I only rarely handled his penis. Mine he touched once with his fingers; and that made me shiver so much that I think he was frightened. But with alternate stirrings, and still pressures, we mounted. My right hand got hold of the left half of his bottom, clutched it, and pressed his body into me. The smell of the sweat began to be noticeable. At length we took to rolling to and fro over each other, in the excitement. Quite calm things, I remember, were passing through my brain. "The Elizabethan joke 'The Dance of the Sheets' has, then, something in it." "I hope his erection is all right"—and so on. I thought of him entirely in the third person. At length the waves grew more terrific; my control of the situation was over; I treated him with the utmost violence, to which he more quietly, but incessantly, responded. Half under him and half over, I came off. I *think* he came off at the same time, but of that I have never been sure. A silent moment: and then he slipped away to his room, carrying his pyjamas. We wished each other "Good-night." It was between 4 and 5 in the morning. I lit a candle after he had gone. There was a dreadful mess on the bed. I wiped it clear as I could, and left the place exposed in the air, to dry. I sat on the lower part of the bed, a blanket round me, and stared at the wall, and thought. I thought of innumerable things, that this was all; that the boasted jump from virginity to Knowledge seemed a very tiny affair, after all; that I hoped Denham, for whom I felt great tenderness, was sleeping. My thoughts went backward and forward. I unexcitedly reviewed my whole life, and indeed the whole universe. I was tired, and rather pleased with myself, and a little bleak. About six it was grayly daylight; I blew the candle out and slept till 8. At 8 Denham had to bicycle in to breakfast [in Cambridge] with Mr. Benians [his tutor], before catching his train. I bicycled with him, and turned off at the corner of —, is it Grange Road? —. We said scarcely anything to each other. I felt sad at the thought he was perhaps hurt and angry, and wouldn't ever want to see me again.—He did, of course, and was exactly as ever. Only we never referred to it. But that night I looked with some awe at the room—fifty yards away to the West from the bed I'm writing in—in which I Began; in which I "copulated with" Denham; and I felt a curious private tie with Denham himself. So you'll understand it was—not with a *shock*, for I am far too dead for that, but with a sort of dreary wonder and dizzy discomfort—that I heard Mr. Benians inform me, after we'd greeted, that Denham died at one o-clock on Wednesday morning,—just twenty-four hours ago now.

# ▼ YOU HAVE FIXED MY LIFE ▼

[WILFRED OWEN & SIEGFRIED SASSOON]

Wilfred Owen (1893–1918) was not successful in his attempts to be either an academic or a cleric (he finally rejected the orthodox church when he recognized his homosexuality). In 1913 he became a poorly paid English tutor in France, and in 1915 he returned to England to enlist in the Artists' Rifles, and was then commissioned into the Manchester Regiment. At the Somme he suffered shell-shock and was sent to the War Hospital in Edinburgh in summer 1917. There he met the poet Siegfried Sassoon (1886–1967), and his friendship with Sassoon marked the turning-point of Owen's poetical development.

When Sassoon said goodbye to Owen at the Conservative Club in Edinburgh in November 1917 he gave him a sealed envelope containing £10 and the London address of Oscar Wilde's lover Robert Ross, through whom he met Osbert Sitwell, Arnold Bennett, H. G. Wells and many other writers. He hero-worshipped Sassoon, and the result was some very moving war poetry: "My subject is war, and the pity of war." He returned to the front, but was wounded and invalided home in July 1918. After a spell in hospital he was back with his battalion at Amiens in September, and he was awarded the Military Cross for conspicuous gallantry in October.

Owen's experiences in the war were not always unbearably painful, as he noted in a letter to his cousin Leslie Gunston on October 15, 1918: "There are two French girls in my billet, daughters of the Mayor, who (I suppose because of my French) single me out for their joyful gratitude for *La Délivrance*. Naturally I talk to them a good deal; so much so that the jealousy of other officers resulted in a Subalterns' Court Martial being held on me! The dramatic irony was too killing, considering certain other things, not possible to tell in a letter." There at the line west of the Oise-Sambre Canal, near Ors, Owen was killed during a dawn attack across the canal on November 4, 1918, together with one other officer and twenty-two other ranks. The war ended one week later. His eloquent *Poems*, permeated by an erotic identification with his comrades, were published posthumously in 1920, edited by Sassoon and Edith Sitwell.

Years later Sassoon wrote that "W's death was an unhealed wound, & the ache of it has been with me ever since. I wanted *him* back—not his poems." Most of the letters Owen wrote from the front were to his mother, but he also wrote to Sassoon between November 1917 and October 1918; unfortunately Sassoon destroyed many of the letters. Owen's mother burned "a sack full" of his papers, apparently at his own request, and his brother Harold for many years prevented research into Wilfred's private life.

WILFRED OWEN TO SIEGFRIED SASSOON

*Mahim, Monkmoor Road, Shrewsbury*
*5 November 1917*

My dear Sassoon,

When I had opened your envelope in a quiet corner of the Club Stair-case, I sat on the stairs and groaned a little, and then went up and loosed off a gourd, Gothic vacuum of a letter, which I "put by" (as you would recommend for such effusions) until I could think over the thing without grame. [Sassoon cannot explain this word.]

I have also waited for this photograph.

Show some rich anger if you will. I thank you; but not on this paper only, or in any writing. You gave—with what Christ, if he had known Latin & dealt in oxymoron, might have called Sinister Dexterity. I imagined you were entrusting me with some holy secret concerning yourself. A secret, however, it shall be until such time as I shall have climbed to the house-tops, and you to the minarets of the world.

Smile the penny! This Fact has not intensified my feelings for you by the least—the least *grame*. Know that since mid-September, when you still regarded me as a tiresome little knocker on your door, I held you as Keats + Christ + Elijah + my Colonel + my father-confessor + Amenophis IV in profile.

What's that mathematically?

In effect it is this: that I love you, dispassionately, so much, *very* much, dear Fellow, that the blasting little smile you wear on reading this can't hurt me in the least.

If you consider what the above Names have severally done for me, you will know what you are doing. And you have *fixed* my Life—however short. You did not light me: I was always a mad comet; but you have fixed me. I spun round you a satellite for a month, but I shall swing out soon, a dark star in the orbit where you will blaze. It is some consolation to know that Jupiter himself sometimes swims out of Ken!

To come back to our sheep, as the French *never* say, I have had a per-fect little note from Robt. Ross, and have arranged a meeting at 12.30 on Nov. 9th. He mentioned staying at Half Moon St., but the house is full. . . .

What I most miss in Edinburgh (not Craig & Lockhart) is the *conviviality* of the Four Boys (L. *vivre*—to live). Someday, I must tell how we sang, shouted, whistled and danced through the dark lanes through Colinton; and how we laughed till the meteors showered around us, and we felt calm under the winter stars. And some of us saw the pathway of the spirits for the first time. And seeing it so far above us, and feeling the good road so safe beneath us, we praised God with louder whistling; and knew we loved one another as no men love for long.

Which, if the Bridge-players Craig & Lockhart could have seen, they would have called down the wrath of Jahveh, and buried us under the fires of the City you wot of.

To which also it is time you committed this letter. I wish you were less undemonstrative, for I have many adjectives with which to qualify myself. As it is I can only say I am

Your proud friend, Owen

---

*Scarborough*
*27 November 1917*

I sit alone at last, and therefore with you, my dear Siegfried. For which name, as much as for anything in any envelope of your sealing, I give thanks and rejoice.

The 5th have taken over a big Hotel, of which I am Major Domo, which in the vulgar, means Lift Boy. I manage Accommodation, Food, and Service. I boss cooks, housemaids, charwomen, chamber-maids, mess orderlies and—drummers.

There were 80 officers when I came, or 800 grouses daily. . . .

---

*A depot, A.P.O. S.17, B.E.F. France*
*Sunday, 1 September 1918*

Dearest of all Friends,

Here is an address which will serve for a few days.

The sun is warm, the sky is clear, the waves are dancing fast & bright . . . But these are not Lines written in Dejection [opening lines of Shelley's "Stanzas, written in dejection, near Naples"]. Serenity Shelley never dreamed of crowns me. Will it last when I shall have gone in Caverns & Abysmals such as he never reserved for his worst daemons?

Yesterday I went down to Folkestone Beach and into the sea, thinking to go through those stanzas & emotions of Shelley's to the full. But I was too happy, or the Sun was too supreme. Moreover there issued from the sea distraction, in the shape, Shape I say, but lay no stress on that, of a Harrow boy, of superb intellect & refinement; intellect because he hates war more than Germans; refinement because of the way he spoke of my Going, and of the Sun, and of the Sea there; and the way he spoke of Everything. In fact, the way he spoke—

And now I am among the herds again, a Herdsman; and a Shepherd of sheep that do not know my voice.

*Tell me how you are.*

With great & painful firmness I have not said you goodbye from England. If you had said in the heart or brain you might have stabbed me, but you said only in the leg [Sassoon annotates this letter: "I had told him I would stab him in the leg if he tried to return to the Front."]; so I was afraid.

Perhaps if I "write" anything in dug-outs or talk in sleep a squad of rifle-men will save you the trouble of buying a dagger.

Goodbye W. E. O.

---

Very dear Siegfried,

Your letter reached me at the exact moment it was most needed—when we had come far enough out of the line to feel the misery of billets; and I had been seized with writer's cramp after making out my casualty reports. (I'm O.C. D Coy).

The Batt. had a sheer time last week. I can find no better epithet: because I cannot say I suffered anything; having let my brain grow dull: That is to say my nerves are in perfect order.

It is a strange truth: that your [book of poems] *Counter-Attack* fright-ened me much more than the real one: though the boy by my side, shot through the head, lay on top of me, soaking my shoulder, for half an hour.

Catalogue? Photograph? Can you photograph the crimson-hot iron as it cools from the smelting? That is what Jones's blood looked like, and felt like. My senses are charred.

I shall feel again as soon as I dare, but now I must not. I don't take the cigarette out of my mouth when I write Deceased over their letters.

But one day I will write Deceased over my books. . . .

Ever your W. E. O.

# ▼ SOUL WINDOWS ▼

[COUNTÉE CULLEN & ALAIN LEROY LOCKE]

The black American poet Countée Cullen (1903–46) was the poet laureate of the Harlem Renaissance. His homosexuality is central to his work, although most African-American scholars ignore it or suppress it. His attitude to his homosexuality was as mixed as his attitude to his blackness: simultaneously affirmative and denunciatory, celebratory and troubled. He wrote poems for his lovers, and dedicated poems to his closest gay friends: Alain Locke, Harold Jackman, Carl Van Vechten, and Leland Pettit. Though closeted, he was well known in the gay underground. His first confidant was Alain Locke, a misogynist professor at Howard who had many contacts in Harlem. His relationship with Cullen was close but probably not sexual—a characteristic gay friendship of love and trust built partly upon sharing a secret. Cullen acted as Locke's pimp in the latter's pursuit of the more famous and more openly gay black poet Langston Hughes.

Cullen was only nineteen when he experienced self-recognition after reading Edward Carpenter's pioneering anthology of gay love, *Iolaüs*, at the suggestion of Locke. In his letter thanking Locke for directing him to this book he mentions his relationship with Ralph Loeb, which, though important for his own coming out to himself, lasted for only a month. He explained to Locke on April 5, 1923 that he felt "compelled to relinquish all hope in that direction. . . . I am afraid to attempt to bend the twig the way I would have it go, lest my way be the wrong way for it." But he had already moved on to a white lover, Donald Duff, an equally serious affair that again lasted little more than a month. Duff was a pacifist, on the literary fringe; he died on December 7, 1942, Pearl Harbor day, and Cullen dedicated his poem "Tableau" to him:

> Locked arm in arm they cross the way,
>     The black boy and the white,
> The golden splendor of the day,
>     The sable pride of night.
>
> From lowered blinds the dark folk stare,
>     And here the fair folk talk,
> Indignant that these two should dare
>     In unison to walk.
>
> Oblivious to look and word
>     They pass, and see no wonder
> That lightning brilliant as a sword
>     Should blaze the path of thunder.

Cullen's early failures at sustaining a gay relationship perhaps caused him to turn to women, and he married Yolande DuBois in 1928. Their marriage soured within six months, and she divorced him when he told her he was gay.

Cullen's lifelong soulmate was the handsome West Indian Harold Jackman (1900–60), whom he had known from 1923. They were called "the David and Jonathan of the Harlem twenties," but it is not absolutely certain that their relationship ever became sexual, though they were both gay. Cullen found an "adjustment" (his code word for sex) in the arms of Llewellyn Ransom from 1924, a "gift" sent to him from Locke. Other lovers included Leland B. Pettit, the organist of the All Saints Cathedral Choir, who was said to have committed suicide over some boy, an incident fictionalized in Blair Niles's powerful novel *Strange Brother* (1931). Cullen had a succession of French boyfriends following a trip to Paris in 1927; his love letters to them, and their replies, are held by Tulane University, New Orleans. Lastly, from 1937–45 he had a secret affair with Edward Atkinson, fourteen years younger than he, whom he met with regularly on Friday evenings; their secret correspondence, full of cyphers and codes which need interpreting (Cullen usually begins his letters "D.B.," meaning "Dearest and Best"), is held by Yale University.

---

Countée Cullen to Alain Leroy Locke

*234 W. 131 St.,*
*New York City*
*March 3/[19]23*

My dear friend,

I am feeling as miserable at this writing as I can imagine a person feeling. Let me explain—The Monday following our Saturday evening together I secured Carpenter's "Iolaüs" from the library. I read it through at one sitting, and steeped myself in its charming and comprehending atmosphere. It opened up for me Soul windows which had been closed; it threw a noble and evident light on what I had begun to believe, because of what the world believes, ignoble and unnatural. I loved myself in it, and thanked you a thousand times as as many delightful examples appeared, for recommending it to me. Tuesday young Loeb was to have come to see me. He did not come. I was keenly disappointed. He wrote no letter. Thursday morning I wrote to him, asking him to attend a concert with me to-morrow (Sunday) afternoon. It is now Saturday night and, although there has been time a-plenty, I have not heard from him. So what I had envisioned as a delightful and stimulating comaradie is not to be. I believe the cause may be defined as parental, for I feel certain that the attraction was as keenly felt by Loeb as by me. I know you will understand how I feel. But I suppose some of us erotic lads, vide myself, were placed here just to eat our hearts out with longing for unattainable things, especially for that friendship beyond understanding. If you wish to write Ralph Loeb his address is 39-41 West 129 St.—But don't mention me! Speak for yourself.

I have just written to Langston asking him to come here for that Poetry recital on March 21. I told him you would be here on that night (I am not sure of that, but I ask you to bend every effort to be here on that date. Your presence will be helpful; some will be there for curiosity, but I want someone there who is interested in me for my self's sake.) And besides, Langston *might* come.

May I not hear from you before then? And in your own handwriting?

Yours most sincerely,

Countée P. Cullen

P.S.—Sentiments expressed here would be misconstrued by others, so this letter, once read, is best destroyed.

P.P.S.—Send your poem when you write.

Countée P. Cullen

# ▼ NOT BY THE MIND ALONE ▼

[HART CRANE & WILBUR UNDERWOOD]

In 1920 in Washington Hart Crane (1899–1932) met Wilbur Underwood, a minor government official with an interest in the arts. He was charming and gossipy, and they often went to pre-Broadway tryouts. Underwood became the confidant to whom Crane wrote long letters about his secret sex life, described in graphic details, until his death. Most of these letters remain unpublished.

Crane cruised the Cleveland parks late at night, and was especially fond of truck drivers and sailors, whom he educated into the mysteries of sex and literature. To Underwood he wrote in 1923, "The first night brought a most strenuous wooing and the largest instrument I have handled. Europa and the bull are now entirely passé. As this happened only two nights ago, I am modest and satisfied. Still, I am uneasy. I fear for all the anticlimaxes that are surely now in store for me." Early in 1923, when Crane was in his twenty-third year, he met a young man at a concert; after the young man took Crane to a vaudeville show they began a brief but overwhelming affair, referred to in the letter of February 20, 1923.

In 1924 Crane lived at 110 Columbia Heights in the shadow of Brooklyn Bridge, with Emil Opffer and Opffer's father. Emil was a good-looking ship's writer, who was regularly away from home for ten-day stretches, during which Crane was jealous. It was here that Crane worked on the *Voyages* poems, written for Opffer, and began the last part of his major poem *The Bridge*, about which many books of interpretation and evaluation have been written. Crane described their relationship as a "blood-brotherhood"; around 1960 (thirty-six years after the affair) Opffer told Crane's biographer John Unterecker that Crane was passionate, ecstatic and sometimes violent, but "It was never *dirty*." Crane threw himself overboard ship on a return voyage from Mexico. His life (and suicide) haunted the imagination of gay writers for the next two generations, just as Whitman's life inspired his own generation.

---

HART CRANE TO WILBUR UNDERWOOD

*[Cleveland*
*Feb. 20, 1923]*

Dear Wilbur:

Those who have wept in the darkness sometimes are rewarded with stray leaves blown inadvertently. Since your last I have [had] one of those few experiences that come,—ever, but which are almost sufficient in their very incompleteness. This was only last evening in a vaudeville show with ——.
—— has manifested charming traits before, but there has always been an older brother around. Last night—it sounds silly enough to tell (but not in

view of his real beauty)—O, it was only a matter of light affectionate stray touches—and half-hinted speech. But these were genuine and in that sense among the few things I can remember happily. With —— you must think of someone mildly sober, with a face not too thin, but with faun precision of line and feature. Crisp ears, a little pointed, fine and docile hair almost golden, yet darker,—eyes that are a little heavy—but wide apart and usually a little narrowed,—aristocratic (English) jaws, and a mouth that [is] just mobile enough to suggest voluptuousness. A strong rather slender figure, negligently carried, that is perfect from flanks that hold an easy persistence to shoulders that are soft yet full and hard. A smooth and rather olive skin that is cool—at first.

Excuse this long catalog—I admit it is mainly for my own satisfaction, and I am drunk now and in such state as my satisfactions are always lengthy. When I see you ask me to tell you more about him for he is worth more and better words, I assure you. O yes, I shall see him again soon. The climax will be all too easily reached,—But my gratitude is enduring—if only for that *once*, at least, something beautiful approached me and as though it were the most natural thing in the world, enclosed me in his arm and pulled me to him without my slightest bid. And we who create must endure—must hold to spirit not by the mind, the intellect alone. These have no mystic possibilities. O flesh damned to hate and scorn! I have felt my cheek pressed on the desert these days and months too much. How old I am! Yet, oddly now this sense [of] age—not at all in my senses—is gaining me altogether unique love and happiness. I feel I have been thru much of this again and again before. I long to go to India and stay always. Meditation on the sun is all there is. Not that this isn't enough! I mean I find my imagination more sufficient all the time. The work of the workaday is what I dislike. I spend my evenings in music and sometimes ecstasy. I've been writing a lot lately. . . . I'm bringing much into contemporary verse that is new. I'm on a synthesis of America and its structural identity now, called *The Bridge*. . . .

---

HART CRANE TO GORHAM MUNSON

*[Cleveland]*
*March 2nd, '23*

. . . And now to your question about passing the good word along. I discover that I have been all-too-easy all along in letting out announcements of my sexual predilections. Not that anything unpleasant has happened or is imminent. But it does put me into obligatory relations to a certain extent with "those who know," and this irks me to think of sometimes. After all, when you're dead it doesn't matter, and this statement alone proves my immunity from any "shame" about it. But I find the ordinary business of earning a living entirely too stringent to want to add any prejudices against me *of that nature* in the minds of any publicans and sinners. Such things have a wholesale way of leaking out! Everyone knows now about B—, H— and others—this list is too long to bother with. I am all-too-free with my tongue and doubtless always shall be—but I'm going to ask you to advise and work me better with a more discreet behavior.

HART CRANE TO WALDO FRANK

*Brooklyn, N. Y.*
*April 21st, '24*

Dear Waldo:

For many days, now, I have gone about quite dumb with something for which "happiness" must be too mild a term. At any rate, my aptitude for communication, such as it ever is!, has been limited to one person alone, and perhaps for the first time in my life (and, I can only think that it is the last, so far is my imagination from the conception of anything more profound and lovely than this love.) I have wanted to write you more than once, but it will take many letters to let you know what I mean (for myself, at least) when I say that I have seen the Word made Flesh. I mean nothing less, and I know now that there is such a thing as indestructibility. In the deepest sense, where flesh became transformed through intensity of response to counter-response, where sex was beaten out, where purity of joy was reached that included tears. It's true, Waldo, that so much more than my frustrations and multitude of humiliations has been answered in this reality and I promise that I feel that whatever event the future holds is justified before hand. And I have been able to give freedom and life which was acknowledged in the ecstasy of walking hand in hand across the most beautiful bridge of the world, the cables enclosing us and pulling us upward in such a dance as I have never walked and never can walk with another. . . .

Dear dear Rat, it seems as though our life together grew into a deeper union every day. What we need is to settle down and feel the world together.

Horrot, mister this is a Rat although it may look more like a turtle!

A page from F. O. Matthiessen's letter of April 28, 1925 to Russell Cheney, with typical blend of playfulness and emotion.

# ▼ RAT AND THE DEVIL ▼

[F. O. MATTHIESSEN & RUSSELL CHENEY]

The highly respected cultural historian and Harvard professor F. O. Matthiessen (1902–50), met his future lover the painter Russell Cheney aboard an ocean liner in 1924. In short order they became an indissoluble bond, and for twenty years they always lived together for several months each year, although they were often separated from one another when Matthiessen had to do scholarly research or when Cheney's painting took him abroad or his ill health (tuberculosis) took him to sanatoriums. During these periods they wrote more than 3,000 letters, only a tenth of which have been published. Matthiessen's magnum opus was *American Renaissance: Art and Expression in the Age of Emerson and Whitman*, a landmark revaluation of American literature and culture (which was required reading while I was at university). He later became engrossed by the causes of the political left.

Cheney was twenty years older than Matthiessen, who was searching for a father, but their relationship can only be called a marriage. There were occasional lapses of fidelity, followed by excoriating confessions. In their correspondence, Cheney adopted the name Rat, and Matthiessen the name Devil. Cheney sketched Matthiessen as a devil at the head of his letters, with horns and forked tail, and sometimes Matthiessen attempted similar caricatures, with less success. Matthiessen was uneasy about the sordid and promiscuous gay subculture, which he avoided; he proudly told his closest friends about his love for Cheney, but they lived in a closet, or at least a cocoon of their own making. Although he told Cheney they were living the life described by Whitman, it is characteristic of his "straight" facade that he never discussed Whitman's gay themes in his critical essays on the poet. He felt that his life with Cheney—stable, monogamous, non-effeminate, largely faithful, all-embracing—was "entirely new—neither of us know of a parallel case. We stand in the middle of an uncharted, uninhabited country. That there have been other unions like ours is obvious, but we are unable to draw on their experience. We must create everything for ourselves. And creation is never easy."

Cheney died in 1945 of a heart attack following an asthma attack, age 63. Matthiessen could not bear the loneliness after such intense love and companionship, and killed himself five years later, age 48. It is clear that Matthiessen had posterity in mind as he wrote and that he hoped these letters would become a testimony to gay love and an important resource for other gay couples to draw upon. They should have been published immediately after his death, but the exact nature of his suicidal depression was not made public knowledge and it was felt prudent to delay publication of the letters for almost thirty years.

RUSSELL CHENEY TO F. O. MATTHIESSEN

*Vénétia-Hotel*
*Paris, le 18 Sept. [1924]*

Well, it's true, isn't it? Our union is complete. Love is stronger than death, stronger than sin—even than old habits. . . . I've wanted to pick up and fly (literally not figuratively) over there for a couple of days, before I go down to Venice. There are lots of things to get straight, yet I kid myself— but you said and I agreed that we both have work to do. When you come to me in December this turmoil will be subdued and our feet will follow the pleasant paths of peace together. I can say my prayers like a kid now when I go to bed and get up. I haven't for twenty years—the peace and fulfill- ment you have brought my soul indeed pass all understanding. . . .

Now, Boy, I better quit. Some day the first letter I ever had from you will come in. My God, feller, do you happen to realize how short a time ago we waved Max [Foster] good bye on the pier there. And I will go to Venice, and you will go to Oxford. But what's that to us, with December before us. Good bye now. I love you and will live as though you were at my side.

    Rat

---

CHENEY TO MATTHIESSEN

*Vénétia-Hotel*
*Paris, le Saturday*
*[Sept. 20, 1924]*

Dearest Dev—

Well, you're in for a bad time. . . . Oh, God damn it, Dev, I'm going to say right along everything that comes into my head. I love you better than anyone in the world. I mean it. I put your picture into that empty half of the frame with my mother's picture. I have never filled it before. I have never loved anyone as I loved her before.

That's the truth so help me God. I love you as I love her and by God. . . . how am I going to tell you. . . . Oh, I haven't "done anything," but I've drunk too much. . . . off on the loose and God damn it, I walked the streets. Me! here I've been living in a fool's paradise. . . .

Your letter came just as my friend Henry Poor came to take me out for all day. I couldn't read it till I stole the time to do so down in the Museum. Couldn't read the letter, but there it was in my pocket, and I'd slip my hand in and hold it, and a couple of times I'd hold it against my cheek, the sense of being with you strong.

Finally I did read it, the first part so darn well giving me all those fellers. Tell you the truth, I had it all, all the quality of your relations with each before—except the steady growth of you and Mitch [Russel Wheeler Davenport]. But you added a lot and cleared things up. I'm with you that way. When you get here, we'll go into absolutely everything and clear it up. Well, comes the second part of your letter. As I read it in a corner of the Museum, to me it was like being whirled up and down in an elevator. First, when you said how you could walk through the streets, and not be looking at everyone. I did for a day after I left you and now I don't any more—oh, you've got a great feller in your life.

It's not so though, Boy, I've slipped just so much farther every day— till last night, here I was between one and two, up and down the likely street, like a dead leaf blown before the wind. Well, I didn't speak to anyone or look at anyone, but darn it I was there. I wasn't home in my bed going to sleep with my soul at peace and one with you, as I have every night before. . . .

Well, I plan to go to Venice, Tuesday night. I wish I had done what I longed to do and gone over for Sunday with you. . . .

MATTHIESSEN TO CHENEY

*[London
Sept. 23, 1924]*

. . . Little by little the largeness of what has happened sweeps over me. I thought I realized it all that last night together; but first the intellect sees, and then when it has created its imaginative symbolism it gives the whole man something to live by. I saw very clearly that night and called it a marriage. The imagination has since been working, and I live body and soul in this new relationship.

Marriage is a mere term; only as a dynamic vivid thing does it dominate life. That is: you can visualize marriage or you can live it. Now I am living it.

Marriage! What a strange word to be applied to two men! Can't you hear the hell-hounds of society baying full pursuit behind us? But that's just the point. We are beyond society. We've said thank you very much, and stepped outside and closed the door. In the eyes of the unknowing world we are a talented artist of wealth and position and a promising young graduate student. In the eyes of the knowing world we would be pariahs, outlaws, degenerates. This is indeed the price we pay for the unforgivable sin of being born different from the great run of mankind.

And so we have a marriage that was never seen on land or sea and surely not in Tennyson's poet's dream! It is a marriage that demands nothing and gives everything. It does not limit the affections of the two parties, it gives their scope greater radiance and depth. Oh it is strange enough. It has no ring, and no vows, and no wedding presents from your friends, and no children. And so of course it has none of the coldness of passion, but merely the serene joy of companionship. It has no three hundred and sixty-five breakfasts opposite each other at the same table; and yet it desires frequent companionship, devotion, and laughter. Its bonds indeed form the service that is perfect freedom. . . .

How many, when reading this, would think so? Ah there's the mockery of it: those gates of society are of iron. And when you're outside, you've got to live in yourself alone, unless—o beatissimus—you are privileged to find another wanderer in the waste land. And perhaps even you think what I have written mawkish? It is infinitely difficult to make the medium of expression adequately clothe your emotions. But I have thought at length on this—between snatches of Goldsmith, and walking in St. James's Park at sunset. If you dislike it, say so, and I will leave such expression to be conveyed by the touch of my hand. But it is an integral part of me.

    Love
    —Dvl

---

MATTHIESSEN TO CHENEY

*[Oxford, England]*
*February 5 [1925]*

Dearest Rat

I wonder if you know how perfect these last letters of yours have been? They take me right to the heart of your painting, to the heart of your life. It's just as though we were sitting in the room there together, talking over the new canvas, my hand in yours. Have I any idea how I share in everything you do? Only through knowing that your heart and mind are always with mine.

It is strange how certain moments of our trip come back and back. Probably the one moment I cherish above all others, the one when I seemed the very closest to you was on that night in Taormina after you had been sick, and I had gotten myself into an unbalanced emotional state imagining that I had been grating on your nerves. We sat on the bed talking the whole thing over until the petty tangle in my brain was unsnarled and I was unbelievably secure once more. Then, after the light was out, we were in each others arms and I said: "I love you, Rat." "Say it again, Devil" you breathed, holding me tight. "I love you, Rat." "Say it again," "I love you." "Say it again." "I love you. I love you." . . .

Somehow in passionately pouring out those words, and in feeling you just as passionately accept them, my whole soul felt that it had expressed itself. Perhaps I was fully conscious for the first time that you had taken eagerly all that I wanted to give. It's hard for a feller to realize that he is loved as much as he loves. . . .

Good-bye till to-morrow, dear Heart. God bless you.

    Pic

# ▼ DEAR SIR! ▼

[LAWRENCE OF ARABIA & "SIR"]

T. E. Lawrence (1888–1935), commonly known as Lawrence of Arabia, dedicated *Seven Pillars of Wisdom* (1926) "to S.A.," the handsome Arab boy Dahoum nicknamed Sheik Ahmed, with whom he shared his quarters for three years, who died of typhus in 1918. In this famous study of the Arab revolt against the Turks he acknowledged that the soldiers, rather than use the "sordid commerce" of public prostitutes "began indifferently to slake one another's few needs in their own clean bodies—a cold convenience that, by comparison, seemed sexless and even pure. Later, some began to justify this sterile process, and swore that friends quivering together in the yielding sand with intimate hot limbs in supreme embrace, found there hidden in the darkness a sensual co-efficient of the mental passion which was welding our souls and spirits in one flaming effort." Rumours about his private life have supplied a dozen biographies.

In August 1992 the London *Daily Telegraph* uncovered new evidence to suggest that Lawrence of Arabia was indeed actively gay, but a reader contradicted this with a statement from a man who shared barracks with Lawrence who claimed that Lawrence was not a homosexual, merely a masochist. In *Seven Pillars* Lawrence had said that "Several, thirsting to punish appetites they could not wholly prevent, took a savage pride in degrading the body, and offered themselves fiercely in any habit which promised physical pain or filth." The story is well known that in 1917 Lawrence was captured as a spy at Der'a, south of Damascus; Hajim Bey, the governor, tried to make love to him but Lawrence resisted, upon which he was turned over to a gang of soldiers to be tortured and raped. Pain, humiliation and ecstasy released the beast within, which "journeyed with me since, fascination and terror and morbid desire, lascivious and vicious perhaps, but like the striving of a moth towards its flame."

After the war he joined the Royal Air Force as a lowly private in order to escape from himself as well as from the fame he felt was unearned. But in order to recapture the experience of the beating he received at Der'a, Lawrence invented an uncle, "R," who gave instructions for the discipline of "Ted," i.e. Lawrence personifying himself as a naughty nephew. Engaged for these purposes was John Bruce, a young Scots friend who had enlisted in the Tank Corps at the same time as Lawrence in 1923. Another service companion sometimes attended as a witness of these floggings, which took place over a period of twelve years: he confirmed that Lawrence was beaten with a metal whip upon the bare buttocks until he ejaculated. Lawrence in his diary occasionally noted, for example, "30 from Jock," his nickname for Bruce; the numbers, from 30 to 75, presumably indicate the number of lashes administered. Bruce sold his story to the *Sunday*

*Times* in 1969, which was serialized as "The Secret Life of Lawrence of Arabia." The following letters were written to the companion who passed the instructions to Bruce, called "Hills"; both he and Bruce claimed to believe that "R" really existed. These letters are in effect the love letters from a slave to his master.

---

T. E. LAWRENCE TO "SIR"

*25 Oct 1934*

Dear Sir,

I am very much obliged to you for the long and careful report you have sent me on your visit to Scotland with Ted; and for your kindness in agreeing to go there with the lad and look after him while he got his deserts. I am enclosing a fee of three pounds which I hope you will accept as some compensation for your trouble and inconvenience.

From what you tell me, and from the reports of those who have examined Ted since, it is clear that he had a sound thrashing, which was after all what he wanted. I hope he will take the lesson to heart, and not make it necessary for us to repeat it. Please take any chance his friendship for you gives, to impress upon him how wrong it is for him, at his age and standing, to force us to use these schoolboy measures against him. He should be ashamed to hold his head up amongst his fellows, knowing that he had suffered so humiliating and undignified a punishment. Try and drive some sense into his head. [Details of the whippings follow.] . . .

Hills [Bruce] reports that after the birching Ted cried out quite loudly, and begged for mercy. Can you confirm this, and do you recollect in what terms his plea was made? . . .

One last question, too, if you say Yes to the main principle—are we at the end of our troubles with the lad? If not, must we give Hills his free hand, or will limited measures suffice? Can Hills be trusted again, or must I look elsewhere? And in that case, do you think your friend would be available or suitable?

With further thanks for your kindness.

Believe me
Yours very sincerely,
R

---

*16 November 1934*

Dear Sir,

I must apologize for having taken so long to answer the additional report you were good enough to send me. Your information was exactly what I needed and I am most grateful.

You have aroused my curiosity by your remark that from your service with Ted you know something that might replace corporal punishment in making him behave himself. You must understand that this is a matter of the first importance to me and to Ted. By his wishes which I must respect, according to my promise, we are prevented from meeting; but if you can get your information on paper, you would put me further into your debt.

I note what you say about Hills, and it only confirms my own impression. You will recollect how he came to go to him this time. Ted's punishment at X had proved not enough, due to the inadequacy of a belt for use upon a grown lad, and not through any fault of yours or your friend's. Unfortunately you could not arrange another dose at the time, and while we were thinking about it Ted allowed himself to give offense upon quite another subject. It was with this second offence that Hills dealt with last month. . . .

I do not know, of course, what your hinted remedy is worth, as a corrective. If it proved effective I might save you and me from a repetition of his punishment. I gather that your friend is not yet available, and it is not fair to the lad himself to keep such a punishment hanging over him for month after month. Yet it is equally impossible for me, having solemnly promised it to him. I always do what I promise, and I have brought Ted to know it. So will you please try to take me into your confidence on this alternative; and please also enquire into the arrangements of the friend who helped you last time, so that we may fall back on him, if necessary.

Yours sincerely,

R

---

*11 January 1935*

Dear Sir,

Your letter showed me that I was perhaps being rather hard on Ted, by repeating that punishment at short interval. So upon reconsideration I informed him that it will be indefinitely postponed. I asked him to give you prompt notice that your help would not be immediately required. We will hold our hands and watch to see if the lad justifies this kindness.

I need not say that I am very much obliged to you for being ready to take the further responsibility. I shall call upon you with confidence if Ted again makes it necessary. Please let me correct one misapprehension in your letter, however. Unless he strips, the birch is quite ineffective. The twigs are so light that even the thinnest clothing prevents their hurting. I fully understand your reluctance to strip him; so I was making up my mind to ask you to use either your friend's jute whip (which you mentioned to me in a former letter) or a useful little dogwhip which I could send you by post.

If the emergency arises, I shall agree to Ted's coming to you in flannels.

Yours sincerely,

R

Jean Marais (*b*. 1913) in a publicity still from one of his films.

# ▼ MY BEAUTIFUL ANGEL ▼

[JEAN COCTEAU & JEAN MARAIS]
*Translated from French by Alexandra Trone*

Jean Cocteau (1889–1963) was a master of literature, poetry, theatre and film. In his unsigned autobiography *Le livre blanc* he acknowledged that he recognized his love of youths when at a very young age he first saw a fresh farm boy bathing naked, and fainted in an ecstasy of joy and fear at the sight of his penis in the midst of its dark patch of pubic hair. Cocteau speculated that his father, who killed himself at the age of forty-nine, had suppressed homosexual inclinations and never understood the uneasiness at the root of his personality.

At the Grand Condorcet school in 1903 Cocteau fell in love with Pierre Dargelos, the thirteen-year-old school vamp, who had "the beauty of an animal . . . that insolent beauty which is only heightened by filth." Shortly afterwards, Cocteau was expelled for "disciplinary reasons," but the image of Dargelos haunts *Les Enfants terribles* and his first film *Le Sang d'un Poete (Blood of a Poet)* (1930). He was sent to another school, but absconded for the port of Marseilles, where he indulged in drugs (he was a life-long opium eater) and sexual affairs with sailors and rough trade. Around 1906 he joined the circle of youths patronized by Edouard de Max, flamboyant aesthete and actor in Paris. When he accompanied Max to a costume ball in 1907 as an oriental princess, with his hair dyed red and in ringlets, a ring on every finger and toe, and a train embroidered with pearls, he was rebuked by Sarah Bernhardt: "If I were your mother, I would send you home to bed."

It was through Max that Cocteau's first books of poetry were published, and he was introduced to the powerful literary and theatrical worlds. By 1917 Cocteau's friends included Proust, Gide, Stravinsky, Picasso, Diaghilev and Nijinsky, and he was now famous enough to have his own young protégés. His first lover was Raymond Radiguet, fifteen when they met in 1918, with whom he had a passionate affair until Radiguet's death from typhoid in December 1923. After a year's solace in opium, Cocteau acquired a succession of young lovers from 1925 onwards, mostly eighteen-year-old blonds, who would live with him for periods of two or three years before being succeeded by another reincarnation of Radiguet.

*Le Livre Blanc* first appeared in 1928, then was reissued in 1930 with powerful erotic drawings by Cocteau. Its descriptions of sex with working-class young men are extraordinarily erotic even in our own jaded age, and it quickly became a gay underground classic. But it is essentially a "white paper" on injustice, an early sexual-political analysis of how guilt and shame are internalized in response to the homophobia of peer groups and the agents of social oppression such as teachers: "My misfortunes are due to a society which condemns anything out of the ordinary as a crime and forces us to reform our natural inclinations.''

The first half of the book documents the dynamics of self-oppression, for example how the narrator pretends to share the heterosexual enthusiasms of his school friends and thus "began to falsify my nature," leading to affairs with women. The second half of the book is an affirmation of homosexuality, when he realizes he has taken a wrong turning and "vowed that I would not get lost again." But it also shows how most gay relationships during this period were "doomed to failure" because of self-loathing and social injustice. The book concludes with a bitter sarcasm upon the Christian church, when the narrator "confesses" to the Abbé "I am happy but in a way that the Church and the world disapprove of" and is rejected: "I thought how admirable was the economy of God. It gives love when one lacks it, and, in order to avoid a pleonism of the heart, refuses it to those who have it." The last pages are swamped by self-pity, but nevertheless express one of the key sentiments that prompted the Gay Liberation movement: "I will not agree to be tolerated. This damages my love of love and of liberty.''

Cocteau's major relationship later in life was with Jean Marais (b. 1913), the young actor for whom he had written the role of the son in *Les Parents terribles* (1938). He had met Marais the previous year, when Marais was twenty-four years old. He was a very beautiful young man, and at the beginning of his career was cast in several roles primarily because of his physique; he became a successful film star (he is the very attractive Beast in Cocteau's film *La Belle et la bête*, 1946) and theatre director (he continues to direct Cocteau's plays). He and Cocteau lived together until 1947, when they both found other young protégés, but they remained friends throughout life. From the late 1950s Cocteau, the Enfant Terrible of the French literary establishment, was heaped with honors, became a member of L'Academy Française and was elected The Prince of Poets. The following letters to Marais—here translated into English for the first time—cover their initial romance and their decision to live together.

---

JEAN COCTEAU TO JEAN MARAIS

*[1938]*

My Jeannot,

It is Christmas, the most wonderful Christmas of my entire life. Your heart, your body, your soul, the happiness of living and working with you are all in my stocking. One subject might be "the useful present," of which I disapprove. As superfluous. I shall look only at the hands that give it. My Jeannot, I can never tell you often enough: thank you, thank you for your creative genius, thank you for our love.

Your Jean

*19, place de la Madeleine*

My adored Jeannot,

I have come to love you so (more than anything in the world) that I have given myself an order to love you only as a father and I want you to know that it is not because I love you less, but more.

I was afraid—to the point of dying—of wanting too much, of not giving you your freedom and of monopolizing you as in the play [*Les Parents terribles*, first performed at the théâtre des Ambassadeurs in Paris in 1938]. And then I'm afraid I might suffer horribly if you were to fall in love and if you didn't want to hurt me. I told myself that if I left you free you would tell me everything and that I should be less miserable than if you had to conceal the slightest thing from me. I cannot say that this was a decision that was very difficult to take—because my adoration is mixed with respect —it is religious in character, almost sacred—and because I give you all I have it in me to give. But I fear that you imagine that there is a certain reserve between us, a certain uneasiness—and that is why I am writing to you instead of speaking, from the bottom of my heart.

My Jeannot, I tell you again that you are everything to me. The very idea of inhibiting you, of taking advantage of your wonderful youth, would be atrocious. I was able to give you some glory and that is the only real result of that play, the only result that counts and that warms me.

Think—you will meet someone of your own age whom you will conceal from me or whom you will stop yourself from loving for fear of driving me to despair—I should be furious with myself until the day I died. It is undoubtedly preferable to deprive myself of a small part of my happiness and to gain your confidence and become courageous enough so that you feel freer than you would with a daddy or a mummy. You must have guessed my scruples and my distress. You're a sharp little Jeannot who knows a thing or two. It is only that I had to explain my attitude to you, so that you might not for a second believe that there is the shadow of a shadow between us. I swear to you that I am fair-minded and chivalrous enough not to be at all jealous and that this obliges me to live in agreement with the god we pray to. This god has given us so much that it would be wrong to ask more of him. I believe that sacrifices find their rewards, don't reprimand me, my beautiful angel. I see by the way you look at me that you know that no one loves you more than I do—and I should be ashamed to put the slightest obstacle in your way. My Jeannot adore me as I adore you and console me. Press me to your heart. Help me to be a saint, to be worthy of you and of myself. I live only through you.

---

Jeannot darling,

I beg you to read this letter as it was written, with your lovely soul and with our love, and don't find the shadow of jealousy, loneliness, the bitterness of age, etc. in it. I pledge my word. I am very, very, miserable, my

Jeannot, because luck helped me to make you famous and now everyone loves you . . . Only the fashionable set is on the lookout for the tiniest mistakes and congratulates itself on them. Now, the fact that you incessantly go out with boys of your own age is splendid. If it were Mercanton, Gilbert [Mercanton and Gilbert Gil, young actors], etc., I would see it only as straightforward, as work, as joy. What your innocence prevents you from being aware of is that the little gang you go out with all the time is, in the eyes of other people, a gang of blackmailers, of idle kept boys, unworthy of you and whom your presence elevates while it debases you. I don't tell you this because I've been told it. I tell off anyone who talks to me about it. I am telling you because I wanted to analyze my distress, to know where it came from and whether its motives were low.

No. I'm sure I'm right. Note that I am not asking you to turn your back on these new friends. I ask you to exercise the same reserve that I exercised when I used to associate with them in the past. Occasionally waiting for a signal before rushing off to see them.

D.'s conversation isn't for you. His tastes aren't for you. His lifestyle isn't for you. You make him out to be a prince charming. But in my eyes and in the eyes of others he's only a poor kid without much of a place in the world and lazy in the face of destiny.

Take heart. Open your eyes. Think. Think of my work, of our plays, our projects, our purity, the straight line we walk—and balance against that my frightful anxiety at knowing that you are always absent from your room and that you have fled to those haunts that are degrading to you without your being aware of it. Don't be angry with me for being so frank. I had a hard struggle before writing these lines. It would be easier for me to take advantage of your kindness and to keep quiet. Meditate on these lines and find the answer in yourself. Don't invent one for me. Live it.

Your Jean

PS. Jeannot *the folly of lovers is immense*, vegetable, animal, astral. What should I do? How can I make you understand that I no longer exist apart from you.

---

*Our house*
*July 1939*

Thank you my Jeannot for having admitted it to me. If I had found it out through the boasts or the indiscretions of that gang of "ladykillers," I think I should have died of it. As things are it doesn't matter and you are even more admirable in my eyes.

My Sunday was spent in dreams, in work, in loving. Pardon me for having complained. My love for you is such, my desire for you is such that I forget the circumstances. You know, as when you kissed Édouard on his paralysed mouth. That should help you to understand.

Jean I loved you so badly, I was so stupid, so ridiculous. I deserve all that won't happen to me because heaven protects heavenly loves.

My Jeannot I believe you. I know, I feel that you adore me as I adore you and that no one in the world is happier than we are. But look: I love life. This Sunday was life. You inspired me and I inspired you. We lived fast and kilometres above the little Nancy boys and the Paris–New York gossip. I should like our love to be excessive continually. Like the works. Always sharp, scandalous, brutally forceful. You understood perfectly well that I explain myself so badly that you could not have answered. We understand one another without speech, by the waves that emanate from us. My Jean, make allowances for one madly in love who has decided never to be cured of his madness, never to be prudent.

---

*19 place de la Madeleine*

My beloved Jeannot,

I'm so bad at speaking to you that I want to explain my stupidities to you better. Not for anything in the world would I wish to resemble the "others" or wish you to think I was "jealous." My Jeannot, I didn't know that one could adore another being as I adore you. I'm angry at fate, not at you. Imagine this dream: to adore one another without a single shadow, unreservedly, without a single false note. That, alas, is impossible. As for me, I thought that I could free myself and, since boys and women still want me violently, that we could each go our own way. But, in my soul and in my body, there is no longer a way I can go. The idea of touching anyone but you, of speaking tenderly to him, revolts me. I recoil from it. Don't think that implies that I'm blaming you. You're free and, since bad luck prevents us from living that dream, I should be mad to trammel you, your youth, your élan.

My rebellions, my pain come only from a miserable animal reflex. The idea of you in the arms of another or holding another in your arms is torture to me. Only, I want to get used to it and I want to know that in your infinite kindness you will be grateful to me.

I ask you above all not to feel embarrassed or constrained about anything and, since I find mysteries even more killing than lies, I ask you to judge the extent of my pain and to make it tolerable. One gesture, one word, one look from you is enough. I am not "jealous" of the one you love, I envy him and what hurts is that I am not, that I no longer am, worthy of that immense joy. I experienced that pain yesterday. I was as downcast as you about the troubles concerning Denham [a young man in the sky blue pyjamas whom Marais found in his theatre box one evening and of whom he writes in *Histoires de ma vie*]. I would have hated anyone who had thought me capable of being pleased about them.

In short, since I am deprived of love and nearly deprived of air to breathe, I should like to become some sort of a saint. Because the alternative would be vice and I object to that. My beautiful angel, I tell you again that I adore you. I want nothing but your happiness.

Your Jean

---

*19, place de la Madeleine*

My Jeannot,

I love you. All your reactions demonstrate nobility of soul and heart. I thank you for all the happiness you give me and the happiness of which you deprive me.

You are my angel. Without you I should lose my head in the midst of all these troubles with both theatre and film.

I should have given everything I had to have you in love with me but since it was not to be, save the secret place in your heart and in the senses of your heart for me.

Love me

---

My Jeannot,

Thank you from the bottom of my heart for having saved me. I was drowning and you threw yourself into the water without hesitation, without a backward look. What is admirable about it is that all this cost you dear and you wouldn't have done it if the impulse hadn't been sincere. So you have given me a proof of strength, a proof that all the lessons of our work have borne fruit. In love you can't run with the hare and hunt with the hounds and there is no such thing as a small love. You tended to believe in André's [André Goudin, Jean Cocteau's secretary] system: "One collects a face," etc. That's wrong. Love is Tristan and Isolde. Tristan is unfaithful to Isolde and it kills him. In just one minute you understood that our love couldn't be weighed against a sort of regret, a sort of baseless sorrow. I shall never forget those two days and that terrible 14th of July when I tempted fate and when I didn't know where to live anymore. We shall find our island of love again and our factory for the production of beautiful works of art. I adore you.

Write me two lines. Your short letters are my fetishes.

Jean

May I ask one little nonsense of you? For me waiting is like an illness. If you get in late, just telephone—a short phone call so that I hear your voice.

# ▼ JUST LIKE HOME ▼

[J. R. ACKERLEY & IDEAL FRIENDS]

Joseph Randall Ackerley (1896–1967) was the archetypal gay littérateur. His personal and professional friends were all part of the homosexual literary set: E. M. Forster, Goldsworthy Lowes Dickinson, Paul Cadmus, Christopher Isherwood, William Plomer, Francis King, James Kirkup, Stephen Spender, W. H. Auden, John Maynard Keynes, and a host of others. During his twenty-four years as literary editor of the BBC's magazine *The Listener* he helped to consolidate the homosexual hegemony of British intellectual and literary life during the 1930s and 1940s. His play *Prisoners of War* (1925) was outspokenly pro-gay, as were his other books and poems. He loathed philistinism and censorship, and delighted in shocking people with homosexuality: "I think that life is so important and, in its workings, so upsetting, that nobody should be spared, but that it should be rammed down their throats from morning to night. And may those who cannot take it die of it; it is what we want."

*Hindoo Holiday* (1932), based upon his experiences as secretary to the gay Maharajah of Chhatarpur in central India, was heavily edited to avoid libel, but Ackerley left detailed notes for its full reconstruction some day. The publisher Frederic Warburg warned "The day after you publish [*My Dog Tulip* (1956)], the police will be round to arrest you for practising homosexuality." He cut the scene in which the narrator goes to bed with the East End lad, but he fully annotated a copy hoping that it would be republished uncensored. Like most upper-middle-class gay men during this period he fell in love with young (basically heterosexual) working-class men. Sex with 200–300 petty criminals, prostitutes and Guardsmen failed to turn up his "Ideal Friend."

*We Think the World of You* (1960) documents his longest affair, with Freddie Doyle, a sailor-deserter and petty thief, whose family Ackerley supported for four years before the jealousy of Freddie's wife made it impossible for them to continue meeting. Ironically it was E. M. Forster's boyfriend the policeman Bob Buckingham who arrested Freddie for theft, not realizing he was Ackerley's boyfriend. The fictionalized autobiography also documents how Ackerley's love was transferred from Freddie to his Alsatian bitch Queenie, whom Ackerley took over when Freddie was sent to prison. Ackerley became an obsessive animal rights advocate, and his almost erotic love for Queenie embarrassed most of his friends. His posthumously published autobiography *My Father and Myself* was written in his last depressing years and concentrates more upon his lack of fulfilment than the humorous enjoyment of experience that was typical of most of his life.

The first letter below is from the boy who became devoted to Ackerley in India, reporting the death of the Maharajah's principal favourite. The second letter comes from a Danish medical student, Ackerley's lover who was arrested in Copenhagen for having sex with a sixteen-year-old and was allowed to escape imprisonment only on condition that he consent to a surgical "cure" by having one testicle removed and replaced by the testicle of a heterosexual man.

---

MAHADEO NAYAK TO J. R. ACKERLEY

*October 1924*

Sorry.

My dear Sahib,

I am extremely sorry to write you that your beautiful *bachcha* [baby, i.e. Rāghunāndi] after the serious illness of two month lost his breath 12 October. He was suffering by thysis. At first he was under Treatment of Doctor and after that of Vaid Raj. No doubt his death is always piercing and pinching my poor heart.

May God rest his gentle soul.

Oh! my dear sahib *now I am alone* in this world (or in Bundelkhand, Chhatarpur). I have nothing; and I have no lovely friend except *you*. So you are not here, what can I do. Now I am in *Great trouble* or (in danger). I have nobody to love me. If you love me *you must come here. I want to cry to meet you with both hands in your neck.*

My hand was could not write you this sorryful letter. Why I always write you pleaserful letter. How can I write you such . . . letter.

Now I want to finish my letter. Now I am crying.

I am your unfortunate and
Bad luck
Mahadeo Nayak

---

JOHANNES TO J. R. ACKERLEY

*January 31, 1927*

I think that the outcome of an operation is very problematical (do you know anything about it?) but now I'm obliged to submit to operation, although I do not want it now. It will be very interesting to see the outcome —if I will be able to feel the same for women as now for men!—I doubt, and you need not be jealous of one or another girl. *You* I'll never be able to forget—10 operations, I feel sure, were not able to alter my love to you.

---

J. R. ACKERLEY TO FRANCIS KING

*Athens*
*21/6/60*

Dearest Francis,

I am flying out of Athens tomorrow, returning to Marseille and Provence, thence home. Another letter before I go. I've enjoyed myself here, though in a baffled and frustrated way: my true misfortune was that *you* are not here. . . .

[—] both saved and destroyed my life—at least I think so. I had just begun an affair with a boy of 16, and [—] told me that there was a law against tampering with the under-aged. Of this, I had no inkling, and the news unnerved me. The hotel had regarded the boy, when I had taken him in that day, with what I thought too deep an interest; nevertheless I had got him to my room and we had both had an enjoyable time for a couple of hours. He was a street boy (from Piraeus)—as with Lolita, he did the picking-up, one of a group of naughty boys who operate round the Rex cinema in Venizelos; but he had a nice, affectionate nature, was gay, considerate, active, not grasping and exceedingly prettily made, and, by the sun, coloured. I meant to keep on with him throughout my stay, and had a date with him for the next day—but [—]'s remark unnerved me. [—] had also said "Don't enter *with* the boy"—but I *had*: since I could speak no Greek, he no English, it would have been hard to concoct any other plan, my phrasebook does not help.

I should now provide an elaborate description of the set-up of the Palladion Hotel, which is, as perhaps you remember, on Venizelos, down by Omonia. Enough to say that sometimes, too rarely, at the reception desk a girl or two functioned: sometimes the manager and an older more authoritative sort of man whom I took to be the proprietor were added. In fact, usually there seemed far *too* many people about, to welcome one and get one into the lift. I must add that everyone was, and continued to be, extremely friendly to me—most attentive—and the "proprietor" kept saying that he hoped I found staying there "just like home"—in spite of my rejoinder (which I don't suppose he understood) that it was from "home" that I was attempting to escape. At any rate, so far as I recall, when I slipped in with my boy, only the two women were functioning.

Anyway, I was unnerved; I did not keep my appointment with the boy the next day, though he did, I saw him from across the road, smartly dressed in a provocative way, arsing about with the other boys who haunted the "Rex." Sorry though I was, I decided to avoid him in the future. (I saw him some days later, very gay and naughty, no heartbreak!)

Four days later, as Henry Reed and I were returning from lunch at Vassily's (Henry was in the Alpha Hotel), another boy offered himself, also very pretty. He too could speak no English, but managed to convey that he was a Turkish tourist from Ankara—a story which I have subsequent reason to disbelieve. He was a little older than boy No. 1, either 17 or 18, smartly dressed in a cheap way. Henry soon made himself scarce, I conveyed to the boy that I lived in a hotel down the road, he said he would like to go in with me, and in we went. A *bad* moment? *Everyone* was in the foyer, proprietor, manager, two female receptionists, and two of the positively hideous pages the hotel seemed to have thought it wiser to select. Much polite fussifiction, "how do you do?" to me, lift pressed for me, nervous conversation from me, everyone most civil, the manager himself rode us up to my floor, more nervous conversation from me. The boy and I entered my room. My dear, we had not been there *two* minutes before the phone rang. I picked it up—muffled, muddled voices, excited tones—then it emerged that it was a call for the boy in my room. Perplexedly, I handed the phone to him. More excited conversation—of which I understood not a word, but certainly heated, the sort of "so what!" tone, then he put the receiver down, said "The Police!" in an agitated way, added "give me 3 drachmas," I gave 5, grabbed his little hold-all, and positively fled.

*What* was it all about? What did he want 3 drachmas for? Who *on earth* had known he was in my room? Would he return? Well, I could write a lot more about it—speculation etc.—but I won't. He didn't return. I questioned the manager, very friendly, no change. "Someone phoned saying he had seen a young boy enter the hotel in company with an Englishman. He wished to speak to the boy. Of course, I had to put him through!"

Well, there seem to me three possibilities only: (the boy himself *must* have been innocent, for he reaped nothing from it but 5 drachmas); (i) a jealous discarded friend of the boy's had seen our pick-up and dished us, (ii) the police had seen us, and dished us, (iii) the proprietor himself, pretending to be a policeman, had dished us. I think the first rather fanciful and reject it. Which of the other two was right I haven't a clue, but it didn't matter, they had the *same* effect—I simply *couldn't* afterwards, take *anyone* else into the hotel *at all*. Whoever was watching me, I was a watched, or at least noticed man, either the proprietor had discreetly informed me (he was as nice as pie afterwards) that he wasn't going to have things like that in his hotel, or the police had seen and phoned (scouting round afterwards I observed that the kiosk exactly opposite the entrance to the hotel had a phone). So although I have felt as sexy as the devil I have simply had to give everything up since: I incline to adolescents, as you know, and they incline towards me. But I don't think I would dare to take even an adult in—a sailor, for example. So my life in Athens has been ruined. And how I have wished you were here! I've thought of changing my hotel—but to what? [—] told me he lived in a louche hotel—a sort of brothel—wonderfully cheap, on the Plaka, and I think I found it in his absence. I have visited a dozen hotels observing the set-up, managerial faces, asking for prices, but I didn't move. I have only two or three more days here anyway—and how, after all, should I know whether a hotel that admitted whatever *he* liked without bother (does he like the brutal?) would also admit what *I* like, the very young, against the law, without bother? And it is so terribly hot, one really does want a shower in one's room: so does one's boy, and how nice it is to see him taking a shower. Perhaps I should have moved to the Grande Bretagne where, I am told, anything may happen, and indeed it is the middling, family hotel, like the Palladion, which is the difficulty. One wants one so poor and tiny that there are no public rooms for entertaining friends, or one with public rooms so many and so vast that no one can keep track of one's activities.

Dearest Francis, perhaps next year, or the next, you and I could rent an apartment in Athens for the spring. How delicious that would be. I do think the Athenians most attractive and wonderfully endowed. Last time I came I was not in the humour, not awake, I am wide awake now.

Anyway (i) how could I get away from [—], who was determined not to get away from me? and (ii) too much time was spent among tattered English and American queens in Zonar's and in those tiresome tavernas (not visited at all this trip) which cater only for those who like he-men and Tarzans! I don't think you ever took me to a Secondary or even Public School or Borstal. My tastes, I now realise, lie in that direction.

    Best love

      Joe

[A long "P.S." has been cut here]

Ralph Hall (1913–1987) as a young man *ca.* 1930s.

Captain Montague Glover (1898–1983) as a young officer, *ca.* 1918. Photos by Montague Glover from *A Class Apart* by James Gardiner.

# ▼ I'LL BE WITH YOU TONIGHT ▼

[RALPH HALL & MONTAGUE GLOVER]

Montague Charles Glover (1898–1983), an officer from the middle classes, was awarded the Military Cross for bravery during World War I, and worked as an architect during most of his life, often for the government. He had many affairs with builders, road-workers, dockers, labourers, young military men and "renters" in Trafalgar Square, but for fifty years lived with a cheerful working-class lad from London's East End, Ralph Hall (1913–1987), fifteen years younger than he, whom he met around 1930. Monty was a keen and skilful photographer, and every year of his and Ralph's life is documented in loving snapshots. Ralph was poorly educated, and absolutely devoted to Monty. He read Agatha Christie thrillers, collected British Empire stamps, and posed for Monty in fields of corn like a pastoral faun, for he was strikingly good looking.

Ralph was drafted into the Royal Air Force in 1940, and for four years he sent Monty hundreds of love letters—the same sort of letters that countless boys sent to their sweethearts back home to bolster their spirits during the war. There are also numerous photographs of Monty's other tricks, especially during the 1930s, dressed in military uniforms and boxing shorts from Monty's closet, powerfully fetishistic set-pieces. He had a flat in London near the barracks, but he and Ralph led a seemingly idyllic life in Little Windovers, the house Monty had designed and built in the village of Balsall Heath in Warwickshire.

Monty retired in 1953 and he and Ralph lived in tranquil domestic bliss at Little Windovers for another thirty years until his death in 1983. When Ralph died in 1987, the house and contents were put up for sale by his relatives, and Monty's unique "gay family album" recording the life of an ordinary gay couple in the 1940s–1970s—digging in the garden, enjoying a cup of tea in bed—and his diaries, letters, photographic negatives and scrapbooks of "found" homoerotic images from newspapers and magazines, were discovered in two cardboard boxes in the local auction rooms by James Gardiner, a collector of visual ephemera, and partially published in 1992.

---

RALPH HALL TO MONTAGUE GLOVER

*RAF Waddington*
*10 November 1940*

My dear,

We had a raid the other night. It was about an hour raid and they did no damage, my dear. They put about twenty bombs on the turnips in the field at the back of the block and the place seem to lift off the ground and the next morning we had another one but we brought it down my dear, I did not go out as they did not call us out. The cake has just arrived my darling and it is lovely and I will be able to have some for tea on sunday. I have been on three night running this week my dear and I have just been told that I am on again tonight. Well it all is a lifetime my dear. The lads all love our cake my Darling, we had some for tea my dear.

I will be with you tonight Darling
Love Ralph

---

*20 November 1940*

My dear Monty

I have just got your letter telling me about the raid at Coventry and I was glad to hear that it is allright at home. With your letters dear you are always speaking to me and I read them over and over again my dear. The lads say that they think we are going out soon, one just said that and came in dear. So you say you went round the site with me and I can see you now walking round. I go back all over the days we had at Richmond and Esher and Drunken Bidford and Leamington along the river. Do you remember the old days when we first started darling. I went back all over it again last night. What a time we had in them days and I am sorry to say I am crying I cannot hold it back no more my Darling. I love you my old Darling. I do miss you ever such a lot my dear as you know my dear. I hope this finds you in good health my dear and all the rest at home. I get over to you as soon as I can my Darling. I love you Monty. Lots of love to my old Darling Monty. I miss you. Goodnight dear,

Ralph xxxxxxx a ring of them for you.

---

*9 May 1941*

My darling,

How can you forgive me for forgetting your birthday you know I wish you all the best in the world my darling. I thought it was the 12 of this month darling. But I tell you the truth darling I would have forgotten as I have been troubled by this going overseas. Darling you don't know how I miss you darling. I might as well tell you the truth. I have been letting myself go and I have been crying over you Darling and calling out for you. The lads say who is Monty? to me and I say what do you mean and they say I was calling out for you in my drunkenness Darling. You old darling I am going to get drunk again tonight too darling and I am with you down at the Bear in Esher darling and please forgive me darling for what I have done darling and forgot your birthday darling, you know I love you darling ALWAYS DARLING Goodnight my love and I will be with you for ever and ever you old Darling and the one and only
RALPH TO MONTY XXXXXXXXXXXXX

*[from aboard ship,*
*ca. October 1941]*

My darling,

I wish you could have seen me off but it was impossible to. I hope you got my telegram allright and the last letter. We are passing a lot of islands you and I done in the crosswords my dear. A lot of the lads are feeling sick and I feel sorry for them my dear. . . . On the night I sent the telegram I was off the next morning, and off like a shot as they say. And I was thinking of you my dear in your office and at home and all the rest my darling. The wrist watch has gone again my dear, it just starts when it likes every hour, I dropped it. I am just bedding down for the night my darling and dont I just wish I was with you, old darling. I can see you lying there sweetheart. Goodnight darling XXXXX All the lads are guessing where we are going darling. I only know I am going away from the man I love, the one and only you old darling. But I know I will come back darling to you, and it will only be a dream darling . . .

---

*Hut 192 Heliopolis*
*23 March 1942*

Darling,

I would love to be in the garden today. It is just like English spring and I know what it is like down your end, the lads tell me all the news when they come out. The garden should be looking nice when this reaches you my Sweetheart. My work is just finished for today and it is 9 o'clock the 20 march and it is just started to rain and it is very cold at night. I hope you are in good health my darling and all at home and I wish I was coming on the boat to you darling. I miss you so much Monty xxxxx you old sweetheart of mine. . . .

---

*18 December 1942*

Hallo Darling,

. . . You dont know how much I miss you . . . I kiss the photo every night. so you are in bed with me after all. I would rather have you with me. I was up the blue in the desert for a week and was it hell. Just sand and more sand. Lets get back to the old days my dear as soon as this war is over. . . . Cairo is just a smell. I cant think of a good thing to say about it at all so lets get home. . . .

---

*[Egypt]*
*19 December 1942*

Darling

I have not had a letter from you yet and the lads that came out here with me have had a lot. I hope everything is all right at home. Look after yourself darling and try to do something for me, you know what I mean my darling. Think of me Monty, You are the only one that ever gave me a frill and you still do. Darling I can see me and you on the bed now you old darling and well be there again dont worry my darling. It is six days before Xmas. Just think of me in the desert with the lads on guard. You are all-ways in my thoughts and I know you will think better of me when this war is over you old darling. Dont I wish I was there with you now darling. I am feeling so strong tonight my sweet. I would love you all night darling.

I am in the guardroom waiting to do my 4th guard my dear and I can see you all at home round the table for Xmas and I know you will miss me darling. This is a XMASxxxxxGIFT from your one and only darling. You dont know how much I miss you Monty. I love you darling so think good of me my sweethart.

    All my love and a merry Xmas

    and a HAPPY NEW YEAR TO THEM ALL

        LOVE

           Ralph

---

*[Telegram, December 1942]*

GREETINGS TELEGRAM to MR GLOVER

MY DARLING

    ALL LETTERS ARE ARRIVING AND WHAT LOVELY LETTERS. ALL MY LOVE AND BEST WISHES FOR XMAS DARLING

        RALPH TO MONTY I MISS YOU DARLING

# ▼ WE'RE A FUNNY PAIR ▼

[W. H. AUDEN & CHESTER KALLMAN]

Although Wystan Hugh Auden (1907–73) emigrated to the United States just before World War II and eventually became an American citizen, he always retained his roots in upper-class England, and his poetry reflects the intellectual ideals of Oxford University and the religious commitments of Anglicanism. Auden, Christopher Isherwood and Stephen Spender were an inseparable trio who represented the new spirit of literature during the 1930s and 1940s. All were deeply influenced by the freedom of the Weimar Republic, specifically its decadent homosexual subculture, which they experienced first-hand. Auden lived on Furbingerstrasse in Berlin near the Cosy Corner, a working-class gay bar where he and Isherwood during 1929 searched for more than just "copy." Auden's diary for this period (he knew of 170 boy brothels) is considered too obscene for publication; he deliberately provoked his regular partner Pieps into beating him up.

But while Isherwood never went much beyond the affirmation of individual personal liberty, Auden espoused wider political causes and his poetry concentrated on anti-Fascism, unemployment, and class differences. The cool aloofness of his work may be due partly to the view that the "great poet" (which he consciously desired to be) cannot reveal personal, specifically homosexual, commitments, which are seen somehow to delimit universal themes and to detract from the intensity of purpose necessary for great reforms. His very explicit poem "The Platonic Blow"—"It was a Spring day, a day for a lay, when the air / Smelled like a locker-room, a day to blow or get blown"—is not included in the authorized edition of his works. See the text in *Gay Roots Vol. 1* (San Francisco: Gay Sunshine Press, 1991).

His many poems celebrating his love for Chester Kallman (1921–75) do not reveal his lover's gender. Kallman was an opera queen whom Auden met in New York in 1939, and they collaborated on the libretto for Stravinsky's *The Rake's Progress* and other works. Kallman in fact deliberately set out to seduce Auden, by sitting in the front row of a college audience for a reading by Auden and Isherwood, flirting and winking at them, and then meeting them afterwards and offering his body to Auden several days later. In due course they became lifelong companions, but Kallman continued to enjoy numerous adventures with rough trade whereas Auden held to the ideal of monogamous marriage. The first couple of years of their relationship were fraught with acrimony and separations, until Auden gave up demands for "fidelity" and settled for what he could get. The first letter below is a "Christmas present" to Kallman. (All of Kallman's letters to Auden have been lost.)

W. H. Auden to Chester Kallman

*Christmas Day. 1941*

Dearest Chester

Because it is in you, a Jew, that I, a Gentile inheriting an O-so-genteel anti-semitism, have found my happiness:

As this morning I think of Bethlehem, I think of you.

Because it is you, from Brooklyn, who have taught me, from Oxford, how the most liberal young man can assume that his money and his education ought to be able to buy love;

As this morning I think of the inn stable, I think of you.

. . .

Because the necessarily serious relation of a child to its parents is the symbol, pattern, and warning of any serious love that may later depend upon its choice, because you are to me emotionally a mother, physically a father, and intellectually a son;

As this morning I think of the Holy Family, I think of you.

. . .

Because even *les matelots* and *les morceaux de commerces* [i.e., sailors and trade] instinctively pay you homage;

As this morning I think of the shepherds, I think of you.

Because I believe in your creative gift, and because I rely absolutely upon your critical judgment;

As this morning I think of the magi, I think of you.

Because it is through you that God has chosen to show me my beatitude;

As this morning I think of the Godhead, I think of you.

Because in the eyes of our bohemian friends our relationship is absurd;

As this morning I think of the Paradox of the Incarnation I think of you.

Because our love, beginning Hans Andersen, became Grimm, and there are probably even grimmer tests to come, nevertheless I believe that if only we have faith in God and in each other, we shall be permitted to realize all that love is intended to be;

As this morning I think of the Good Friday and Easter Sunday already implicit in Christmas day, I think of you.

---

*Wystan's Day*
*[i.e. February 21, 1949, Auden's birthday]*

. . . I've never noticed, *darling*, any reluctance on your part to confine experiences, operatic, intellectual, etc., to me. (If you've never gone with a lover to *Tristan*, it wasn't because of me, but because Miss Butch preferred jazz. *Entre nous*, I would have minded that less than the great *gang* of chaps that always were at the Met.) If I'm anxious for you to approve of Keith [Vaughan] it's not because you are the Beatrice for whom I cherish a grotesque passion, but because you are the one comrade my non-sexual life cannot do without. Expressions like "bowing out" and "disappear" are twists of the knife which, as you know only too well, you beast, hurt. Still I adore you and I suppose you must deserve it.

---

*March 15, 1949*

I know you won't believe it but there was honestly no malice, conscious or unconscious, in [Keith's] being at 27th Street on Christmas Eve. He was Billy's friend (not in that sense) long before I met him, which was through Billy. Do you think I should have refused to go to Billy's for Christmas or that I should have gone but refused to take him with me?

As to our relationship, I'm sure that you have a pretty good idea of how it is. I am Poppa to him; he, unfortunately, cannot be Big Brother to me, only Young Brother. . . . I can talk to him and educate him—he cannot educate me. I'm not being catty about him, because you would realize at once if you met him, how decent he is. Once again, darling, what do you expect of me? One night stands with trade? I have neither the taste, the talent, nor the time.

A chaste fidelity to the Divine Miss K? [i.e., Chester] Miss God, I know, says that, but I haven't the strength, and I don't think you, sweetie, have the authority to contradict me. If it is wrong, at least I don't behave badly to him as I do to you. Enough. We're a funny pair, you and I.

# ▼ CROSSING BRIDGES ▼

[STANLEY HAGGART & HARRY HAY]

Harry Hay (born 1912), father of the gay liberation movement and founder of the Mattachine Society, met the handsome interior decorator Stanley Mills Haggart in 1935, when the latter came backstage after a performance of Gogol's *Clean Beds* in which Harry played second lead, and Harry fell for him instantly, "with a chemistry the like of which had never happened before." But Stanley's formidable mother, who hung on to their position as the foremost family of Kansas even after moving to California, resented her son's friendship and did what she could to keep the men apart.

After six months of growing strain, Stanley vanished, and was persuaded by his mother and brother to see a psychologist in an attempt to "cure" his homosexuality, and he succumbed to their urgings to get married. A year and a half after disappearing, Stanley, realizing his mistake, tried to salvage his real love. A short note to Harry ("Harry, you win. I have learned my lesson.") was followed by a letter written during his honeymoon, and then a flood of letters at the rate of nearly one a day, which Harry Hay's biographer calls "a testament to an ultimately tragic affair." The two men were eventually reunited in 1938, but Harry had become increasingly active in meetings of the Communist Party and the two men were politically incompatible. Hay "abandoned" Stanley, whose homely domestic ideals he regarded as unrealistic, and Stanley in due course made a new life-match.

---

STANLEY HAGGART TO HARRY HAY

*October 23, 1937*

You know me well enough to know that I will go to any lengths if I feel I am right—if I feel I have something to do. A few weeks ago my latest effort was to marry Phyllis Ward. Does that shock you to know this—and that I am now crossing the Atlantic with her—married to her? My awakening has been horrible and the agony had been almost more than I can bear. To go back a bit, I got your letter 2 days before the ceremony. Your letter has struck deep down into the very depths of me—has cut through all pretenses. . . . To think it had to take a marriage with its wedding night experience to show me where my real affinity lies. Every cell in me screamed out in protest at my desecration of my body. At that time I knew that I belonged to you and you to me. . . . I need your help in straightening this mess out. And it is a mess—frightful. Phyllis loves me terribly and is such a fine girl. I told her yesterday of my feelings for you and she realizes from my behavior that a part of me which she had wanted for herself belonged to you. Our marriage was and is a perfect setup . . . wrong in every way.

The reason is that I belong with you, and you with me. Neither of us seems able to help it. Goodness knows I have done everything possible to keep us apart. Why? I don't know. But I'm trembling now over the thought of being with you soon.

[Stanley explained that the marriage had been encouraged by a doctor in England who counselled the couple.] . . . He wanted to know whether I was homosexual through birth or if it was acquired. Phyllis (not her fault) made me decide that I could be "normal" and he urged our marriage. Just because of this lack of truth, this mess has come about. [He worried about his and Harry's prospects as a couple.] . . . I know the difficulties in our way if we go onwards together. I will have none of my present life to back me up—all will desert me. My life with you would have to be enough so that I would not care—would willingly abandon everything for you. But my darling I have that sweet certainty that if we were close enough together nothing else would count.

---

*[Undated]*

Sweetheart—

I left [my brother] Lawrence yesterday and am halfway across Kansas— on my way to you. Society has already begun to collect its price for our love. I was forced to break with my brother and his wife and the hurt of it sends me to you with tears in my eyes. I'm crossing my bridges to you my beloved—and my eyes are steadily on you—my heart is with you.

---

*[Undated]*

Some of my thoughts today went into song—and lifted an untrained voice up to that level where one exists when inspired. For I love you, Harry. . . . I gasp with expectancy over the thoughts of our being together in a home —for ever. That's what I want. Every nook and cranny of the rooms will be inspired. The walls will burst and surge with the vibrations of our merging.

# ▼ REACHING DEEP
## INTO THE HEART'S CORE ▼

[HERBERT HUNCKE & NOAH]

Herbert E. Huncke was born in 1915 in Greenfield, Massachusetts and died on August 8, 1996 in New York City. Hitting the road at the age of twelve, he lived a life on the fringes of American society as a hustler, addict, and petty criminal. He travelled around the country from 1934–39, riding the rails with the last of the hoboes and living by his wits, finally finding his psychic home among the drifters of Times Square. In the mid-1940s he met William S. Burroughs and gave him his first shot of morphine. Soon Huncke became a part of the intimate circle of Burroughs, Jack Kerouac, and Allen Ginsberg, who all looked to Huncke as a sort of guide to the underbelly of New York City.

Dr. Alfred Kinsey interviewed Huncke for his groundbreaking study of sexuality, and even paid him two dollars for every interviewee he'd bring by. The prototypical hipster, Huncke introduced Kerouac to the carney term "beat," meaning beaten down to an almost euphoric state of exhaustion, which Kerouac later adapted into "Beat Generation." Kerouac said of Huncke, "He is the greatest storyteller I know, an actual genius in my mind." He was an old-style raconteur, with graceful and refined manners who could charm like no other.

Though he is more well-known for appearing in works like *On the Road*, *Junky*, and *Howl* penned by his more famous associates, he was a prolific and striking writer in his own right. His memoirs are poignant and rich in detail, authentic and non-judgmental descriptions of people he's known and places he's seen, including prison, where he spent a total of thirteen years. *The Herbert Huncke Reader* was published in 1997 by William Morrow and Company.

In 1964 Huncke was arrested for possession of narcotics and sentenced to one year in New York's Hart's Island, though he would be released after six months. The following letters were written during his incarceration there to a young friend (apparently in his twenties) named Noah with whom he had fallen in love. Huncke had hung out and done drugs with Noah before he was imprisoned. (Thanks to Benjamin Schafer, editor of the above mentioned *Herbert Huncke Reader* for providing biographical information and the text of the letters.)

---

HERBERT HUNCKE TO NOAH

*February 19, 1964 [letter unsent]*

Noah,

Skimming thru the news today the movie review on the Jonas Mekas film [*Guns of the Trees*] and particularly noted Ginsberg's name. Received an exceptionally moving letter from Paul. Words flow from his pen creating passages of sheer beauty. He is a great person and gains strength and stature seemingly before one's eyes. How fortunate I am knowing both of you. His woven of fine-spun threads of gleaming silver and gold. Yours of hard cobalt—glorious reds—umber and angry yellows. It is strange how each induces the same hypnotic trance—while reaching deep into the heart's core—searching out the same truths—declaring the same convictions—exposing repeatedly the wonder of the organic basic qualities of the mystery of the soul. Trying to reach each of you from here—in this old building of three floors—constructed in a sort of H form—each floor a huge dormitory housing many, many men of all ages—but mostly old— the misfits and maladjusted—the derelicts and lost—the tired and hungry —on this beautiful little island—where sea gulls also make their home— and the wind sometimes sweeps them in their flight toward the sea while their screeching becomes the sound of keening women—rather like peering toward a winter sun seen faintly thru a veil of pale gray clouds. Also it is difficult retaining an impersonal (the very idea of anyone at anytime even pretending to be impersonal is, of course, ridiculous) attitude. Nevertheless it behooves me—at this point—to pay lip service—so to speak— to the commanding forces. I can only hope you understand. I had a very impressive dream recently in which I saw you standing at the prow of a ship. You sailed past me. I called to you—asking your destination and you smiled at me but did not answer. I looked away for a moment—feeling very sad and lonely and I thought I will not show my concern—so I quickly looked back and you were surrounded by many people and you had changed someway—so that I had difficulty recognizing you. All of a sudden—I know you were happy and I was glad.

    Huncke

---

*March 16, 1964 [letter sent]*

Noah—it seems our positions have become similar in a rather vague sense. I also find it difficult writing letters these days—particularly to you. Of course my reasons are perfectly obvious. I am in jail. My present environment presents a limited scope. I have no news. . . . Your letter was both a pleasant surprise and somewhat disturbing. As much as you may dislike living at home—I can't help but feel it is in all probability for the better at least until you feel you have developed some degree of self-reliance and can no longer stand the restrictions. From what you said in your letter it does sound as though they are making an effort to extend themselves. Remember—it doesn't lie entirely up to them. You also must make concessions. In fact—since basically yours is the most tolerant attitude—in the final analysis—you must carry the heavier part of the load. Hell Noah, I can't talk to you—it seems—without coming on like a dim-witted-advise-dishing-out old fool. It is utterly impossible for me to say any of the things —I know in my heart—should be said—if there is any hope of retaining your friendship. You—the one person I most desire to speak truthfully to— are the one I am the most evasive with. Why? Of one thing I am sure—it is certainly not because of the Allen G. and Peter O. type thing. . . . It is something much more than that. Anyway, try and bear with me. I can't honestly say I consider Monroe and Bill Heine the best company you might choose. Actually—I'm envious—and only feel thusly because I'm not there with you—although envy isn't the only reason. Frankly I'd worry less were I on the scene because—in my opinion you are pretty vulnerable—when all is said and done—and I'd feel better if I were there to run interference—so to speak. Boy—if I deliberately set out to make you reject me—I couldn't do much better. Regards to Diane. Be as good to her as you can, Noah— she needs love. For that matter—don't we all? Incidentally, with enough of the right chemical substance, the idea of traveling . . . sounds like a great idea. I don't care how the raunchy the note—or short—send it anyway.

    Huncke

P.S. This is the first of two letters composed to you—saying essentially the same things. maybe I'll send the other tomorrow.

    H.

# ▼ RELAX, MAN ▼

## [NEAL CASSADY & ALLEN GINSBERG]

To sum up the gay "line of succession," Walt Whitman slept with Edward Carpenter, who slept with Gavin Arthur (1901–72), who slept with Neal Cassady, who slept with Allen Ginsberg (1926–97), who generously shared the mantle of gay poetry among the Beat Generation in the 1950s. Ginsberg's great poem *Howl* (1956) was one of the most shocking poems of that generation—"I saw the best minds of my generation destroyed by madness, starving hysterical naked, / dragging themselves through the negro streets at dawn looking for an angry fix"—but also one of the most liberating, a watershed for gay liberation—"who howled on their knees in the subway and were dragged off the roof waving genitals and manuscripts, / who let themselves be fucked in the ass by saintly motorcyclists, and screamed with joy. . . ." By the 1960s Ginsberg was preoccupied with Buddhist wisdom, and he became a leading figure in the Flower Power movement, lecturing in American universities against the Vietnam war and chanting his mesmerising Hare Krishna Mahamantra.

Allen Ginsberg's first important relationship was with Neal Cassady, and their letters chart an odyssey, geographically as well as spiritually, ranging across America, South America and India. Cassady had been the companion of Jack Kerouac (1922–69) in his travels, described in Kerouac's *On the Road* (1957). Cassady was basically heterosexual in a homosexual milieu; his life was full of pathos, and prison; he died in 1968. Cassady and Ginsberg were together in Denver June through August 1947, before Ginsberg went to Dakar and Cassady went to New York. Ginsberg went to New York that fall hoping to rendezvous with Cassady, but Cassady had returned to San Francisco a couple of days earlier to get married. There was a painful separation, but eventually they renewed their correspondence and remained friends through the 1960s, and occasionally even slept together. Ginsberg's early letters to Cassady do not survive, probably because Cassady destroyed them when he eventually married. Carolyn Cassady did not know of this correspondence until the letters were being prepared for publication in 1977, when she described them as a "testimony to the tenacity of deep and enduring love."

---

NEAL CASSADY TO ALLEN GINSBERG

*Denver, Colorado*
*March 14, 1947.*

Dear Allen;

    . . . My life is, at the moment, so cluttered up I have become incapable of relaxing long enough to even write a decent letter, really, I'm almost unable to think coherently. You must, then, not only forgive, but, find it within yourself to understand & in so doing develope a degree of patience until I am able to free myself enough to become truly close to you again.

On your part, you must know, that any letdown in your regard for me would upset me so much that, psychologically, I would be in a complete vacuum. At least for the immediate future I must request these things of you. so *please* don't fail me. I need you now more than ever, since I've noone else to turn to. I continually feel I am almost free enough to be a real help to you, but, my love can't flourish in my present position & if I forced it now, both you & I would lose. By God, though, every day I miss you more & More.

Understanding these things I hope, nay, in fact, know you must pour out more affection now than ever, rather than reacting negatively & withering up so that all is loss, or would be, between us.

Let us then find true awareness by realizing that each of us is depending on the other for fulfillment. In that realization lies, I believe, the germ that may grow to the great heights of complete oneness. . . .

I shall find a job tomorrow & perhaps by losing myself in work again I may become more rational & less upset & unnerved by the emotional shock of returning. Write soon I need you. I remain your other self.

Neal.

---

Neal Cassady to Allen Ginsberg

*Denver, Colorado*
*March 30, 1947.*

Dear Allen,

. . . I don't know how to say this, but you've hit the nail on the head. No more sacrament, no more directing my efforts in the nervous, stupid, neurosis you have outlined so well. I understand perfectly Allen and by god, you're right! Man, from here on out it'll be a breeze. Really, the formulation you gave is just what I needed. I'm overwhelmed with joy, I feel a sense of relief, I almost know peace again! All of this just thru understanding and agreeing with you. . . .

What you say on "Play" is honestly what I've been doing, or striving for, all my life, therein lies our, or my, confused sense of closeness. Also, I fear, therein lies our strength of tie to each other, I say I fear, for I *really don't* know how much I can be satisfied to love you, I mean bodily, you know I, somehow, dislike pricks & men & before you, had conciously forced myself to be homosexual, now, I'm not sure whether with you I was not just forceing myself unconciously, that is to say, any falsity on my part was all physical, in fact, any disturbance in our affair was because of this. You meant so much to me, I now feel I was forcing a desire for you bodily as a compansation to you for all you were giving me. This is a sad state and upsets me for I want to become nearer to you than any one & still I don't want to be unconciously insincere by passing over my non-queerness to please you. Allen, this is straight, what I truely want is to live with you from Sept. to June, have an apt., a girl, go to college, (just for French to sit in on classes etc.) see all and do all. . . .

---

NEAL CASSADY TO ALLEN GINSBERG

*Denver, Colorado*
*April 10, 1947*

. . . I don't care what you think, that's what I want. If you are able to un-derstand and can see your way clear to shepharding me around the big city for 9 months, then, perhaps, go to Europe with me next summer thats swell, great and wonderful, exactly what I want, if not—well, why not? Really, damn it, why not? You sense I'm not worthy of you? you think I wouldn't fit in? you presume I'd treat you as badly or worse? You feel I'm not bright enough? you know I'd be imposing, or demanding, or trying to suck you dry of all you have intellectually? Or is it just that you are, almost unconciously, aware of enough lack of interest in me, or indifferance to my plight and need of you, to believe that all the trouble of helping and living with me, would not be quite compensated for by being with me? I can't promise a darn thing, I know I'm bisexual, but prefer women, there's a slimmer line than you think between my attitude toward love and yours, don't be so concerned, it'll fall into line. Beyond that—who knows? Let's try it & see, huh? . . .

Relax, man, think about what I say and try to see yourself moving toward me without any compulsive demands, due to lack of assurance that I love you, or because of lack of belief that I understand you etc. forget all that and in that forgetfulness see if there isn't more peace of mind and even more physical satisfaction than in your present subjective longing (whether for me, or Claude, or anybody) I know one cannot alter by this method, but come to me with all you've got, throw your demands in my face, (for I love them) and find a true closeness, not only because what emotionality I have is also distorted by lonliness, but also because I, logi-cally or not, feel I want you more than anyone at this stage.

I'm really beat, off to bed, and a knowledge of relief, for I *know* you must understand and move with me in this, you better not fight against it or any other damn thing, so shut up, relax, find some patience and fit into my mellow plans.

Love & Kisses, my boy, opps!, excuse, I'm not Santa Claus am I? Well then, just—Love & Kisses,
          Neal

ALLEN GINSBERG TO NEAL CASSADY

*New York*
*[Fall 1947]*

Dear Neal:

. . . I think you know what is coming in this letter, it is serious; if you don't want to I won't ask you to read further or to reply for that matter.

You know or (at the moment) I am smarter than you & cleverer in ways and I don't want to be smart or clever at this point, even subtle. I must admit that I have known more or less consciously that all the "purity" of my love, its "generosity" and "honour" was, though on its own level true, not at all my deeper intention toward you, which was and is simply a direct lover's. If we were equal and I were as strong as you in the relationship "I could afford to be"—I would naturally flow into common generosity. But we are not, for all my purity and abnegation is a stall and a sell out, and all my "gifts" to transmit, if they were to be any use to you which I really thought they would be, were unimportant in my mind and subsidiary to my main beggary. I would have been capable of continuing it, before, even to the point of renouncing any sexual claim on you as I did in my last letter; but that I know and knew was possessiveness taking the palatable & generous form. I had no clear ideas in mind when I told you to come back, except to follow out my agreement to the letter, though perhaps not in spirit, and wait for you to pity me again and sleep with me. . . .

I do not know how I can hope for any love for you because my own love is one compounded of hostility & submission. I don't understand and can't, your own emotions, even when explained only because my drive is so blind that I cannot comprehend even intellectually the possible realism of your statements. And I can't well plead a case of love for you truly because at my most sweet or straight or good-goody or sacrificing or demanding, I am always conscious below of stabbing you in the back while I lead you or deceive you. This is not so much conscious as merely known, by both of us, I suppose. . . .

I don't know what I can do Neal now. You know you are the only one who gave me love that I wanted and never had, as you have—this does not humiliate me any more—a number of others, and I sometimes wonder about them. What must I do for you to get you back? I will do anything. Any indecencies any revelations any creation, any miseries, will they please you. Or will they frighten you as this does? I mean to bend my mind that knows it can destroy you to any base sordid level of adoration and masochistic abnegation that you desire or taunt me with. This has style, and it is now so much vomit. Or do you look on it as such? I do not care what I think really, I hate & fear you so much that I will do anything to win your protection again, and your mercy.

I am lonely, Neal, alone, and always I am frightened. I need someone to love me and kiss me & sleep with me; I am only a child and have the mind of a child. I have been miserable without you because I had depended on you to take care of me for love of me, and now that you have altogether rejected me, what can I do, what can I do? . . . I blame you yet I still ask for the whip. . . .

I have never asked you for a true favor, a gratuitous gift from you but small ones once or twice when I was driven to it by your love & purposeful or unconscious frustration of me. I have always been obedient & respectful, I have adjusted my plans to yours, my desires to your own pattern, and now I do ask—I pray—please neal, my neal, come back to me, don't waste me, don't leave me. I don't want to suffer any more, I have had my mind broken open over and over before, I have been isolate and loveless always. I have not slept with anyone since I saw you not because I was faithful but because I am afraid and I know no one. I will always be afraid I will always be worthless, I will always be alone till I die and I will be tormented long after you leave me. I can't give up now for this time the one chance I have of serving not being served, the last time, my only time. Already I am aging, I feel my life is sterile, I am unbloomed, unused, I have nothing I can have that I will ever want, only some love, only dearness & tenderness, to make me weep. . . . I have descended depths beyond depths into my own personality, even to the point of exhibition, of self-pity that is not self pity but knowledge of tragedy. Neal, how can I change, what can I do? Don't you see that I cannot be composed, I cannot reconcile myself, because there is no other reality but loneliness for me and before I am dragged back into isolation I will clasp and grasp and claw in fright even at you without consciousness—even I—and I am afraid that I cannot survive if I have to go on into myself. . . . Is not my state so wretched that you who once loved me cannot think of me without guilt. Or if it is guilt that will call you, then guilt, I am not so strong that I can afford to choose my weapons. Didn't you first come to me, seduce me—don't you remember how you made me stop trembling in shame and drew me to you? Do you know what I felt then, as if you were a saint, inhuman, to have touched me so, and comforted me, even deceived me a moment in my naieveté to think I was loved. I remember that night, and it is so sad now in my mind, to think that it did happen, if once, that I think of death and only death afterwards. Do you think I am lying again? I don't mean Death as suicide, I mean the unknown, the unforseen, the horrible.

I would go on and on but in my eye I am afraid that all my emotions will only bore you and that you will turn from me with every pleading phrase, I am afraid that you could and this leaves me now as I end, speaking to you, sitting here, waiting in silence, speaking to you no more o god neal please Come back don't be harsh on me I can't help this I can only apologise and beg and beg and beg.

Allen Ginsberg

# ▼ EROS AND HONESTY ▼

[PIER PAOLO PASOLINI & FRANCO FAROLFI]
*Translated from Italian by Stuart Hood*

Pier Paolo Pasolini (1922–75) was a transgressor. His teaching career was ruined in 1949 when political enemies publicized his homosexuality, leading to his trial for seducing three teenage boys, expulsion from the Communist Party and loss of his teaching post. His life on the sexual fringes in Rome is portrayed in his early novels *Ragazzi di Vita* and *Una vita violenta*, and most notably in his provocative film *Salo, or The 120 Days of Sodom*, an analysis of Fascism in terms of sexual sadism. The erotic films *Trilogy of Life* made him famous in the 1970s, and portrayed a world of sexual innocence, paralleling his own longing for an uncomplicated life with "bands of twenty-year-old youths who laugh with their innocent male voices and take no notice of the world around them, continuing along their lives, filling the night with their shouts." His film work, such as the mystical-ideological *Teorema*, was complemented by numerous controversial articles advocating political and religious reform. A large volume of his homoerotic poetry, including a cycle written for Ninetto Davoli the cute actor who appeared in his films, has not been published.

Pasolini had many brief encounters in the suburban cinemas of Rome, in Trastevere, on building sites, and regularly on the via del Tritone. In November 1975 he was murdered by a piece of rough trade he had picked up in Ostia, seventeen-year-old Pino the Frog, who beat him with a nail-encrusted board and then ran over him with a sports car. The Communists claimed he was killed by the Fascists, who had staged the encounter with the hustler to discredit him. This is probably wishful thinking by intellectuals who find a politically motivated death less disturbing than sexual violence. The letters selected relate to Pasolini's first public disgrace which led to his repudiation of hypocrisy, and are written to Franco Farolfi, his "dearest companion" in his first year at the Galvani *liceo* in Bologna, where Pasolini's family moved in 1937–38; and to Silvana Mauri, the only woman Pasolini said he "could have loved," a kind of Madonna figure to him, who had written to express her grief at the trial reports in the newspapers.

---

PIER PAOLO PASOLINI TO FRANCO FAROLFI

*[Casarsa*
*September 1948]*

Dear Franco,

You don't know what a comfort and what sort of happiness you gave me with your letter. I have been on the point of answering a thousand times to the one in which you alerted me to your illness and have never been capa-

258

ble of doing so, not from cowardice but from selfishness. Perhaps I was happy, who knows, I don't remember. Now that at least potentially you too are at peace and full of life I can treat you as an equal and reply to you even in the maddest. The first thing to say to you is this: I feel as never before my friendship for you, I very much desire to see you. . . .

I have come to the end of that period in life when one feels wise for having overcome crises or satisfied certain terrible (sexual) needs of adolescence and of first youth. I feel like trying again to give myself once more illusions and desires; I am definitely a little Villon or a little Rimbaud. In such a state of mind if I were to find a friend I could even go to Guatemala or to Paris.

For some years now my homosexuality has entered into my consciousness and my habits and is no longer Another within me. I had had to overcome scruples, moments of irritation and of honesty . . . but finally, perhaps bloody and covered with scars, I have managed to survive, getting the best of both worlds, that is to say eros and honesty.

Try to understand me at once and without too many reservations; it is a cape I must round without hope of turning back. Do you accept me? Good. I am very different from your friend of school and university, am I not? But perhaps much less than you think . . .

Dear Franco, thank fate for your reappearance (by the way are you bald? I warn you that you reappeared to me "blond"), I am full of freshness and expectancy.

An affectionate hug,
Pier Paolo

---

*[Casarsa*
*31 December 1949]*

Dearest Franco,

I shall write to you at length in a few days; meanwhile two words. I have lost my teaching post because of a scandal in Friuli following a charge made against me of the corruption of minors.

Fortunately we wrote to each other this autumn so the business will cause you less surprise. The thing that cost me the ruin of my career and this tremendous biographical jolt is not in itself very serious; it was all a put-up job due to political reasons. The Christian Democrats and the Fascists seized the occasion [brief membership in the Communist Party] to get rid of me and did it with repugnant cynicism and skill. But I'll tell you about that another time.

Today is the last day of the year; I have nothing before me, I am unemployed—absolutely without any hope of work; my father is in the physical and moral condition you know of. A suicidal atmosphere. I am working furiously at a novel on which I am building all my hopes including practical ones; I know they are mad hopes but in a kind of way they fill me. In my condition I naturally could not come to Parma. Who knows now when we shall see each other again and I am very sorry because I still feel that I am very fond of you.

    A kiss,

        Pier Paolo

---

PIER PAOLO PASOLINI TO SILVANA MAURI

*Rome*
*10 February 1950*

Dearest Silvana,

    . . . I cannot yet manage to pass judgement on myself not even, as would be easy, to give a negative judgement, but I think it was inevitable. You ask me to speak to you truthfully and *with a sense of shame*; I shall do so, Silvana, but when we *talk*, if it is possible to talk with a sense of shame in a case like mine: perhaps I have partly done it in my poetry. Now since I have been in Rome I just have to sit at my typewriter for me to tremble and not know even what to think; the words seem to have lost their meaning. I can only tell you that the ambiguous life—as you rightly say—which I led in Casarsa I shall continue to lead in Rome. And if you think about the etymology of ambiguous you will see that someone who leads a double existence can only be ambiguous.

    . . . it is not possible for me nor will it ever be possible to speak of myself with shame: and instead it will be necessary often to stand in the pillory because I do not want to deceive anyone—as basically I deceived you and other friends who talk about an old Pier Paolo or of a Pier Paolo who has to be a new self.

I do not know what to understand by hypocrisy but now I am in terror of it. Enough half-words—the scandal has to be faced, I think St. Paul said . . . I think in this connection that I want to live in Rome precisely because here I shall be neither an old nor a new Pier Paolo. Those who like me have been fated not to love according to the rules end up by overvaluing the question of love. A normal person can resign himself—that terrible word—to chastity, to lost opportunities, but in me the difficulty in loving has made the need for love obsessive: the function made the organ hypertrophic when, as an adolescent, love seemed to me an unattainable chimera: then when with experience the function had resumed its proper proportions and the chimera had been deconsecrated to the point of being the most miserable daily matter, the evil was already inoculate, chronic and incurable. I found myself with an enormous mental organ for a function which by now is so negligible that only yesterday—with all my misfortunes and my fits of remorse—there was an uncontainable despair for a boy sitting on a low wall and left behind for all time and in all places by the tram as it went along. As you see I am talking to you with extreme sincerity and I do not know with how much shame. Here in Rome I can find more easily than elsewhere the way of living ambiguously, do you understand? and at the same time the way of being entirely sincere, of not deceiving anyone as I would end up doing in Milan: perhaps I am telling you this because I am discouraged and place you by yourself on the pedestal of someone who is able to understand and feel for me: but the fact is that up to now I have not found anyone as sincere as I would wish. The sexual life of others has always made me ashamed of mine: is the wrong all on my side? It seems impossible to me. Understand me, Silvana, what I have most at heart is to be clear to myself and to others—with a clarity that has no half measures, is ferocious. It is the only way to make me forgive that terrifyingly honest and good boy which someone in me continues to be. . . . I intend to work and to love, both desperately. But then you will ask if what has happened to me—punishment, as you rightly call it—has been of no use to me. Yes, it has been of use but not to change me and even less to redeem me; but it was of use to me to understand that I had touched bottom, that the experience had been exhausted and I could begin from the beginning but without repeating the same mistakes; I have liberated myself from my iniquitous and fossil perversion, now I feel lighter and my libido is a cross, no longer a weight that drags me down to the depths. . . . There are moments when life is open like a fan, you see everything in it, and then it is fragile, insecure and too vast. In my statements and in my confessions try to catch a glimpse of this totality. My future life will certainly not be that of a university professor; by now I bear the mark of Rimbaud, or Campana [Dino Campana, 1885–1932, called "an Italian Rimbaud," who died in a mental home] and also of Wilde, whether I want it or not, whether others accept it or not. It is something uncomfortable, annoying and inadmissible, but that is how it is; and I, like you, do not *give in*. . . . I have suffered what can be suffered, I have never accepted my sin, I have never come to terms with my nature and have not even become used to it. I was born to be calm, balanced and natural; my homosexuality was something additional, was outside, had nothing to do with me. I always saw it alongside me like an enemy, I never felt it within me. Only in this last year I let myself go to some extent; . . . the search for an immediate pleasure, a pleasure to die in, was the only escape. I have been punished for it without pity. But this too we shall talk about or else I shall write to you about it more calmly, now I have too many things to say to you; I shall add right away in this connection a detail: it was at Belluno when I was three and a half (my brother was not yet born) that I felt for the first time that most sweet and violent attraction which then remained within me—always the same, blind and sinister like a fossil.

It did not yet have a name but was so strong and irresistible that I had to invent one myself: it was "teta veleta" [perhaps meaning "hidden tit"] and I write it for you trembling, so much does this terrible name invented by a child of three in love with a boy of thirteen frighten me—this name which belongs to the fetish, the primordial, the disgusting and the affectionate. . . .

---

*[Rome*
*February 1950]*

Dear Franco,

I have taken a long time to reply to you and am now doing so because it would be shameful if I postponed it again. But I do not feel like talking to you about my case, I am fed up with it, overburdened. Perhaps you are dramatizing the scandal a little too much; its importance is purely practical in that I am left without a job, without hope of work, and with my family in the condition you know of. Yes, the most serious problem is now that of finding any kind of job, even as a worker. . . . As for the scandal, I have digested it; after all I had a right to this scandal, didn't I? In this world incredible things like this happen. Think what a frightening mechanism can form in the brain of an unfortunate like me: sex-prison, love—having one's face spat at, tenderness—the brand of infamy. . . .

And you? Your girls, about whom you talked to me so candidly without knowing that for me every word on the subject was a mortal wound? Have you solved it, the insoluble problem of sex? It is a figure which increases in a geometric progression with each unit you subtract from it; only with death will the zeros turn up. . . .

# ▼ THE PROMISED LAND ▼

[WILLIAM BURROUGHS & KIKI]

The growth of respectability in American (and British) life in the late 1940s and 1950s probably contributed to the pressure cooker which burst in the Gay Liberation movement in the 1960s. Many gay men realized how futile it was to attempt to achieve a facade of conventionality in the face of such rigorous monitoring of lifestyles that were at all different from the norm. William Burroughs (1913–1997), like many, simply turned traditional behaviour on its head, and sought for paradise in places like Tangier, from where he wrote to Allen Ginsberg on December 13, 1954: "It's like I can't breathe in the U.S., especially in suburban communities. Palm Beach is a real horror. No slums, no dirt, no poverty. God what a fate to live there!"

In places like Mexico, Peru and Morocco, amongst junkies, queers, and expatriates, a whole generation of drop-outs from middle-class America found the freedom to be themselves and the energy and inspiration to revitalize American (and European) literature. In 1955 Burroughs used his own letters and fragments of letters, including gay love letters, in a chapter of *Naked Lunch*, cutting them up and rearranging them in the "mosaic" technique for which he became famous. Burroughs and Ginsberg wrote frequently to one another, sharing their drug-induced insights and experimental writings, and their experiences with boys. Burroughs, who felt that Ginsberg's relationship with Neal Cassady was "a cul-de-sac of the soul," had far more satisfactory affairs because he did not demand that the indigenous boys fall madly in love with him in return. His relationship with his boy Kiki in Tangier, discussed in the letters below, lasted for three years, until Kiki was murdered by a jealous former lover in September 1957, a Cuban singer (a "frantic old fruit") who found him with a girl.

---

WILLIAM BURROUGHS TO ALLEN GINSBERG

*May 12, 1953*
*Gran Hotel Bolívar*
*Lima, Peru*

Dear Allan,

. . . Lima is the promised land for boys. I never saw anything like it since Vienna in '36. But you have to keep an eye on the little bastards or they'll steal all your fucking valuables. (I lost my watch and $15 in the service.) Oh well the watch didn't run anyway. I never had one that did. I have not seen here any queer bars (hope I don't see any), but in the bars around the Mercado Mayorista—Main Market—any boy is wise and available to the Yankee dollar. Last night I checked into a hotel with a beautiful Indian to the great amusement of the hotel clerk and his friends. (I don't think the average U.S. hotel clerk would be amused at such an occurrence.) Yes, they have Yage here and a short trip from Lima. I plan to go when I finish the Yage section. . . .

WILLIAM BURROUGHS TO JACK KEROUAC

*[August 18, 1954*
*Tangier]*

Dear Jack,

. . . Kiki has confiscated all my clothes and intends to cure me of the habit. I also have various new, substitute preparations prescribed me by a good German Jewish, refugee doctor. So I have hopes of success with Kiki here to care for me, and to provide the appropriate amenities when I start coming off in my pants (I have no pants)—spontaneous orgasms being one of the few agreeable features of the withdrawal syndrome. And not limited to single orgasm, one can continue, with adolescent ardor, through three or four climaxes. Usually you are too weak to go out and find a "love object" as the analysts call them. (When you are coming off the junk, I mean, you don't feel up to looking around for sex.) Sounds so passionless, like, "I found a pretty hot 'object' last night." I find myself getting jealous of Kiki—he is besieged by importunate queens. In fact I am downright involved, up to my neck in Maya [illusion]. He is a sweet kid, and it is so pleasant to loll about in the afternoon smoking tea, sleeping and having sex with no hurry, running leisurely hands over his lean, hard body, and finally we doze off, all wrapped around each other, into the delicious sleep of a hot afternoon in a cool, darkened room, a sleep that is different from any other sleep, a twilight in which I savour, with a voluptuous floating sensation, the state of sleep, feeling the nearness of Kiki's young body, the sweet, imperceptible, drawing together in sleep, leg inching over leg, arm encompassing body, hips hitching closer, stiffening organs reaching out to touch warm flesh.

Jack, I would think twice before giving up sex. It's a basic kick and when it's good as it can be it's *good*. . . .

WILLIAM BURROUGHS TO ALLEN GINSBERG

*August 26 [1954*
*Tangier]*

Dear Allen,

. . . Most definitive reason to stay here is Kiki. Lately I want him with me all the time. I found out last night that I love him. He comes in late last night. I had been sleeping, still drowsy, not digging exactly what he says. Suddenly I realize he is describing in ghastly detail the designs he proposes to have tattooed on the beautiful, copper-brown skin of his chest, and shoulders and arms. I run my hands over it by the hour while he purrs in sleep like a contented cat.

So I had hysterics, cried and kissed and begged him not to do it. "It's like you were going to put a plug in your lip, or a ring in your nose, or knock out your front teeth to put in gold teeth—" (Some of the Arabs do this)—"It's a desecration!" He was finally impressed by my intensity. I gave him my last sport coat, and my other pair of pants (I have nothing left now but my combat jacket, one pair of slacks, and that odd sort of costume jewelry cheap brown coat from the chic-est shop on Worth Ave. in Palm Beach), and ten $ I could ill-afford, to *promise* me *never* to have himself tattooed. I was shocked into an awareness that in a way I love him. Now I know I should not allow myself to be emotionally involved. He doesn't understand and looks at me in bewilderment when I embrace him with special intensity.

It is so exasperating. I can't really get near him. I feel all-out attempt to do so would be disastrous for me. I know I should let matters rest in status of liaison, fond of him in an off-hand way, but no involvements, and no risk of hurt. But it's so dull like that. I notice the sex is much more enjoyable since I feel some variety of love for him.

---

WILLIAM BURROUGHS TO JACK KEROUAC

*Dec. 7, 1954*
*Tanger [sic]*

Dear Jack,

Just a line to tell you I am back in the Promised Land flowing with junk and boys. The trip was rough, but by sheer will power I managed to sleep straight through to Gibraltar, waking up only to eat occasionally. Been spending 15–20 hours a day in bed with Kiki catching up on my back screwing. He is really a treasure, my dear. So sweet and affectionate but at the same time indubitably male. . . .

Colin Spencer (*b.* 1933) in a photo of June 1956 taken by Billy the Vicar at the pool of the Villa Bantoc, Cap Ferrat, France.

# ▼ MY HEART IS BREAKING ▼

[COLIN SPENCER & JOHN TASKER]

Colin Spencer (born in London in 1933) has written nine novels, notably *Anarchists in Love* (1963) and *Poppy Mandragora and the New Sex* (1966), several plays, and a dozen books about food, including a history of vegetarianism, *The Heretic Feast*, and *The Faber Book of Food* (1994). He is a journalist and broadcaster, and an occasional contributor to Britain's *Gay Times*. He met John Tasker in Brighton in 1957 while studying at the art school (he later got a good job illustrating for the *Times Literary Supplement*). Both aged twenty-four, they shared a love of literature and the theatre, and had a passionate affair. But Spencer felt "suffocated" by their living together, and soon he was having other affairs (usually with wealthy elderly gentlemen, for he was a very beautiful young man), and he left for Paris. Later at the Villa Bantoc, Cap Ferrat, Billy, his sugar daddy, took nude photos of Spencer by the pool, but asked him and his other young guests to remain out of sight when Somerset Maugham came to tea.

Spencer and Tasker again lived together for six months in Vienna, in a flat paid for by a closet gay American diplomat whom Spencer obliged with a striptease, but again Spencer required a "breather" from the relationship. They exchanged passionate love letters until Spencer married the archaeologist Gillian Chapman in October 1959. He wanted a family and a son, but recognized later that his marriage was also "my rebellion against what society did to gay people. Sadly, I fought it with a conventional weapon. I can remember clearly wanting John, but clearly not wanting us as a gay relationship."

Tasker went to Australia and became a very successful theatre director, but never lived with anyone again. He died of cancer in 1988, and had made arrangements for Spencer's letters to be returned to him after his death. Spencer re-read their correspondence of thirty years earlier, and decided to publish it in atonement for having thrown away his only true love. His introduction to *Which of Us Two? The Story of a Love Affair* (1990) is full of bitter recrimination: "However much I now analyse my motives I am still left with the vile suspicion that I murdered a love that should have been nurtured, that I destroyed that which should never have been destroyed. I had the youthful temerity to think such a fiery and intense relationship could occur again, grow perhaps even more powerful through the years; but nothing like John ever did appear again, or had any chance, for if Gods exist I have shown myself to be a wastrel and could not be trusted."

COLIN SPENCER TO JOHN TASKER

*18:vi:57*

My Dear John,

I suppose it is difficult for you as it is for me to write this letter, what to say and how much to say, the adroit inference that is self-consciously planned. It is all vastly complicated and I can't pretend to understand a quarter of it. One has, of course, a few clues. (1) I miss you. That is only natural, I suppose, but worse, I feel miserable without you and regret the times I was unkind and certain. That again is only human. (2) I keep on seeing you everywhere I go in Brighton, your head or hands or body appear suddenly, flash forward and then I hear your voice. I am full of ghosts. And then there is (3) it is not enough to remember, but my mind insists upon recreating moments we should have experienced and wondering if life is going to allow us to. Like midnight bathing . . .

I bathed naked in a warm and darkened sea in the early hours of this morning and this afternoon bathed in the same sea, naked again. I'm brown all over. . . .

I am too dazed and quite unable to make plans. I hope we shall be able to see each other again soon.

    C.

---

JOHN TASKER TO COLIN SPENCER

*London SE 14*
*[19 June 1957]*

My Dear Colin,

It seems very strange to see your name beginning this letter. All last week I took pleasure whenever there was an immediate contact between us. That meant judging your mood of that moment, watching your first reaction. That, I take most delight in, the moment when an idea bridges two people, an electric moment when a word, an idea, without necessarily being deep, joins one to another, when the word doesn't have to be formed and spoken, then it is even more exhilarating. That happened between us many more times than once I think.

In comparison a letter is a poor substitute. What I thought might happen is happening. I already distrust and disbelieve all that I felt we achieved when we were together. Why? I'm not quite sure. Perhaps there wasn't a strong link forged? Perhaps it's an unconscious effort at protection in case *you* no longer believe in it. . . .

Send me a sane letter. Or even flippant. Not earnest like this one.

    Warmly, love,

        John.

COLIN SPENCER TO JOHN TASKER

*[21 June 1957]*

My Dear John,

What a strange and curious letter.

Why should you be afraid of such a normal reaction to last week? We may well go down in a cataclysm of thunder, guts and tears and having nothing at the end of it all to remember. I don't think life bothers or even worries about what we secretly want. It gives us something quite different from what we asked for. And then of course one can always play that delightful game of adaptability. When one is about ninety, bald, paunchy and addled (and maybe wise) one can't cry like the young or long like the frustrated because one has "adapted" to oneself. And that is probably a living death. Which is all to say that if you want something enough, scream for it until you get it, don't, don't be reasonable. Love is rare enough after all, for one to tear one's own guts out in order to get it. And we all play that game in some degree or other. You know I believe, think, feel, that something real did happen last week. I don't think I've doubted it once. But I think it can die through undernourishment quickly.

So if you can, and if you can bear to see me washing, ironing, packing, why don't you come down next weekend? I leave on the Monday.

C.

---

JOHN TASKER TO COLIN SPENCER

*London SE 14*
*[23 June 1957]*

Dear Colin,

. . . I was in a daze all last week. I couldn't get you from my mind, I was more than miserable. And I felt frustrated, that we were so far apart and that, at that moment, if we had been together we could have been very happy. I found myself looking for you in the streets, in cafés, at the theatre, hoping by some strange quirk of chance you had been able to come up to town. . . .

Colin, liebchen, I never doubted what happened last week. I simply couldn't stop wondering if it had affected you as it had me. I was afraid to say—I want to be with you—see, here I'm shying, because I really want to say, I love you. And that is true. I *want* us to find time to explore that because we would be very happy very often.

Last week, for the first time for *many* months I gained confidence in myself. That was your work. You did it in many ways. Summer started last week.

I'm coming down at the weekend if it's still all right. I'll give you a hand in packing and preparing. Please, though, not too much of that. Leave some time for lying in the sun, bathing and being happy. . . .

John

COLIN SPENCER TO JOHN TASKER

*Lido di Venezia*
*8:vii:57*

Darling—

I love you, I love you, I love you and I miss you and I want you and I don't like it at all. All the things I have I find I want to share with you and then you're not there.

The heat is intolerable, the sea like a hot bath, at night sleep is almost unbearable and at the moment I still haven't seen Venice, but I will in an hour. So I'll write tomorrow and tell you the first impressions. Oh, darling, why are you such a long way away? Last week I wasn't sure of anything. This week I'm sure of too much. But I simply want to be with you. I think I enjoyed those last two days as I have never enjoyed anything before.

Write to me quickly for I'm starved of hearing from you, parched and desolate.

Love,
C.

---

JOHN TASKER TO COLIN SPENCER

*London*
*[July 1957]*

My dear Colin,

. . . Sweet, I want us to be so very happy. And I want us to be resilient to mistakes and upsets and difficulties. We know each other as yet under ideal conditions—lots of free time, sun, money to spend. I want so to strengthen the bonds between us so that they could take the strain when conditions are far from perfect. And I want to see that area of common ground on which we meet extend and grow. It would kill me to watch it shrink away.

And I want to learn to accept you as you are without in any way wanting to change you into what I might want you to be. For me that will be hard!

I love you sweetheart. Darling. Very much. Come back very soon.

My love, my thoughts and even more.
John

---

COLIN SPENCER TO JOHN TASKER

*Croydon*
*16:xii:57*

My Darling,

I have never known this ever before—I cannot think of anything else all day and most of the night, but you. Do you believe me? I wouldn't write it if it wasn't true—I'm sunk in a perpetual gloom writing letters to you in my mind longing for the sound of your voice and the touch of your body.

I think it is driving me a little mad. And when I say every minute, I mean literally that. I can't write a thing, if I force myself I feel I am breaking inside—the only time I forget *you* is sometimes at the theatre or the cinema but three-quarters of that time is spent in things which jar you back into my memory. I need you, need you desperately. I feel my heart is very slowly breaking and with such pain.

John, are you coming back here soon after Xmas? I'm only a little nearer to getting a job, but I think I'm having an interview at the BBC tomorrow —I only hope I land something worthwhile. And where are you going to spend Xmas? I can't send you a present now, it's too late. I hope you'll be in Schwarz but I don't know the address, and I'm frightened this letter will take a long time in the Xmas rush and you won't get it for some time— I'm terrified too that my going away has lost you for ever.

Please sweetheart, I want very much to make you happy and if you come back I'll do everything I can for you even to drowning all the sugar dads that ever was in a large sack like a litter of kittens.

I'm abysmally unhappy without you. I'm quite sexless too, I haven't come for a week and I don't think I've had a hard on either. My body belongs to you and wants you as much as I hope your body needs mine.

One more thing: if you find it and think it really impossible for you to leave Vienna. Then somehow we must think again and I'll get out there. I know, I've just got to be with you. I know it more every day.

I don't want *us* to be destroyed. Because of my fault we have come perilously near it.

I love you with all my body, with all my heart and I think now it must be, with all my soul.

     Colin

---

JOHN TASKER TO COLIN SPENCER

*August '59*

Colin Colin my dear dear Darling,

If I don't keep writing to you I'll go round the bend. Oh sweetheart, I couldn't go to sleep at all last night, I lay there thinking of you and you married and the end of everything we stood for and I writhed and tossed in bed the whole night. Somewhere about dawn I must have finally gone to sleep for an hour.

Sweetheart, what what what is happening to us? Darling, time and time again you've written that you wanted to come out here [Australia], that this would be a big adventure, that the last anniversary would be the last one apart and then this letter, this terrible one that burns a hole in my pocket, and that like some crazy hypnotized thing I must read and read again.

Darling, your decision—can I really call it a decision?—affects us tremendously, nullifies what I hoped would be a fruition of two years together, would be recompense for all this intense pain and longing and

272 / Colin Spencer & John Tasker

loneliness.

Darling, could you really love me and still rush into this? You've been seeing Jill how long now again? Is it so urgent that you must marry immediately? If only for me, for the barest peace of mind I can have, please delay it a little. Please. These roots you speak of, that you need. What are they essentially? Security? Love? Understanding? Belonging? These you had with me. Surely you don't want to *settle* down already, a married man with a house and all the attendant pulls that castrate work? You know that with me you did your best work, that it came to a kind of fruition with me. All that exciting vital life we'd planned—Australia, the islands, the States, Europe, Italy. Does that come to nothing? For us both those few days in Italy meant so much because *we* were together. We give things meaning. Jill can too I'm sure, but can she give you that deep meaning *and* coat everything done and seen and touched with that glaze of *fire* that we did? You said that you didn't find that bonfire with her. You said we had lit one which shouldn't go out. Darling, don't let it go out. We lit a fire which illumined everything and, oddly enough, was a guiding light to others. There is so much to be done and now you are the only person I can do it with. How can you be so cruel as to qualify us; I am the only *boy* you have ever loved so deeply. Only *boy*! But not counting girls? Not counting Jill? Darling, that is an untruth. A terrible blatant untruth. Be honest. What was *is*—yes is still—vivid and savage is between us, joining us. And darling, it is not to be found again. I have this nether region, neither dark, nor light. Living and half living it certainly is. Darling, you can't suddenly not be in love with me. Did you lie or exaggerate in those loving letters that came so recently?

Please darling, come here to see me. If only for two weeks. I've already set things in motion so that you can easily come for the shortest time. Darling, this you owe to me. Please have enough sensibility to wait and to try to see me. . . . Can you imagine how hurt I am now? And have you no responsibility towards me? To me who is as much a part of your body as your arms, as much a part of your being as the air you breathe? Darling, do not let me go mad.

# ▼ WE'LL CHANGE THE WORLD ▼

[ALLEN GINSBERG & PETER ORLOVSKY]

Allen Ginsberg (whose correspondence with Neal Cassady is in a previous selection) met Peter Orlovsky (born 1933) in San Francisco in 1954. It was the first time Ginsberg had an affair with someone who was not primarily heterosexual, and their relationship was unusually frank and open, "completely giving and taking." Ginsberg immediately determined that Orlovsky would be his "life-long love; I was completely enamored and intoxicated—just the right person for me, I thought." Orlovsky has been an ambulance attendant, psychiatric nurse, and handyman in a wide range of jobs to earn money for very extensive travels. He describes himself as a "nut tree farmer, poet-teacher-singer" at the Jack Kerouac School of Disembodied Poetics at the Naropa Institute in Boulder, Colorado.

What Ginsberg called their "marriage" lasted from 1954 to Ginsberg's death in 1997, though its terms changed over more than forty years, surviving the upheavals of freaking out on drugs in the 1960s through the strains caused by Ginsberg's worldwide fame. It went through many phases and they ended up "independent" though together, with Orlovsky sleeping mostly with girls but sometimes again with Ginsberg. "But the origin of our relationship is a fond affection. I wouldn't want to go to heaven and leave Peter alone on earth; and he wouldn't leave me alone if I was sick in bed, dying, gray-haired, wormy, rheumatic."

---

ALLEN GINSBERG TO PETER ORLOVSKY

*Chambre 25*
*Paris 6 France*
*January 20, 1958*

Dear Petey:

O Heart O Love everything is suddenly turned to gold! Don't be afraid don't worry the most astounding beautiful thing has happened here! I don't know where to begin but the most important. When Bill [Burroughs] came I, we, thought it was the same old Bill mad, but something had happened to Bill in the meantime since we last saw him. . . . but last night finally Bill & I sat down facing each other across the kitchen table and looked eye to eye and talked, I confessed all my doubt and misery—and in front of my eyes he turned into an Angel!

What happened to him in Tangiers this last few months? It seems he stopped writing and sat on his bed all afternoons thinking and meditating alone & stopped drinking—and finally dawned on his consciousness, slowly and repeatedly, every day, for several months—awareness of "a benevolent sentient (feeling) center to the whole Creation"—he had apparently, in his own way, what I have been so hung up on in myself and you, a vision

273

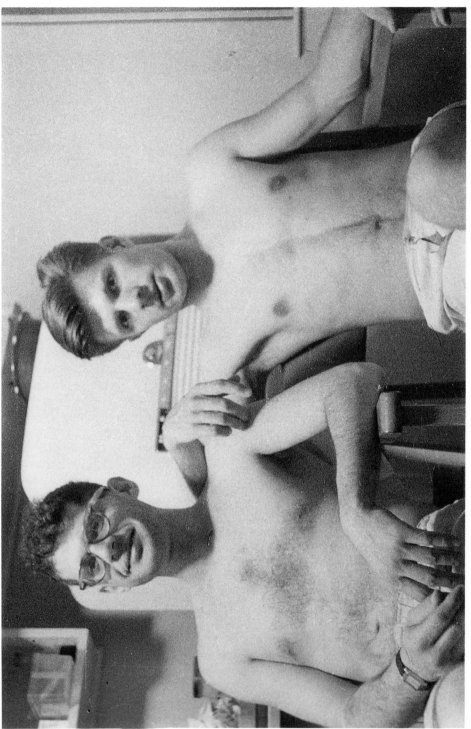

Allen Ginsberg and Peter Orlovsky, San Francisco, 1955.

of big peaceful Lovebrain—said it gave him (came sort of like a revelation slowly) courage to look at his whole life, me, him more dispassionately. . . . We talked a long time got into tremendous rapport, very delicate, I almost trembled, a rapport much like yours and mine, but not sexual, he even began to dig my feelings about that, my willingness but really I don't want to, has stopped entirely putting pressure on me for bed—the whole nightmare's cleared up overnight, I woke this morning with great bliss of freedom & joy in my heart, Bill's saved, I'm saved, you're saved, we're all saved, everything has been all rapturous ever since—I only feel sad that perhaps you left as worried when we waved goodby and kissed so awkwardly—I wish I could have that over to say goodby to you happier & without the worries & doubts I had that dusty dusk when you left . . . —Bill is changed nature, I even feel much changed, great clouds rolled away, as I feel when you and I were in rapport, well our rapport has remained in me, with me, rather than losing it, I'm feeling to everyone, something of the same as between us. And you? What's happening inside Dear Pete? I read Bill your poems, I'll type them & send them soon, everything is happening so fast. I feel like I can write even. Are you OK? Write me happy letter, don't be sad, I love you, nothing can change love, beautiful love, once we have it. . . .

---

PETER ORLOVSKY TO ALLEN GINSBERG

*[On board ship*
*returning to New York]*
*Jan 22, 58*

Dear Allen:

On the ship, close to home, at night, full turky stomache sadness on my face but finally read through the brothers K[aramazov] & see the same madness in my famiely. Have been very quite, sick half the time from the bellybutton waves but eating marvously & to boot havent smoked much at all & to boot have this nice typewritter to type to yo . . . . I know I goofed with Bill being so silent as if crying inside my throught, yes I gess I am meek, like you say. But at the end of eternity theres nothing to be imbarresed about. . . . Love Bill like I love you, be a chair for him to sit on and for him to talk prouldly from—Bill seems more like a brother now then a farther with stern eyes in Tangers. Bill got roses in his teeth. I took a one hour shower yesterday & used to much water that the hall was soken wet twenty people nocked on my door in fright but I kept singing along till cleaned & wash all dirty clothes. Have had two wet dreams so far, did not masterbate once & feel good about that for I must stop that habit for its insulting to my cock. . . . On the frist day out I saw land in the sky & thought it was real. It was only till I left you & Bill to get on train did I feel lonely sadness pains and crying in my throught but now I feel better. tho when I left you I felt our friendship was like sunset dust floating & seper-

ating away—young young young saw flying fish with red boots on. . . .
Someone wants the typewritter so must move on off. I feel very good &
confident things will work out well. . . .

---

PETER ORLOVSKY TO ALLEN GINSBERG

*[New York]*
*Feb 10, 58*

Dear Allen:

Great piece of news this morning; got job in Psychiatric MST—start
work Thursday—all dressed in white again—felt great relief when found
out I could work there—of course its a far cry from dream ambulance attendant job I said I would get on pay—but $60 is ok . . . I have to get bite
to eat honney—I cant continue write now—can you read my handwritting
—no patience—darn coffee at apt—?? go go go go—help—tea with limon
—but I do feel good and so dont worry dear Allen things are going ok—
we'll change the world yet to our dessire—even if we got to die—but OH
the world's got 25 rainbows on my window sill. . . .

---

ALLEN GINSBERG TO PETER ORLOVSKY

*Feb. 15, 1958*
*London*

Dear Peter:

Got your letter yesterday, was so happy to receive it and your sweet sex
talk. I had been running around with mad mean poets & world-eaters here
& was longing for kind words from heaven which you wrote, came as fresh
as a summer breeze & "when I think on thee dear friend / all losses are restored & sorrows end," came over & over in my mind—it's the end of a
Shakespeare Sonnet—he must have been happy in love too. I had never
realized that before. . . .

O.K. I'll wrap this up. Write me soon baby, I'll write you big long poem
I feel as if you were god that I pray to—

   Love
      Allen

---

ALLEN GINSBERG TO PETER ORLOVSKY

*[London]*
*Feb. 24, 1958*

Dear Peter:

. . . Sure miss you, as if a golden soul of me were still there, to think on,
floating six feet above ground across the Atlantic (I feel your ball of soft
fire in the room a near presence summoned up by a thot sometimes)—keep
thinking of Shakespeare sonnet "But when I think on thee dear friend /
all losses are restored and sorrows end." Got all your letters now, including last airgram Feb. 19. . . . I'm making it all right here, but I miss you,

your arms & nakedness & holding each other—life seems emptier without you, the soulwarmth isn't around, only lots of energy, I do a lot—as in England I read wildly & saw lots of people & did something to hop poesy there, it will have an effect I'm sure once they broadcast that BBC record, open the floodgates in London maybe, for new feeling in poetry there—it's all so deadened now & insincere. But I feel alone without you Peter, I already daydream with tears of how sweet we'll be, meeting again, in summer, it seems a short time off. . . .

Bill thinks new American generation will be hip & will slowly change things—laws & attitudes, he has hope there—for some redemption of America, finding its soul. But we are so run by competition and deception, there is no possibility of men being true, even to their dear wives—you have to love all life, not just parts, to make the eternal scene, that's what I think since we've made it, more & more I see it isn't just between us, it's feeling that can [be] extended to everything. Tho I long for the actual sunlight contact between us I miss you like a home. Shine back honey & think of me. Find anybody in NY? Maybe also we have some mad balls in NY when we end the summer. . . .

Goodbye Mr February.
as tender as ever
swept with warm rain
love from your Allen

---

PETER ORLOVSKY TO ALLEN GINSBERG

*[New York]*
*April 22, 58*

Dear Allen:

. . . Hi Allen—hay-ho doll—come on over and blow me you sexy ass of yours under the sheets that I feel all the time—right there between my hands—I miss the shoe shine you'd give my cock!—God—you know I've layd nobody since we last made it together—God for all I know my cock may be getting rusty like a dusty kings crown in dewy dungen—I'm sick of all this crying—the world is never going to end all this sadness—I'm going to marry good woman & grow my own love army . . .

---

PETER ORLOVSKY TO ALLEN GINSBERG

*[New York]*
*June 23, '60*

Dear Allen with dark Indian Death Eyes:

. . . I also thought, Yesterday, that you (in yr last letter said our Peyote High scared you when I laffed) feel I do harm to myself if we seperated & you get married (children) or I get mad at you & so I think now what ever we do (weather I turn into cockerroch cralling along 1st Ave coblestones & get Xed by truck) (both get married or just you) (as you fell in love

with John Weiners or bring back new boy friend from Lima as you want
to go away alone by yr self to india hill cave—or sit on my cock & talk it
over & lay down & do it again, as you get married & I take care of yr baby
while you blink in Jungle Storms or open the door & say "Now Peter you
just cant stay around & do notheing all the time"—or be happey to each
other at important times—maybe I am yr Child & you dont know it
Allen—Allen I love you, Allen, Please Allen give me a sapey (sap)
kiss—. . .

Write me more if you want I sail yr heart
       Love from 33 st. P.O. Peter
             by by now

# SOURCES AND ACKNOWLEDGMENTS

[This is to be considered as part of the Copyright page]

The editor wishes to express his gratitude to Alexandra Trone for her translations of letters by Federico Gonzaga and Pietro Aretino, Heinrich von Kleist, Johann Joachim Winckelmann, Johannes von Müller, and Jean Cocteau; and to Paul Schalow for his translation of the letter from a Buddhist priest. The editor and publisher are grateful for permission to reprint copyright material, as acknowledged in the following list.

**J. R. ACKERLEY:** Reprinted from *The Letters of J. R. Ackerley*, ed. Neville Braybrooke (London: Duckworth, 1975) by permission of Gerald Duckworth & Co. Ltd. Letters to Ackerley from Mahadeo Nayak and Johannes, from Peter Parker, *Ackerley: A Life of J. R. Ackerley* (London: Constable, 1989). **Hans Christian ANDERSEN:** *Hans Christian Andersen's Correspondence*, ed. Frederick Crawford (London: Dean & Son, 1891). **St. ANSELM:** To Gondulph and William, from St. Anselm, *Cur deus homo* (London: The Ancient & Modern Library of Theological Literature, [1889], prefatory Life signed R. C., probably Richard William Church, Dean of St. Paul's) [Text modernized for the present book]. **W. H. AUDEN:** Reprinted from *Auden in Love* by Dorothy J. Farnan (London and Boston: Faber and Faber Ltd., 1984) by permission of the publisher. **Brother AUGUSTINE:** *Norfolk News* (England), September 17, 1864. **Marcus AURELIUS and FRONTO:** *The Correspondence of Marcus Cornelius Fronto*, ed. C. R. Haines, 2 vols. (London: William Heinemann; New York: G. P. Putnam, 1919). **BAUDRI of Bourgeuil;** and **A SPANISH MONK:** Trans. copyright © 1984 Thomas Stehling, *Medieval Latin Poems of Male Love and Friendship* (New York and London: Garland Publishing, Inc., 1984). **William BECKFORD:** *Life at Fonthill 1807–1822, With Interludes in Paris and London, From the Correspondence of William Beckford*, trans. and ed. Boyd Alexander (London: Rupert Hart-Davis, 1957). **BO JUYI:** Trans. Howard S. Levy, *Translations from Po Chü-i's Collected Works*, 4 vols. (repr. New York, 1971); and Arthur Walley, *The Life and Times of Po Chü-i* (London: George Allen & Unwin, 1949). **Ernest BOULTON, Frederick William PARK, et al.:** William Roughead, *Bad Companions* (Edinburgh: W. Green & Son, 1930). **Rupert BROOKE:** Paul Delany, *The Neo-pagans: Friendship and Love in the Rupert Brooke Circle* (Macmillan London, 1987). **BUDDHIST PRIEST** to Okajima Uneme, trans. Paul Gordon Schalow, copyright © 1997 Gay Sunshine Press, Inc. **William BURROUGHS:** From *Letters of William S. Burroughs: 1945–1959* by William S. Burroughs, edited by Oliver Harris, copyright © 1993 by William S. Burroughs; Introduction copyright © 1993 by Oliver Harris; used by permission of Viking Penguin, a division of Penguin Books USA Inc. **Lord BYRON:** to Elizabeth Pigot, from Thomas Moore, *The Letters and Journals of Lord Byron*, rev. ed. (London: Chatto & Windus, 1875); and *The Works of Lord Byron: Letters, 1804–1813*, ed. William Ernest Henley (London: William Heinemann, 1897); to John Edleston and Francis Hodgson from *Byron's Letters and Journals*, ed. Leslie A. Marchand (London: John Murray, 1973). **John CHURCH:** *Religion & Morality Vindicated, Against Hypocrisy and Pollution; or, An Account of the Life and Character of John Church the Obelisk Preacher, Who Was Formerly A Frequenter of Vere-Street* (London, 1813). **Jean COCTEAU:** Jean Cocteau, *Lettres à Jean Marais*, © Albin Michel 1987, used by permission of the publishers Les éditions Albin Michel, Paris; English translation by Alexandra Trone. **Francisco CORREA Netto:** Translated by Luiz Mott and Aroldo Assunçao, "Love's Labours Lost: Five Letters from a Seventeenth-Century Portuguese Sodomite," in *The Pur-*

*suit of Sodomy: Male Homosexuality in Renaissance and Enlightenment Europe*, ed. Kent Gerard and Gert Hekma (New York: Harrington Park Press, Inc., 1989), pp. 91–101. Reprinted by permission of The Haworth Press, Inc., New York. **Baron CORVO (Frederick Rolfe):** *The Venice Letters*, ed. Cecil Woolf (London: Cecil & Amelia Woolf, 1974). **Hart CRANE:** *The Letters of Hart Crane 1916–1932*, ed. Brom Weber (New York: Hermitage House, 1952). **Countee CULLEN:** From the Alain Leroy Locke Papers, published by permission of the Moorland-Spingarn Research Center, Howard University, Washington, D.C. **F. Holland DAY & NARDO:** Estelle Jussim, *Slave to Beauty: The Eccentric Life and Controversial Career of F. Holland Day* (Boston: David R. Godine, 1981). **ERASMUS:** *The Epistles of Erasmus from His Earliest Letters to His Fifty-First Year Arranged in Order of Time*, trans. Francis Morgan Nichols, 3 vols. (London, New York and Bombay: Longmans, Green, and Co., 1901, 1904, 1918). **Marsilio FICINO:** *Della Divine Lettere del Gran Marsilio Ficino*, tradotte per M. Felice, 2 vols. (Venice: Gabriel Giolito de' Ferrari, 1563), English translation by Rictor Norton. **Edward FITZGERALD:** James Blyth, *Edward Fitzgerald and "Posh": "Herring Merchants"* (London: John Long, 1908). **Allen GINSBERG:** Allen Ginsberg and Neal Cassady from *As Ever: The Collected Correspondence of Allen Ginsberg & Neal Cassady*, ed. Barry Gifford (Berkeley: Creative Arts Book Company, 1977). Copyright © Allen Ginsberg and Carolyn Cassady. Used by permission. Allen Ginsberg and Peter Orlovsky from *Straight Hearts' Delight: Love Poems and Selected Letters*, ed. Winston Leyland (San Francisco: Gay Sunshine Press, 1980). Copyright © 1980 by Allen Ginsberg and Peter Orlovsky. Used by permission. Photo of Allen Ginsberg p. 274 copyright © Allen Ginsberg. Courtesy of Fahey/ Klein Gallery, Los Angeles. **Federico GONZAGA to Pietro ARETINO:** Alessandro Luzio, *Pietro Aretino nei primi suoi anni a Venezia e La Corte dei Gonzaga* (Turin: Ermanno Loescher, 1888) and Alessandro Luzio, "L'Aretino e il Franco," *Giornale storico della letterture italiana* (Turin: Ermanno Loescher), xxix (1897), 252; English translation by Alexandra Trone. **Edmund GOSSE:** *The Life and Letters of Sir Edmund Gosse*, ed. Evan Charteris (London: William Heinemann, 1931). **Thomas GRAY:** *Correspondence of Thomas Gray*, ed. Paget Toynbee and Leonard Whibley, 3 vols. (Oxford: Clarendon Press, 1935). **Stanley HAGGART:** Excerpts from *The Trouble with Harry Hay: Founder of the Modern Gay Movement*, by Stuart Timmons, copyright © 1990 by Stuart Timmons. Reprinted by permission of Alyson Publications, Inc. **Ralph HALL:** Reprinted by permission of the publishers from *A Class Apart* by James Gardiner, published by Serpent's Tail, London and New York, 1992. **Alexander HAMILTON:** *The Works of Alexander Hamilton*, ed. John C. Hamilton (New York 1851); Allan McLane Hamilton, *The Intimate Life of Alexander Hamilton* (London: Duckworth, 1910); *The Papers of Alexander Hamilton*, ed. Harold C. Syrett, assoc. ed. Jacob E. Cooke (New York: Columbia University, 1961). **Lord HERVEY:** *Lord Hervey and His Friends 1726–38*, ed. the Earl of Ilchester (London: John Murray, 1950) and Robert Halsband, *Lord Hervey: Eighteenth-Century Courtier* (Oxford: Clarendon Press, 1973). **HILARY the Englishman:** Trans. copyright © 1984 Thomas Stehling, *Medieval Latin Poems of Male Love and Friendship* (New York and London: Garland Publishing Inc., 1984). **Herbert HUNCKE:** Two letters by Herbert Huncke to Noah copyright © 1997 the Estate of Herbert E. Huncke. **Henry JAMES:** Reprinted by permission of the publishers from *The Letters of Henry James* edited by Leon Edel, Cambridge, Mass.: The Belknap Press of Harvard University Press, copyright © 1974, 1975, 1980, 1984, 1987, Leon Edel, Editorial; copyright © 1974, 1975, 1980, 1984, 1987, Alexander R. James, James copyright material. **King JAMES VI & I:** *Letters of King James VI & I*, ed. G. P. V. Akrigg (Berkeley, Los Angeles, London: University of California Press, 1984). **Heinrich von KLEIST:** to Ernst von Pfuel, from *Heinrich von*

*Kleist in seinen briefen*, ed. Ernst Schur (Charlottenburg: Schiller-Buchhandlung Verlag [1911]); to Rühle, from *Heinrich von Kleist's Leben und Briefe*, ed. Eduard von Bülow (Berlin: Verlag von Wilhelm Besser, 1848); English translation by Alexandra Trone. **Hubert LANGUET and Sir Philip SIDNEY:** Languet to Sidney December 24, 1573 trans. Charles Samuel Levy, *The Correspondence of Sir Philip Sidney and Hubert Languet, 1573–1576* (printed Doctoral Thesis, Cornell University, 1963); all others from *The Correspondence of Sir Philip Sidney and Hubert Languet*, trans. Steuart A. Pears (London: William Pickering, 1845). **T. E. LAWRENCE:** John E. Mack, *A Prince of Our Disorder: The Life of T. E. Lawrence* (London: Weidenfeld and Nicolson, 1976). **King LUDWIG II:** Translated by Edward Carpenter (slightly amended) in his anthology *Ioläus* (London: George Allen & Unwin, 1906 enlarged edition, repr. 1929). **MARBOD of Rennes:** Trans. copyright © 1984 Thomas Stehling, *Medieval Latin Poems of Male Love and Friendship* (New York and London: Garland Publishing, Inc., 1984). **F. O. MATTHIESSEN and Russell CHENEY:** *Rat and the Devil: Journal Letters of F. O. Matthiessen and Russell Cheney*, ed. Louis O. Hyde. Copyright © 1978 Louis Hyde. Reprinted by permisson of Archon Books, North Haven, Connecticut. **George MERRILL:** Edward Carpenter, *Selected Writings, Volume 1: Sex*, ed. David Fernbach and Noël Greig (London: GMP Pulishers, 1984). **Herman MELVILLE:** Reprinted by permission of the publishers from *The Letters of Herman Melville*, ed. Merrell R. Davis and William H. Gilman, copyright © 1960 Yale University Press. **MICHELANGELO:** John Addington Symonds, *The Life of Michelangelo Buonaroti* (1893). **Johannes von MÜLLER:** Müller to Bonstetten, from *Briefe eines jungen Gelehrten an seinen Freund* (Tubingen, 1802), English translation by Alexandra Trone; Bonstetten to Müller, from Marie-L. Herking, *Charles-Victor de Bonstetten* (Lausanne, 1921), English translation by Rictor Norton. **Wilfred OWEN:** © Oxford University Press 1967; reprinted from *Wilfred Owen: Collected Letters* edited by Harold Owen and John Bell (1967) by permission of Oxford University Press. **Pier Paolo PASOLINI:** *The Letters of Pier Paolo Pasolini*, Volume I: 1940–1954, ed. Nico Naldini, trans. Stuart Hood (London: Quartet Books, 1992), reprinted by permission of the publisher. **PAULINUS of Nola:** Trans. copyright © 1984 Thomas Stehling, *Medieval Latin Poems of Male Love and Friendship* (New York and London: Garland Publishing, Inc., 1984). **PHILOSTRATOS:** Letters 1, 2, 11, 13 and 46 from *The Letters of Alciphron, Aelian and Philostratus*, trans. Allen Rogers Benner and Francis H. Fobes (Loeb Classical Library; London: William Heinemann; Cambridge, Mass.: Harvard University Press, 1949); **Colin SPENCER and John TASKER:** © Colin Spencer, 1990; reprinted from Colin Spencer, *Which of Us Two? The Story of a Love Affair* (Viking, 1990) by permission of the author. **Earl of SUNDERLAND and Edward WILSON:** *Love-Letters Between a certain late Nobleman And the famous Mr Wilson* (London, printed for A. Moore, [1723]). **TCHAIKOVSKY:** Piotr Ilyich Tchaikovsky, *Letters to his Family: An Autobiography*, trans. Galina von Meck; with additional annotations by Percy M. Young (London: Dennis Dobson, 1981), English translations copyright © 1973 by Galina von Meck. **Mashida TOYONOSHIN:** Reprinted from *The Great Mirror of Male Love*, by Ihara Saikaku, Translated, with an Introduction, by Paul Gordon Schalow, with the permission of the publishers, Stanford University Press. © 1990 by the Board of Trustees of the Leland Stanford Junior University. **Walt WHITMAN:** Fred Vaughan, Lewis Brown and Alonzo Bush letters from *Calamus Lovers: Walt Whitman's Working-Class Camerados* and *Drum Beats: Walt Whitman's Civil War Boy Lovers*, both ed. Charley Shively (San Francisco: Gay Sunshine, 1987 and 1989), used by permission; to Peter Doyle from *Calamus: A Series of Letters Written During the Years 1868–1880 by Walt Whitman to a Young Friend (Peter Doyle)*, ed. Richard Maurice Bucke (Boston: Laurens Maynard, 1897). **Oscar WILDE:**

*Complete Works of Oscar Wilde* (Collins, 1948, 1966); *The Trials of Oscar Wilde*, ed. H. Montgomery Hyde (Penguin, 1948); *The Letters of Oscar Wilde*, ed. Rupert Hart-Davis (1962). Copyright © Estate of Oscar Wilde 1962 by permission of Merlin Holland. **J. J. WINCKELMANN:** J. J. Winckelmann, *Briefe*, 4 vols. (Berlin: Walter de Gruyter, 1952–57); English translation by Alexandra Trone. **Thomas J. WITHERS:** The letters are among the Hammond Papers, South Caroliniana Library, Columbia, SC, and were first printed by Martin Duberman in his article " 'Writhing Bedfellows' in Antebellum South Carolina,'' in the *Journal of Homosexuality* (Fall/Winter, 1980–81), and subsequently reprinted several times.

**SELECT BIBLIOGRAPHY:** In addition to individual biographies, which I will not list here, and the standard reference works such as the *Dictionary of National Biography* and *Chambers Biographical Dictionary* etc., I have also consulted the following anthologies and compendiums specifically covering gay history and literature: *The Alyson Almanac* (Boston: Alyson, 1990); Emmanuel Cooper, *The Sexual Perspective: Homosexuality and Art in the Last 100 Years in the West*, 2nd ed. (London and New York: Routledge, 1994); Martin Duberman, *About Time: Exploring the Gay Past* (Meridian, 1986 and 1991); *Hidden from History: Reclaiming the Gay and Lesbian Past*, ed. Martin Duberman, Martha Vicinus and George Chauncey, Jr. (Meridian, 1990); *Encyclopedia of Homosexuality*, ed. Wayne R. Dynes, 2 vols. (Chicago and London: St. James Press, 1990); Michael Elliman and Frederick Roll, *The Pink Plaque Guide to London* (London: GMP, 1986); Noel I. Garde, *Jonathan to Gide: The Homosexual in History* (New York: Vantage, 1964); *A Queer Reader*, ed. Patrick Higgins (London: Fourth Estate, 1993); Jonathan Katz, *Gay American History* (New York: Thomas Y. Crowell, 1976); *Gay Roots: An Anthology of Gay History, Sex, Politics & Culture*, ed. Winston Leyland, 2 vols. (San Francisco: Gay Sunshine Press, 1991, 1993); A. L. Rowse, *Homosexuals in History* (London: Weidenfeld and Nicolson, 1977); and Leigh W. Rutledge, *The Gay Fireside Companion* (Boston: Alyson, 1989).

RICTOR NORTON is author of the pioneering historical study *Mother Clap's Molly House: The Gay Subculture in England 1700–1830* (London: Gay Men's Press, 1992). He taught one of the earliest courses on gay and lesbian literature (Florida State University, 1971) and co-edited the first all-gay issue of an academic journal (*College English*, 1974). His book *The Homosexual Literary Tradition* was based on his Ph.D. study of homosexual themes in English Renaissance Literature. He then emigrated to London and worked full-time at *Gay News* from 1974 to 1979. Many of Rictor Norton's essays for *Gay Sunshine* on gay history and literature were reprinted in *Gay Roots*, vols. I & II (San Francisco: Gay Sunshine Press, 1991, 1993); and he is also a contributor to the *New Dictionary of National Biography* (England). His most recent book is *The Myth of the Modern Homosexual: Queer History and the Search for Cultural Unity* (London: Cassell, 1997). He lives in London, where he is currently researching the history of gay subcultures in Victorian England.

Published in paperback, there is also
a limited edition of 200 cloth copies.